THE ONLY
GRANT-
WRITING
BOOK
YOU'LL EVER NEED

THE ONLY GRANT-WRITING BOOK

YOU'LL EVER NEED

FIFTH EDITION

ELLEN KARSH & ARLEN SUE FOX

BASIC BOOKS

New York

Basic Books
Hachette Book Group
1290 Avenue of the Americas, New York, NY 10104
www.basicbooks.com

Printed in the United States of America

Originally published by Basic Books in July 2003

Fifth Edition: November 2019

Published by Basic Books, an imprint of Perseus Books, LLC, a subsidiary of Hachette Book Group, Inc. The Basic Books name and logo is a trademark of the Hachette Book Group.

The publisher is not responsible for websites (or their content) that are not owned by the publisher.

Print book interior design by Six Red Marbles.

Library of Congress Cataloging-in-Publication Data

Names: Karsh, Ellen, author. | Fox, Arlen Sue, author.
Title: The only grant-writing book you'll ever need / Ellen Karsh and Arlen Sue Fox.
Description: Fifth Edition. | New York : Basic Books, [2019] | Revised edition of the authors' The only grant-writing book you'll ever need, 2014. | Includes bibliographical references and index.
Identifiers: LCCN 2019020178 (print) | LCCN 2019022254 (ebook) |
    ISBN 9781541617810 (pbk.)
Subjects: LCSH: Proposal writing for grants—United States. | Grants-in-aid—United States. | Fund raising—United States.
Classification: LCC HG177.5.U6 K37 2019 (print) | LCC HG177.5.U6 (ebook) |
    DDC 658.15/224—dc23
LC record available at https://lccn.loc.gov/2019020178
LC ebook record available at https://lccn.loc.gov/2019022254

ISBNs: 978-1-5416-1781-0 (paperback), 978-1-5416-1912-8 (ebook)

LSC-C

10 9 8 7 6 5 4 3 2 1

In memory of

Tess and Rubin Karsh

and

Ruth and Irv Barish

CONTENTS

INTRODUCTION TO THE FIFTH EDITION

ONCE AGAIN we are preparing a new edition of *The Only Grant-Writing Book You'll Ever Need* in a climate of change and uncertainty. One day maybe this won't be the case, but we're starting to have our doubts. As in past editions, our purpose is to help you write the best proposal possible, whatever the climate, to enhance your chances of getting funding for your organization, educational institution, or personal projects. And, as for past editions, we have turned to foundation officers, outstanding nonprofits leaders, and government officials to seek their best advice. Always in the past we have been able to assure you that, even when the search was difficult, there still would be plenty of grants available if you knew how to find the right funder and present your case clearly and forcibly. This still is true for many foundation and government grants, but **we need to sound an alarm** to organizations that depend largely on government grants and contracts.

If you have been reading the newspapers and listening to pundits over the last few years, you are aware that the federal government is engaged in major changes and that budget concerns may force significant retrenchment in many service areas. Many state and local governments traditionally receive and pass on federal funding to

educational institutions and nonprofits. But we hear from government officials that there are likely to be fewer grants and contracts
to state and local governments and to nonprofit organizations over
the coming years. Local governments that have managed to keep
needed programs afloat in the face of recent federal and state cuts
may find it harder and harder to do so. And we hear from foundations watching this process that they are unlikely to be able to pick
up the slack in funding. Although there is hope that such conditions
may change over time, organizations that do not prepare for cuts in
government funding in the near future may not be around to benefit
in the long run.

So a new purpose for this book is to encourage you not only to
perfect your grantsmanship skills to function in an even more highly
competitive era than in the past but also to identify and implement
fundraising methods that do not depend on grants. We will mention,
but not discuss in this book, common fundraising methods that many
of you already use—annual appeals, fundraising events, crowdfunding
and other social media, events and journals, and more. We believe
you need to increase your outreach in your communities to enhance
the unrestricted income that you bring in from these activities. There
are many excellent books and online resources to help you do this.

We also want to introduce you to some innovative, and sometimes controversial, fundraising methods described by our foundation and government contacts, presented in more detail in an
updated introductory roundtable on the funding environment and
in a new chapter, Lesson 18. These methods, increasingly used by
the most far-seeing organizations, include formalizing and increasing
the role of volunteers to enhance existing programs and services,
identifying and implementing opportunities for business enterprises
that serve your mission, collaborating with other nonprofits and local businesses, and implementing fees for service when possible. *Your
grant-writing skills will be as vital in these initiatives as they are
in seeking grants; we will show you how in Lesson 18, in a section
on writing a business plan.*

Many organizations currently use the simplest of these methods—for example, having parents help teachers work with children on reading skills, having volunteers serve meals to seniors, running bake sales and auctions, or collecting a nominal contribution for meals or activities. We touch on these methods and more in Lesson 18 because too many organizations acknowledge that they have done very little to diversify funding. And even these simple methods can be expanded and institutionalized to bring more resources into your organization.

We are suggesting broader approaches as well, incorporating both a planned and systematic use of volunteers and what we will call business-oriented or entrepreneurial sources of income (sometimes called *social enterprise*). In many organizations this will require something of a cultural shift because staff are committed to providing services "for free" to needy individuals and families. Unfortunately, these services are not "free"; they have been supported by government and foundation funding. To continue providing the essential services you know are so vital, you must find new ways to support them.

Because one of the authors of this book is a rabid baseball fan, we are once again using our national pastime to illustrate how organizations can think outside the (grant-writing-only) box when it comes to surviving when money is tight—and, by the way, when isn't money tight?

There probably isn't a baseball fan around who wouldn't agree with this statement: "Boy, has baseball changed." Most readers over 30 grew up never hearing of sabermetrics, a term that came into use in the early 2000s and was featured in a book (which became a hit movie), *Moneyball* by Michael Lewis. To make a long story short, sabermetrics replaces baseball managers' hunches and years of experience with actual statistics. No longer do managers say, "I know that Mighty Casey will hit a homerun now, even though (a) he's a lefty and so is the pitcher, (b) he can't hit a curve ball and this pitcher throws only curve balls, and (c) he's faced this particular pitcher 10 times and struck out all 10 times. He's due." Today there's no way, with all the data and statistics available to the manager, that Mighty Casey would bat against this particular pitcher. The batter would instead be the player with statistics that make him the most likely to have success. Today teams keep track of everything about players— from how hard they hit the ball to how fast the ball comes off their bats to what direction the ball travels. Suddenly "launch angle" is all the rage in baseball. And all this information, these analytics, are loaded onto the managers' tablets and used for in-game decisions, which is why fans watch as fielders shift around before each pitch is thrown so it will be a little more difficult for the batter to get a hit.

But in spite of all these newfangled ways of doing things, baseball itself hasn't really changed: all but a few minor rules are the same as they were back in the day. Still, the successful teams are generally the ones that are using all the latest technology. They are always looking for a way to be better, smarter, more open minded, and more creative. And, as usual, the players are trying to get stronger, healthier, faster, and more skillful.

Like baseball, grant writing[1] really hasn't changed either. The basics are the same. But now most grantmakers look for increased diversity of funding sources, and a winning proposal is likely to include and highlight supplementary strategies the organization is using to bring in money and stay afloat when other funding is scarce (see Lesson 13, on sustainability). The questions on the grant application may look the same as they looked 10 years ago, but the proposal that answers the questions in a way that reflects the entrepreneurial spirit of the organization is the one that has the best chance of getting funded. And although a grant application may not include a question that says "Describe the entrepreneurial spirit of your organization," you will be able to find many places in your proposal where

---

[1] We must mention that although we often use "grant writing" as a term in common usage, strictly speaking, one doesn't write grants, one writes proposals in order to win grants; grants are a reward for excellent proposal writing!

you can easily describe your efforts to "think outside the box"—a phrase funders themselves use frequently. If you're not there yet, Lesson 18 will give you some ideas about where to start.

WHAT'S IN THE BOOK?

The Only Grant-Writing Book You'll Ever Need organizes the whole grant-seeking experience into three parts (preparation, proposal writing, and follow-up) and 18 lessons. Each lesson is designed as a workshop, starting with opening remarks followed by discussion questions and concluding with a short "pop quiz." These questions give you an opportunity to practice what we preach, so we hope you give them a shot. (We provide the answers—with explanations—in Appendix 6 so you can see how you did.)

But there's a lot more to grantsmanship than just the proposal. So we've included a chapter on writing with style; a chapter on "intangibles," with information that's usually not communicated anywhere because you're assumed to know it; and "roundtables" with suggestions from grantmakers, government officials, and nonprofit leaders about what they think it takes to write a good proposal and about how you should approach the economic and social climate in which you're writing.

We'd especially like to call your attention to two items in the book: Roundtable I: Grantsmanship and the Funding Environment, which follows this introduction, and the new chapter mentioned earlier, Lesson 18: When Grant Funding Needs a Boost, Build a Business!, which makes some of the issues and suggestions in this roundtable more concrete.

After the financial meltdown in 2008, and again in 2014, we asked our panelists for views on grantmaking in that environment, and presented them in economy-focused roundtables in the third and fourth editions. For the current edition, we reviewed those roundtables, checked in with grantmakers, and found that most of what our panel had told us is still relevant. So we've kept many of the comments from the earlier editions and added what we've heard more recently about their concerns regarding federal budget cuts and the current climate for grantmaking.

After the roundtable, Part I starts you off with prerequisite lessons: Identifying who you and/or your organization are, what kind of funding you should be looking for, where to look for it, and how to make sense of grant-application packages. We discuss differences (and similarities) in the approach to grants by nonprofits, government agencies and schools, and individual grant seekers.

We also give you some strategies to ensure that you will be a more well-rounded and successful grant writer than ever. Like the baseball player who is always looking for an edge over the competition, you can gain an edge as well. What makes a successful grant writer (besides good writing, of course)? Part I ends with a discussion of intangibles that affect grantsmanship, including some thoughts on the role of a grant writer in the organization.

Part II opens with some rules and guidelines on good writing and the opportunity to practice writing sections of a grant proposal. In the remaining lessons in Part II, we take you through the process of developing each element of a typical grant proposal.

Submitting a proposal isn't the end. In Part III we talk about steps to take after you learn whether you have been approved for funding—or not. This section ends with the new chapter on entrepreneurial approaches to fundraising and on ways in which excellent proposal-writing skills can be transferred to the development of a business proposal.

At the end of each part, we present a lively Funders Roundtable, giving you the responses of a large and diverse group of grantmakers from government funding agencies and foundations to a slew of pertinent questions on the topics and issues covered in that part. Their answers will help even experienced grant writers gain new insight into the grant process and an understanding of what the money people really look for.

We also have updated the appendices. Appendix 1 offers tips to improve your chances of winning a grant (drawn from our own experiences, the comments of our panel of grantmakers, and successful grant seekers). Appendix 2 is a proposal checklist to help ensure you have touched all the right buttons. (We urge you to create your own checklist for each new proposal that you plan to write.) It is followed by an extensive, updated glossary of common terms used in the grants world (Appendix 3). In Appendix 4 we give you some model application forms and letters; in Appendix 5, which is updated and annotated to reflect major changes in some important websites, you will find notes on a few useful sites. Appendix 6 provides the answers to the pop quizzes.

We want to note that the title of this book is aspirational: We do hope that it is the only grant-writing book you'll ever need. Throughout the book, we have tried to demystify the process of developing programs, writing proposals, and winning grants so that anyone—even those with the least experience—can succeed. Although readers with relatively little experience or those changing careers may be the ones who find the book most useful, we are doing our best to provide helpful information—about what the grantmakers are saying, and especially about diversifying funding—to even the most experienced.

ABOUT THE FUNDERS ROUNDTABLES...

As you'll recognize if you're a longtime grant seeker (or work for one), or as you will understand one of these days, experienced proposal writers can become a little presumptuous at times and, at least where grants are concerned, turn into opinionated know-it-alls about how to do it. Because we had written so many proposals and won millions of dollars in grants (we're not mentioning right now how many grants we *didn't* win); because we'd attended so many bidders' conferences where applications were explained in minute detail and participated in so many foundation workshops; and because we'd taken (and given) grant-writing seminars over the years, we got to be pretty sure we knew what the funders wanted.

But we can confide in you: Every now and then we were secretly a little afraid that just maybe we really *didn't* know exactly what grant-makers love or hate. So for each edition, we talked with funders and nonprofit leaders representing foundations and organizations of all sizes in all parts of the country, as well as with government officials. And we got some insights and surprises that made the effort worthwhile for us and, we hope, for you.

Then, because the first edition was in preparation during the attacks of 9/11, we addressed with grantmakers the impact of terrorism on grant funding. Not to suggest we're a jinx, but the second time, just after hurricanes Katrina and Rita, we asked funders about the effects of natural disasters, disaster planning, and other issues on the grants landscape. For the third edition (just after the financial industry's meltdown) and the fourth (prepared after more than a year of federal budget crises), we asked about funding in a volatile economic climate. Now, on top of many more devastating hurricanes and wildfires, we face a federal government that is more than a trillion dollars in debt and promises years of cutbacks in a wide variety of programs. More than ever, we felt the need to know what government and foundation grantmakers had to say about grant seeking, and they very kindly gave their time to answer our questions.

Although we call our conversations "funders roundtables," we didn't really go the roundtable route. Instead, we interviewed each individual alone, following essentially the same interview format. We wanted to give the interviewees the opportunity to frame their answers independently and without being distracted by things other panelists said. In addition, early on we started interviewing successful nonprofit leaders who have invaluable insights into and experience with the grants process.

Many of those we interviewed were perfectly happy to speak on the record, but others felt that they would have to hold back if they were going to be quoted directly, or even if they were only acknowledged by name in the book. Because our purpose was to get their uninhibited good advice, we decided not to quote anyone by name. The grantmakers and others whom we interviewed couldn't have been more forthcoming, more giving of their time, more willing to share their expertise and insights, or more clearly committed to the needs of grant seekers and their communities. Whether we name them in our acknowledgment section or not, we are deeply grateful to all of them.

GRANTSMANSHIP AND THE FUNDING ENVIRONMENT

IN THE BEST OF TIMES, in the worst of times, and in all the time in between, there are always grants to be had (and we hope that will never change). For each of the previous four editions, we focused our interviews on grantmakers' approaches to specific calamities current at the time—9/11, hurricanes Katrina and Sandy, the economic meltdown of 2008 and the ensuing financial crisis—that we thought would affect the availability of grants from federal, state, and local governments and from private foundations and corporations. We had a strong hunch—in fact, we thought it was obvious—that catastrophes of all kinds would diminish grant seekers' chances of obtaining more routine funding. And, not surprisingly, we learned from the grantmakers that this hunch was correct.

For the current edition we decided to take a more holistic view of grantsmanship—to look not only at calamities and catastrophes but to place the grants process in the context of the political, cultural, and social environment as well. As we write, the scene is tumultuous, globally as well as nationally. Immigration; health care; the climate change debate amid increasingly severe hurricanes, tsunamis, and

1

wildfires; a fluctuating stock market; ever-present terrorism threats; the #MeToo and Black Lives Matter movements; and the increase in deadly mass shootings and gun violence are just a few of the topical issues of the day. Moreover, after many years of economic growth since the 2008 financial crisis, there are now fears that a new recession may occur in the not-too-distant future.

With all this uncertainty swirling around, we asked our panel of foundation and government grantmakers, elected and appointed officials, and nonprofit leaders to suggest how grant seekers can present themselves and their groups in the best light—whether there's chaos across the globe or all is right with the world. And one thing should be made very clear before we go any further: You *must* be knowledgeable about what's going on, especially when things seem most chaotic.

One grantmaker we spoke to told us that foundations (like the rest of us) aren't used to dealing with such rapid and unexpected changes in the cultural environment, and they are working hard to figure out how to fund solutions to new problems that seem to crop up daily. We hope that by the time you're reading this book, the scene will no longer be so tumultuous, that the world will be more tranquil and issue free—but don't count on it. Even if some current issues are resolved (or have been relegated to the back burner), there always will be new ones. You need to be sure your organization, your programs, and your grant proposals are as strong as possible to meet new challenges.

THINGS TO KNOW IN ANY ENVIRONMENT

We tried to pin our current panelists down about what a winning grant proposal should look like. They were quick to remind us that although proposals are important, the organizations they represent should be well run and high functioning. Many funders talked about the importance of strong organizational leadership, of nonprofit managers with "relevant skill sets and entrepreneurial vibes," of being technologically savvy and having a strong presence on social media. They warned that organizations should be "well organized and have better data on hand now" (with the easy availability of online research, there is no excuse not to) and "be able to clearly articulate their goals and move the needle toward their mission." In all the lessons throughout this edition, we address (and stress) the points that are so important to funders.

Measuring Impact Is No Longer an Evolving Concept; It Is a Key for Most Funders

Program outcomes and impact on the clients and the community are more important than ever. Your first thought might be, "Haven't outcomes always been important?" The answer is, "Sort of, but sometimes more like lip service," at least for many foundations. (Government grantmakers always have been very strict about measurable results.) Several funders we spoke to for previous editions already had been moving toward focusing on outcomes; their insights are especially relevant now. One panelist explained that she takes a results-based approach to grantmaking: "We're moving from a 'funder' mentality to an 'investor' mentality. We're asking ourselves, 'What do we really want to buy, what are our chances of getting it, how will we know we're getting it, and is this the best use of our money?'"

A number of others said they were looking harder than they used to at the success—and the likelihood of success—of the programs they funded or were considering. "For an organization that helps children," a funder explained, "I want to see the deeper impact on the children's lives. Did you actually keep a child out of a gang? A single example can be meaningful."

"We don't just want to know that you conducted workshops," another panelist said; "we want to know how many people got jobs." "Or," she suggested, "you can ask participants what three things they got out of the workshops and whether you can follow up with them later. We like to fund a program not for one year but for three years. We believe that program activities can take place during the first year and follow-up support should occur in the second and third years." Another grantmaker added, "we're asking for a mid-year report to make sure things are getting done that have been promised. We want to be impactful."

In today's funding climate, the very first question asked of grant seekers is, "How will you know if your program succeeds?" We can almost guarantee you that this emphasis on results will not go away anytime soon, so if you don't currently focus on outcomes for all of your programs, you'd better start.

"Not so long ago," explained a foundation grantmaker, "it was still enough for a nonprofit to justify its need for grant funds by simply saying that the money would fill or serve a need." Groups that were doing "good work" could survive by describing their good work to funders. There was great sympathy for the clients and great empathy for those dedicated professionals providing the services. Sympathy and empathy often led to grant funding."

"Now," one of our panelists said, "there are more evidence-based questions than ever on grant applications. Foundations are asking grant seekers how the impact of their programs can be measured." Another grantmaker explained that "new donors [nicknamed, by more than one funder, the "hedge-fund guys"] generally have no legacy of philanthropy in their families, which is why they think in business-oriented ways...looking for outcomes and data." He added that if nonprofits don't recognize the need to address outcomes and results, they will be "lapped by other organizations." Another funder agreed, suggesting, "There is a 'Disrupt Philanthropy Movement' started by young people of great wealth. They dwell on outcomes."

Grantmakers expect a return on each grant—but they'll help you get there. Because of this strong emphasis on impact, some foundations, you will be relieved to know, fund training in how to identify outcomes. As one panelist explains, "It's such a difficult task—because there is no standard definition of outcome measures." One of the grantmakers was very explicit about the importance of outcomes. "We expect to see a 'rate of return' on each grant. The outcome of a worker training program grant should be jobs. And the outcome of an after-school program grant should be high-school graduation."

You *Must* Diversify Your Funding Sources

Even more than in the past, grantmakers expect you to diversify your funding sources—and to quit relying solely on government and foundation grants. For years, "diversify funding" has been a mantra, or a warning, from grantmakers to the organizations they fund. Especially in periods of economic downturn, it is clear why it is unwise to rely only on grants to keep programs and organizations up and running. As we saw in the years after 2008, foundation money just wasn't there. And in periods of government belt tightening, grants become scarcer, whether at the federal, state, or local level. One panelist noted, "The federal government has been slowly starving over the last few years [and the state has been cutting back too]. So far the city has been able to compensate for the loss—but if there's a recession this won't be possible anymore."

Broaden your horizons. As far as grantmakers are concerned, diversifying funding sources, like identifying program outcomes and impact, will never go out of style. Although we focus on writing grant proposals, we want to remind you to broaden your fund-raising horizons. "Groups should expand their resource pool," a funder suggested. "Stop relying only on foundations for funding." Another suggested that organizations look for individual gifts. "Push the envelope. Be thoughtful, strategic, relational." Others said, "Diversify fundraising strategies; seek earned income as well as grants.... Think about all the options that are open to you.... Think holistically." "Ask for more from the people who have already given" and expand your donor base. Still another said, "If you put all your eggs in one basket [i.e., relying only on government or foundation support], you're probably already in deep trouble."

One expert urged nonprofits to pursue what he called "evergreen" strategies—approaches that would strengthen them in the long term, such as developing planned-giving programs, pursuing earned income, and cultivating major donors, as well as learning new strategies, such as social media and social entrepreneurship. Most panelists said they would be very interested in—and a few would be glad to support—proposals from groups that were creating small (or growing) businesses to generate unrestricted funds, as long as they were in accord with the organization's mission.

And if you still need to seek foundation support (as most organizations always will), find ways to diversify that too. An executive director of a nonprofit figured out a way to bring added funding into his organization, which addresses the needs of seniors. He suggests thinking creatively about diversifying your foundation support: "Maybe a foundation isn't so interested in the elderly," he explained, "but they could be interested in animals—and might be willing to pay for the care of [older people's] pets." Similarly, a grantmaker noted, "Change a program to make it more relevant. Maybe offer a meal; this could open the door to funders who give grants to programs addressing hunger."

Be Creative, Flexible, and Willing to Take Risks

Grantmakers aren't necessarily expecting organizations to do things differently these days, but one defined a successful group this way: "Be flexible, entrepreneurial, willing to take risks. Be willing to fail. Learn from your failures. . . . It can no longer be business as usual." As one grantmaker said (sadly), "Nonprofits have a prevailing attitude: 'If only we can reach the angel who will give us the total amount of money that we need' . . ." Another pointed out that "new solutions must be found to help nonprofits stay solvent. Right now we're in the Einstein definition of insanity. We are doing the same thing over and over again and expecting different outcomes. That has to change."

One panelist explained an obstacle to diversifying funding that is well known to nonprofit organizations. "If you serve poor people," he said, "it's hard to charge money for anything." Another funder explained why she opposes a strategy of diversifying funding by charging fees for the services that had always been provided at no cost: "The people we are helping—the poor people—have been in a depression for a long time." (We should note that other grantmakers were enthusiastic about asking for contributions as long as there was a sliding scale or some other way to make sure no one was denied services.)

Another panelist suggested that "creative fundraising is looking at what's hot and what's not.... People have been doing the same things over and over again. You should be asking yourselves, 'How can I fit into change without changing my mission?'"

A number of panelists noted that "nonprofits tend to be risk averse—they will rarely spend money (they may be hesitant about buying lists of potential donors, for example, or paying for technology support), even if spending money will make them more money in the end." Funders felt that such risk aversion also might get in the way of creative thinking about nontraditional fundraising, such as starting small business enterprises, as one way to bring in unrestricted money.

Because diversifying funding can no longer be an elusive goal— pie in the sky—for organizations, we have included concrete suggestions for some possible initiatives in Lesson 18.

Learn to Be an Advocate!

Grant seekers should become passionate advocates for their organizations and participants. Advocacy is another ubiquitous grant-maker mantra that often goes unheeded. One of our panelists said, "On all fronts, nonprofits need to be bolder, stronger, resilient, and loud.... Nonprofits have to up their game in advocacy." "It's not enough to vote in elections and make the occasional donation to your favorite local candidate's war chest." "Get involved with advocacy; fight for dollars you've always had." "Nonprofits should be forces for good—push up and out by being strong advocates, which is just as important as being good at deliverable services." A panelist from a major umbrella organization noted that civic education and civic engagement should be a major focus for foundations and advocacy groups: "Why did we get to a point when [the federal government] is all about tax cuts and cutting spending? How did we get here, and how could foundations [advocate to] ameliorate the budget cuts?"

One of our grantmakers pointed out that "in policy making, nonprofits are on the menu but not at the table." His advice: "Collaborate more to be stronger advocates." Work with umbrella organizations advocating for your issues to have the most impact. Another funder thinks advocacy is so important that his foundation has started supporting advocacy work. "Groups are now seeking funding to become part of advocacy efforts." He pointed out that foundations are waking up to the need to defend the climate in which their own missions take place. And he adds, "If you are providing for childcare, advocate for childcare." The focus on advocacy, while seemingly obvious, is a reminder not to expect others to advocate for you. And it's up to you to find and collaborate with those groups that are doing similar work and have similar goals.

Get Your Board Moving

Nonprofit boards are expected to take a much bigger role in the life of the organization. Although government and foundation funders always have examined board involvement in the operation and financial support of grantees, in recent years they have become much more concerned about such involvement. Every grantmaker we spoke to talked about the importance of boards. And an executive director of a large, successful nonprofit said that he spends 25 percent of his week talking to board members. "Board development is key," he added. "Make sure board members know exactly what is going on in the organization."

A panelist said, "We look at the diversity of board members and their attendance at meetings. Do they fund the organization, are they present at site visits?" And another asks about the board's financial support. "If it is less than 100%, we need to know why."

"Now is a good time to make sure your board is up to speed so they can talk about your organization smartly," one funder pointed out recently. "You need all the publicity you can get."

Funders suggested that you'd be smart to take full advantage of the skills of members of your board. One grantmaker said, "Look at your board. What are they doing for you?" Another pointed out, "People don't have the human resources skills, the real estate skills necessary to save money by negotiating better leases. This is where the board should come in—to help you." "Instead of looking for big checks from struggling foundations, look toward your community and focus on your board."

Recruit—and Thank—Volunteers

It is surprising to us how little attention some nonprofits pay to organizing volunteer programs. Everyone likes the idea of having volunteers, but too few organizations consider how to best use them. A grantmaker suggested that this climate is a perfect time to encourage volunteers. "Organizations must get much better at handling volunteers, especially when volunteers are really needed." Someone in your organization should be assigned, at least part time, to recruit and coordinate volunteers. One nonprofit leader told us that his organization has five full-time staff members in the volunteer office to make sure that things go smoothly. And, in a significant shift from seeing older adults only as clients in need of services, some senior-serving organizations ask groups of participants to design and run programs that will benefit their peers and the community at large.

Organizations that make good use of volunteers also make sure to thank them. As one nonprofit leader noted, they (like many others) recognize their volunteers' work through an annual Volunteer Appreciation Day, giving awards for their service. And, in addition to its annual awards celebration, another organization adds a summer ice cream social to thank volunteers.

IT IS IMPORTANT TO BE REALISTIC . . .

If There Is a Recession, What Do We Need to Know?

As we mentioned earlier, there have been recurring warnings that a recession is a very real possibility over the next couple of years. Based on the history of the ebb and flow of the economy, our panelists (and some economists) think we are, unfortunately, due. It seems sensible to pay attention to the advice of grantmakers who have lived (and learned) through past recessions. In any case, it's a good idea to think now, when you may be able to find grants for planning and preparation, about what you'll do in a national or regional disaster or a downturn.

Previous rounds of interviews offer some useful strategies for planning ahead. As one panelist told us the last time foundations were hard hit, "The economy forced us to take a pause and look at what we've been doing." Most funders agreed that taking a hard look at their own strategies and practices is a good idea. "We're waiting to see what's happening and what will happen," a grantmaker explained. "[A difficult] economy invites us to be self-critical." They are consistent in saying that organizations that rely on grants should do the same.

Foundations will want to help when—and if—they can. "Look," said a grantmaker, "when the economy is going badly, it is important for the philanthropic sector to help floundering groups that rely on grant funds so it's not a 'survival of the fittest' contest. In a recession, philanthropists need to analyze their giving strategies so they are more responsive to the needs of the groups that are vying for support." Another funder hoped that foundations would take on other responsibilities—advocacy, for instance—and not just write smaller and smaller checks. And recent interviews indicate that although many foundations now talk to one another primarily within interest groups—in education, the arts, or youth, for example—many are increasingly seeing collaborative investment in public policy and advocacy as something they need to do across disciplines.

But, as the last downturn demonstrated, philanthropic organizations aren't immune from world events, so it is a good idea always to remember that grantmakers aren't cash cows.

Governments have their troubles too. Of course, it's not just foundations that will feel the pinch during a recession. State and municipal government agencies—which receive as well as give grants—not only will slash their own funding to local providers but also will have to find new resources for their own missions in the wake of federal cutbacks. This is a challenge some city and county governments had never faced before the 2008 financial meltdown, and some were better equipped than others to address it. One government funder explained, "The mayor [was] pushing agencies to seek alternative funding sources—saying, 'If you want your budget to be whole, you'd better find other funding.'"

A foundation officer noted, "After 2008 it took about three years to restore the endowments of private foundations. Now they're back and bigger. But federal, state, and local government funding levels have not returned to their pre-2008 levels. And given politics being what they are, no one expects them to. Ever." And just in case anyone thinks help is on the way from private philanthropy, a foundation funder warned us that, "We [foundations] can't fill government holes, so cities and states had better not expect us to come to the rescue." (This funder did admit that "once in a while we will come to the rescue if the need is very great and we don't see other options.")

"In a recession or after a major disaster, we'll be asking, more than ever, 'Why do you need the money?'" A grantmaker from a small foundation explained that in a downturn or an emergency, "money feels twice as precious and I want to make very sure that 'best practices' are being utilized by grantees." A funder from a large foundation agreed. "We ask, 'Do you really need that amount of money to do what you say you want to do?' You'd better sell us on why you need the specific amount you're requesting." Another panelist added, "We're looking hard at what we want to do because—pure and simple—we'll have to do less. We're raising the bar. Money is worth more."

How Do Grantmakers Decide How to Cut Back in Difficult Times?

Do they change their priorities? Each time we have interviewed grantmakers, we've asked, "If you cut back on funding, do you focus on fewer causes (for example, food and shelter but not arts and education) or do you cut grants across the board?" Would they change their priorities to focus, for example, on the neediest populations or the neediest areas during recessions or after hurricanes and other natural disasters? We think that some of their responses may help you think about what you—and they—will do if the economy slows again or another hurricane diverts resources away from routine funding.

Surprisingly, most funders did not change their priorities. But some saw an economic downturn as a good time to institute new policies that they were considering anyway. One said, "We will be considering some emergency grants—feeding programs, for instance—but these will not impact the rest of our grant giving." And still another added that in a difficult economy "we are asking other [funders] to join us when a problem is identified. We get the best and the brightest together to address ways to tackle the problem as a group—and we get financial contributions—then we create a special fund specifically to deal with the problem we identified. If hunger is an emergency issue in the community, for example, we will create a challenge grant that we make available to local groups working on this problem in ways we believe are likely to make a significant impact."

It's all about impact. "For us," explained a grantmaker, "there was a decrease in giving right after the [financial] meltdown—we reduced some grants, eliminated others. 'I'll give you a smaller grant so I have enough money left over to give someone else a little something too.' But now, we've moved away from that approach and we're giving fewer, but larger, grants because we want to make the kind of impact that only a greater amount of money can ensure." Another funder also looked at the effects of grant funds: "The economic downturn provided a good excuse to stop sprinkling small amounts of money over a large geographic area and start focusing our attention on one community to make more of an impact."

Recent interviews suggest that as the trend toward larger grants continues, grantmakers, especially government agencies, also are moving toward larger grantees. These larger organizations are seen as better able to sustain their programs over time and to serve larger numbers of people.

Some good news. We asked, "In difficult times, do you support only current grantees or are you willing (and able) to support additional programs that you think are very important?" In light of a move toward larger grantees, common sense suggests that new or small organizations might have a much tougher time getting funding when the economic picture is so dire. We asked funders about this. The good news for current grantees is that most funders will try to continue working with you. The bad news for others is that, if there is an economic downturn or a recession, many funders will only be able to support their current grantees. Still, some funders will suggest other sources for funding or will provide technical assistance. And still others admit that if they are blown away by your idea for a project, maybe—just maybe—they can round up the funding necessary to support it.

If you're small, you'd better be strong. The funders generally agreed that newer, smaller organizations will have a problem in a poor economy, and that it's "a good time for foundations to stop funding organizations that are weak, and not to take on any new grantees." But another respondent was more reassuring: "It's not whether an organization is big or small that decides if it will survive in a tough economy; it's whether it's weak or strong."

"We don't fund teeny start-ups but we do join other grantmakers to fund consortia of small groups," one funder told us. But that doesn't mean new, small groups shouldn't be proactive. One of our panelists said, "Not-for-profits need to communicate—to stay on the radar of a foundation even if they are not receiving funding at the moment. I like to get a personal letter—with so much email, it's difficult to differentiate one group from another."

But one foundation grantmaker was very positive about smaller groups and gives grants over as much as five years to capable, creative, "emerging organizations." "We want our groups to try something new and learn how to tell their story. We're basically funding them to get ready to be funded by [larger foundations]."

Think collaboration. One recent change we noticed as we spoke to funders about the impact of the economy on grantmaking is that a number of them expressed a greater interest in giving grants to umbrella groups, to collaborative projects, or to technical assistance organizations that help not-for-profits increase their overall capacity—all in the hopes of maximizing the reach of the funding. Many grantmakers feel that your organization's ability to accomplish your goals is enhanced by your network of relationships in the community. One put it succinctly when she said, "Collaboration should be seen as a survival mechanism." Another added, "In [a bad] economy, collaborations look better than ever." (She likes to give a grant of, say, $50,000 to be shared by three neighboring organizations to pay for one development director.) An experienced proposal writer noted that "people usually collaborate best with groups they know but have not necessarily worked with, as opposed to perfect strangers." In her experience, "The best way to approach collaboration is not to have a generic conversation about 'how wonderful it would be to collaborate one of these days,' but to say, 'We have a grant application that we all need to work on together that is due on such-and-such date.'" But at least one funder disagrees. "We don't want collaborations that spring up just for funding. If groups have been working together in the past, let the funder know it."

Build your relationships with grantmakers. Grantmakers noted that not-for-profits should make the most of their relationships with funders. One said, "Relationships do matter enormously. It's about trusting you with their money, [knowing that] you can do quality work and be honest in what you say and do." And these relationships matter most in hard times. In response to Katrina, for example, one funder in the New Orleans area said, "We didn't wait for proposals, because the local groups were so overwhelmed. We went out to the shelters, assessed the need ourselves, and made grants immediately, without proposals. Now we're back to our normal process, reviewing proposals and making grants bimonthly." And after Hurricane Sandy, the executive director of a small but well-respected organization in an affected area reported that she had received calls from a number of foundations that knew her organization had the capacity to provide critical relief in its community. As one grantmaker said, "We know who the great groups are—the ones who can handle the money in this situation."

Seize the Moment

As we spoke to funders for each edition, we noticed that even after disasters, some people were trying hard to shine a positive light on things. So we asked this question, even thinking it was a little too Pollyanna-ish: "If a crisis really yields opportunity, as some optimists claim, how would you suggest that grant seekers seize the moment?" Believe it or not, we got some enthusiastic replies. Most of the following comments were made as we prepared earlier editions of the book, but the responses hold true today.

This is a good time to focus on your image. One funder wondered, "How can we take advantage of the [economic] climate to be more vibrant?" Another suggested that it would be a good time for organizations to "tweak their public image—ask colleagues, friends, and relatives whether they think their organizations are presenting themselves—websites, social media, mailed materials, events—in the best light. People not in the field or not involved in an organization's day-to-day activities often have very perceptive things to say. And they may be more willing to say these things now that there seems to be so much at stake."

Along the same lines, a panelist suggested that everyone who works for an organization should have a 10- to 20-second "elevator speech." "If you meet someone at a party or on the bus—or on an elevator—you have no idea who they are (they could be one of those 'hedge fund guys'!), or who they know (they could know a 'hedge fund guy')." "If you can talk about your organization in a clear, concise, heartfelt way, the person you meet may go back to the office and search for more information about the organization because of that very convincing elevator speech. This person may know someone halfway across the world who would be interested in what you are doing." "Thanks to the Internet, interested strangers really *can* find out about your organization in no time at all!" Similarly, another funder suggested, "Get nominated for something. Win awards. Give speeches. Sit on panels. Write blogs. Money is still out there. People are still giving dollars away. Their hearts are still moved." "Develop a public voice," said a panelist. "This is especially true in difficult economic times. Call attention to your work. Write articles."

Comb through your budgets for cost savings. Finally, a foundation grantmaker reminded us that "groups tend to be good at the 'fundraising side' rather than the 'cost-saving side'—that not-for-profits are really built for growth." A difficult funding climate is a good time to address the cost-saving side, with an eye toward streamlining organizations, making them run better and more efficiently in good times and bad.

In Closing

It is not surprising that, in good times and bad, grantmakers want to make sure that organizations applying for grants really, really need the money. They also want to be certain that the money they give will be spent wisely and make an impact. Funders are looking hard at this concern and trying to figure out thoughtful ways of measuring impact. You should be doing the same thing! But be careful. If you're trying to make an impact by being entrepreneurial and innovative, don't lose sight of your group's mission and constituency. Remember who you are and whom you serve.

And remember that grantmakers always are looking for "more bang for the buck." Why wouldn't they? It is up to those writing a grant proposal to show them that you understand the current economic, political, and social climate, that you aren't living in a state of denial, that you don't expect it to be business as usual.

To conclude this roundtable, we have selected two sentiments expressed by grantmakers that can propel you forward in any economic climate:

"You can't wait for a savior. You're a savior."

"Without grantees, we just have money. Grantees are our clients."

PART I

PREREQUISITES

"I JUST GOT A THIRD-GRADE TEACHING JOB IN MIAMI. I need a car to get to school but there's no way I can afford one now. How about a grant? Can I get some funding for a used Prius?"

No.

"My uncle is dying to visit his long-lost cousin in Rome. Can he get a grant to cover the airfare at least? It would mean so much to him."

No.

"I just got married and I don't even know how to boil water! Can I get a grant to study the basics at a cooking school near my house? It would save my marriage."

No.

"My bicycle was stolen."

"I need a dental implant."

"I'm desperate for a smart TV."

No. No. No.

Now, more than ever, the word "grant" is tossed into more conversations than Instagram and Twitter combined. Grants are hot. Just attend a grant-writing workshop anywhere and see the room fill with people from every profession. Grants are exciting—money usually is—and completely misunderstood. Mostly, we hear about grants that have been won, not about grants that have been lost. And we rarely hear how time consuming the grant proposal was to develop and write. Instead, we (*think* we) hear that someone dashed off a grant proposal, pressed the send button, and miraculously got a whopping big check in the mail a few days later.

Recent years have seen a huge increase in applications for non-profit status, apparently because many people believe that all you need to do to get grant money—or get a paid job for something you're doing as a volunteer—is to incorporate as a not-for-profit organization and that there's plenty of money out there for the asking. It seems as if these applicants haven't been listening to the news. We don't want to be discouraging, but if you are one of these new applicants, we urge you to take a step back and look at *who you are, when and why you should look for grants,* and *from whom you should look for grants* before you decide to invest the time, energy, and money that it takes to incorporate, get your nonprofit status, and write your first proposal.

Notice that we said *write your proposal.* We didn't say *win a grant.* Excellent proposals and programs often do not get funded (and awful ones occasionally do) for a variety of different reasons—politics of all sorts, for instance; or the kinds of natural and man-made disasters we've been experiencing, which force some grantmakers to reallocate their resources; or the impact of stock market movement on the portfolios of foundation grantmakers, as occurred during the Great Recession and in less dramatic fluctuations since then. Or they just don't get funded because resources are limited in proportion to the number of applicants. For example, one huge foundation recently received some 40,000 proposals; it awarded 1,400 grants. So the proposal has to be excellent in order to have half a chance of winning any money. And even if you don't win a grant at first, the proposal lets the reviewers form an impression of you and your organization that could help you (or hurt you) when you apply the next time.

Like the lottery, you have to be in it to win it. But unlike the lottery, in the world of grants it is not enough just to be in it. Your application has to be strong; it should represent you and your organization in the best possible light. If you can't do that—because you don't have enough time or enough help to put the proposal together—then *do not apply*, at least not now. Waiting until next year, or next month, is sometimes the smartest thing you can do. Submitting a poorly thought-out, poorly developed, poorly written proposal is sometimes the most damaging thing you can do to your long-term prospects.

LESSON 1

WHO AM I (AND WHAT IN THE WORLD DO I WANT TO DO)?

OPENING REMARKS

More than 20 years ago, the US Department of Education announced that it would fund innovative parent centers to be housed in public school buildings. These centers were supposed to be developed and run by parents, and the types of activities available to parents would be chosen by—you guessed it—parents. To apply for this grant, applicants had to be not-for-profit organizations, not schools. I was a beginning grant writer at the time, and I was assigned to write a proposal for a small parents' organization whose name I can't remember. As I was completing the grant application and getting ready to mail it to Washington, DC, I noticed that it asked for proof of not-for-profit status. I knew nothing about this. I figured these parents surely weren't making a profit, so they obviously had not-for-profit status. What proof did they need except my word? I was wrong. My proposal was disqualified by the Department of Education. No one even read it. —EK

LEADING QUESTIONS

Who Am I?

It is important to know who and what you are before you start trying to raise money. Organizations come in all shapes and sizes, and
they raise money for a wide variety of purposes, from beautifying
city blocks or fielding a Little League team to providing services for
elderly people with Alzheimer's or creating shelters for victims of
domestic violence. Organizations fall roughly into three categories,
with a few subcategories, although there's a lot of overlap. Who you
are and what you want to do pretty much determine where you need
to go for money.

Grassroots organizations usually are small, very local groups
such as block and tenant associations, neighborhood improvement
groups, and merchants' associations. Many do not bother with a formal organization structure, or they may have a minimal structure—a
leadership committee or maybe elected officers. Their interests may
involve block or building security, neighborhood beautification, activities for local preschoolers, or bringing neighbors together for a
holiday party. The kinds of things they want to get funding for might
include walkie-talkies for a block-watchers' group; uniforms, equipment, and perhaps rental of a field for sports activities; buses to take
kids on trips to a museum, a ball game, or the Statue of Liberty; or
money for decorative planters, benches, or other street furniture.

Small grassroots organizations may be able to raise the few hundred or few thousand dollars they need through dues, door-to-door
collections, raffles, bake sales, block parties, flea markets, or donations from local businesses. As they grow, they may start looking
for foundation or government grants to help support their expansion, and to do this they may need to become officially recognized
nonprofit organizations (the parents in our opening remarks were
a grassroots group). Sometimes new grassroots organizations make
the mistake of seeking grants before they are quite ready. Although

certain fundraising activities (such as bake sales) may be appropriate at an early stage in an organization's life, successful proposals for
foundation and government grants must come later.

As panelists noted in Roundtable I, many of the smallest organizations are likely to find funding scarce in times of natural disaster or
economic turmoil. If you are just starting out, you may have to continue relying on volunteers for another few years, or you may want
to consider merging with one or more like-minded groups to create
an organization with greater capacity to carry out your mission (we'll
talk about capacity in Lesson 14).

Social service agencies and other service providers are either *not-for-
profit* (also called nonprofit) organizations, local *government agencies*, or
for-profit businesses set up to address the needs of groups of people of all
ages and types: children (day care, education, after-school programs,
literacy, arts, recreation); teenagers (education, violence prevention,
pregnancy and substance-use prevention, sports, arts and cultural
activities, preparation for high school or college entrance exams,
employment readiness and placement); older adults (senior centers,
home care services); families (citizenship education and immigration
counseling, legal services, domestic-violence prevention, services to
families with children returning home from foster care, employment
training and placement, adult education, language training); communities (police, sanitation, health, environmental protection, disaster
planning, housing/shelter); or the city or region (transportation, water,
sewage). These organizations range in size from a volunteer or paid
staff of one or two serving a very small neighborhood area to huge,
citywide, regional, or even national agencies.

Within the social service category, community-based organizations are groups of any size, whether incorporated or not, whose
mission is to serve the particular geographic or ethnic community
in which they are located rather than an entire city. Cultural institutions (libraries, museums) are one type of service provider and
also may vary dramatically in size. Universities and hospitals may be

among the largest nonprofit, for-profit, or government-run service providers in a community.

Some not-for-profit social service organizations may operate one small program (say, caring for a few young children); larger nonprofits and government agencies may run dozens of programs for all ages and needs. Their funding needs may range from a few hundred to many millions of dollars, and they need to raise money from a number of different sources, including individual donors, private foundations, corporations, and government funding agencies. Some also operate for-profit programs or businesses to help diversify their funding. (We'll discuss some of these enterprises in Lesson 18.)

If service providers are nonprofit groups—as opposed to government agencies—they usually are incorporated under state laws (like any other corporation) and receive tax-exempt status from the Internal Revenue Service. You may hear the term *501(c)(3)*,[2] which refers to the section of the Internal Revenue Code that authorizes this type of organization, or the term *determination letter*, which is the document from the IRS stating that you're tax exempt. You use state

---

[2] 501(c) is the section of the code that authorizes and defines tax-exempt organizations. Subsection 501(c)(3) requires that the organization "be organized and operated exclusively" for defined public purposes "that are beneficial to the public interest," including "relief of the poor...advancement of religion, advancement of education or science," and numerous other activities. Private foundations and public charities also come under this section of the code. Organizations that are tax exempt under this section generally are not permitted to lobby, although they are permitted to circulate information that is nonpartisan in nature. There are other kinds of not-for-profit corporations under the code. The somewhat controversial Section 501(c)(4), for example, governs civic leagues and social welfare organizations such as volunteer fire companies and community associations; 501(c)(5) governs labor, agricultural, and horticultural organizations; 501(c)(6) governs business associations such as chambers of commerce; and 501(c)(7) addresses social and recreational clubs such as college alumni associations, fraternities and sororities, garden clubs, and so on. Churches and other religious organizations, certain schools and colleges, certain hospitals, government units, and certain other entities are established as public charities under another section of the code, Section 501(a)(1).

incorporation papers or an IRS determination letter to prove you're a nonprofit because most foundations and government funders only give to such organizations. (By the way, the terms nonprofit and not-for-profit are used interchangeably in common discussion, but the latter is the technical term in the law and recognizes that the purpose of an organization is "not for profit," although the organization could show a budget surplus or—in its dreams—maintain significant financial reserves.)

As the footnote indicates, many kinds of not-for-profit corporations are defined under the Internal Revenue Code. Nevertheless, 501(c)(3) is the section that covers most social service organizations and the one you most need to be aware of. Contributions to 501(c)(3)s are tax deductible, so individual donors as well as foundations and government entities are more inclined to fund this type of organization. So if you do not represent a 501(c)(3), before you think about getting a grant, you need to think about whether you want to spend the money for lawyers and go through the organizing effort and the paperwork required to form a nonprofit corporation. Although it is possible for an organization to do this on its own (start with your state's secretary of state or department of state and the nearest IRS office), we strongly recommend that you use a lawyer. In many communities a private attorney may provide the service at low cost or for free ("pro bono"). There also are organizations like the Legal Services Corporation or Lawyers in the Public Interest that have local offices and can either advise you on the process or refer you to an attorney who can help.

It may take quite a while to prepare the paperwork necessary for a 501(c)(3) application and for incorporation. It can also take a few months for the Internal Revenue Service to begin to review the documentation, so you should allow enough time for the process to be completed.

But we should remind you that, especially in these times, you should think twice about incorporating just to get grants. Because governments are likely to continue cutting back on their giving and contracting—at least for a few more years—and foundations will not be able to provide enough support to close any gaps, grantmakers are becoming more strategic in their approach, and a new organization may not be well positioned for this. It will be cheaper and perhaps smarter to focus on working with other organizations that have been around a while and have a track record. As we said earlier, just because an organization has completed its paperwork and receives its designation as a 501(c)(3) doesn't mean that winning grants will suddenly become easy. Grantmakers look very hard at potential grantees, and the vast majority of them expect to see a significant track record, a committed board of directors (who provide some financial support themselves), fiscal health, talented leadership, a clear vision, the capacity to implement programs, and the ability to sustain projects, activities, staff, and programs that are grant funded. New 501(c)(3)s have a way to go before they can count on winning grants.

Advocacy groups, which funders say are more important than ever, may be local, regional, citywide, national, or international. They are interested in specific issues, such as trying to convince government agencies to provide more funding for after-school education, or charter schools, or children with disabilities; trying to protect the environment; prohibit abortion; promote low-income housing; support transsexual rights; or make marijuana legal for recreational as well as medical purposes. They may be incorporated as not-for-profit organizations but usually are not 501(c)(3)s because this section of the law specifically prohibits tax-exempt organizations from lobbying the government in most situations. Some foundations will fund their activities, but many are unable to do so. Advocacy groups usually need to raise money from individuals and other organizations that care about their causes. They do submit proposals for grants to those foundations that may share their interests, but are more likely to use mailings, the Internet, social media, telephone solicitation, and other individual approaches for their fundraising.

Advocacy groups normally do not receive funding from government agencies either, but there may be exceptions. Each funding agency makes its priorities clear, and you should seek out funders who want and are able to give grants to the type of organization with which you're involved and the type of project you want to implement. We will talk again and again about how important it is to target appropriate funders based on both what kinds of projects and programs you want to get funded and what kind of organization you are.

Individuals—for example, artists, writers, filmmakers, scholars—are generally interested in getting grants that will fund their projects. They may be associated with a university, research hospital, or cultural institution, which is likely to be the grant recipient, although the individual prepares the proposal. Other individuals seek support for independent projects. Research is costly and time-consuming. Shooting a film (and editing it) costs a fortune. We will talk about specific grants for individuals, how some artists form not-for-profit organizations so they can become eligible for a range of grants, and how others connect with existing not-for-profits that can act as a fiscal conduit (we'll talk about this later too) for foundation and government grants.

Who Gets the Grant?

Grants generally are directed to specific types of organizations. Some federal grants, for example, may be awarded only to a local or state government agency, local education agency (LEA: a board of education, school district, etc.), or institution of higher education. If these are the only eligible applicants for a specific type of funding, other organizations need not apply.

Most private foundations that require a 501(c)(3) do not fund government agencies, although some government agencies have set up their own not-for-profits or work closely with existing not-for-profits in order to accomplish shared goals. The Los Angeles Fire Department Foundation, for instance, supports the Los Angeles Fire Department and was very active during the recent catastrophic fires in California. In New York City, the Police Foundation is a 501(c)(3) that raises money for the police department. The city's Parks Department works closely with the nonprofit Central Park Conservancy to raise supplementary funding for Central Park. Some cities have their own citywide not-for-profits that raise money for special initiatives and for agencies that don't have their own 501(c)(3)s or are not closely associated with local not-for-profit organizations.

There are many legal ramifications for this kind of operation, not the least of which is a real or perceived conflict of interest. For example, a conflict may arise if the 501(c)(3) of a municipality or a government agency receives funds from a corporate source that it is expected to regulate or if the 501(c)(3) is perceived by the public as a way of getting around the city's own funding rules in order to help political allies. This means that the option must be explored thoroughly with attorneys before it is pursued. If you work for a municipal government agency and want to raise private dollars, check with your budget office or legal department to see how it can be done.

POP QUIZ

Throughout this book we will be giving you brief quizzes to let you check what you've learned in each lesson. Answers to the pop quizzes are found in Appendix 6.

Multiple Choice

Select the best answer for each of the following questions:

1. Which is the best example of something that a small grassroots organization might be likely to get a grant or donation to pay for?
    a. Uniforms for the local Little League team
    b. A neighborhood day-care center
    c. A community science and technology museum
    d. A citywide literacy program for immigrants

2. A document known as a 501(c)(3) is:
    a. A license to raise money
    b. Proof of not-for-profit status
    c. A description of a certain kind of government grant
    d. A way for individual donors to hide their true identity

3. Most foundations give grants only to:
    a. Not-for-profit organizations of all kinds
    b. Cultural and arts institutions
    c. Municipal and state governments
    d. Social service agencies and organizations

4. Why is it so important to "know who you are" before writing a proposal?
    a. Because not every person or organization is eligible for every grant
    b. Because you may not be eligible for any grant at all
    c. Because you may need to do a few important things before applying for a grant
    d. All of the above are good reasons

Essay Questions

Take 15 to 30 minutes to mull over the following questions. You may want to write out a paragraph or two and save the brief essay to develop in later lessons.

1. Who are you? Briefly describe your organization and place it in the range of organizations described in this lesson.

2. What single project or activity do you think you or your organization may need money for?

WAIT A SECOND—WHAT IS A GRANT...AND WHERE DO I GET ONE?

OPENING REMARKS

A man called me to find out how he could get a federal grant to build a radio station in his basement to air his music collection. He was sure there was money out there. But he had no organization, no plan, no budget…no, no, no. There is a misconception about grants—that just because grants are available, everybody should apply for one. After all, who couldn't use the money? But the truth is that there are times when you really don't need money. You need volunteers; or student teachers, student lawyers, or student social workers; or donated computers or secondhand books. Or simply a friend to give you a hand in getting a job done. And even if you do need money, there are plenty of fine individuals, organizations, and ideas that have legitimate money needs that are not the least bit appropriate for any kind of grant at all. Sure, you may be able to raise cash through bake sales or raffles, through benefits or scholarships, through donations or gifts. But spend the time and energy to win a grant? Don't bother. —ASF

LEADING QUESTIONS

What Is a Grant?

A grant is an award of money that allows you to do very specific things, usually according to very specific guidelines that are spelled out in painstaking detail and to which you must respond very clearly in your grant proposal.

How Do I Know If I Need a Grant?

At first you may not even know if you need a grant. Before you let dollar signs start dancing in your head, you must have a problem that you (and your organization) want to solve, decide what you need to do to solve it, and figure out how much that might cost. You may work at the YMCA and feel that there is a serious opioid problem in your community that you would like to address through a weekend camping and drug prevention education program for teenagers at the Y. Maybe you're a pediatrician and have noticed a growing number of asthma cases among your preschool patients and want to find out why, or you're a third-grade teacher perplexed by bullying during the school day and you want to get expert help to change this climate. Or you may live on a street where all the trees died of Dutch elm disease and you want to plant new, more resistant ones. Or you want to make a film or compose a symphony or study abroad or write a biography. The question is: What do you have to do to get the results you want?

Some organizations have learned that chasing grants can take them away from their core mission or move an excellent program in the wrong direction (this is called "mission creep"). Funders have constantly reminded us that most successful programs and organizations are not grant driven, they are mission driven. In other words, they are not created, massaged, and manipulated to fit the precise guidelines of a grant that just happens to be available. Rather, you have strong, comprehensive, well-developed programs or plans that show you have made good use of all other available resources. If money is needed to implement or supplement a well-designed program, that is where a grant comes in. But the program is the thing. The better designed the program is to address the need, and the more other funding you have raised or resources you have found to support it, the more likely you are to win grants. The same thing is true for individuals. Some people don't have a commitment to a topic for a film or book; they just have a commitment to getting a grant. But it has to be the other way around, of course.

When Money's Scarce, Aren't Grants Even More Important?

We won't lie to you. At the time of this writing, for various political and economic reasons, we are facing very uncertain times for grant seekers, to put it mildly. Although the economy has improved dramatically since the Great Recession of 2008, the intense debate on the federal budget and additional cuts and expected cuts at the federal level—aggravated in some cases by budget deficits at the state and local levels—have thrown a dark cloud over nonprofit and government service providers, researchers, businesses, and many others assisted by government funding. And, as we noted earlier, many economists (and grantmakers) are expressing concerns about the very real possibility of another recession.

Furthermore, also as noted earlier, cuts at the federal level are likely to lead to additional cuts in spending at all government levels because so much federal money flows through state and local agencies. This means less money for all kinds of projects, from the smallest to the largest.

We aren't trying to scare you; we just want you to think realistically and strategically about resources in coming years. If you're operating primarily with government or foundation grants, it's time to work on diversifying your funding plan to include other resources. We urge you to broaden your support through fundraising mechanisms such as appeals, events, sponsorships, social media, social enterprises (which we discuss in Lesson 18), and even fees from participants if your target population can support small payments.

Most importantly, we believe that no matter how bad the funding climate is, there still will be opportunities for government grants and contracts. It's just that when money is scarce you need to be even more proactive in finding and winning funds to keep your programs going.

Grants and your mission. All fundraising should flow from and support your mission. Remember that it's one thing to do everything in your power to find grants to support your agency's programs; it's something else entirely to pursue grants that distract you from your core mission. If you provide services for senior citizens and then suddenly decide to apply for grants for preschoolers just because there's money available, you may dilute your organization's effectiveness—and raise questions in grantmakers' minds about your strategies.

If community needs are driving you to expand your services, you must do so in a thoughtful, systematic way—never losing sight of your mission. If you are a senior center and know that the community needs children's programs (which no other organization provides), you may think about creating intergenerational activities (bringing together children and seniors) that do not take you so far afield that funders question your ability to do what you say you're going to do. After you have successfully created and operated the intergenerational programs for a while, you may find it easier—and the grantmakers will find it more credible—to branch out into other activities for children.

THE FUNDERS

The federal government and state and local governments give grants (often in the form of contracts) that generally require paperwork, audits, and accountability. Private foundations and corporations give grants. Individuals give grants, usually through a fund or trust set up for that purpose and administered by a bank or foundation.

In many areas of the country, a regional association of grant-makers (RAG) may publish a standard or common application form that grant seekers can use for all participating foundations in that area (many RAGs also publish a common report form). These forms incorporate headings that structure the way the proposal is written and the information that must be included. The forms differ a bit from area to area but are strikingly similar in content. All require the proposer to state a need, describe the program, present a rational budget, provide supporting materials that indicate the organization's capacity to implement the program, and document the organization's not-for-profit status. Each foundation may require additional information, and some no longer use such a form because it does not fit their needs.

Nevertheless, you should see if there is a common application form in use in your area and treat it as a guide or model for your proposals when a foundation you're interested in doesn't provide its own model. You can find common application forms online; a sample appears in Appendix 4.

Government grants are generally announced through requests for proposals (RFPs), notices of funding availability (NOFAs), funding opportunity announcements (FOAs), or other notices that specify the nature and cost of the program that must be proposed. Some government grants allow applicants a substantial amount of leeway to propose programs that address their organizations' specific needs; others are very prescriptive. All include guidelines, due dates, and so much required information that you will start to wonder why the grantmakers don't just write the proposal themselves.

Foundations, on the other hand, tend to be less prescriptive. Most foundations do not issue RFPs, although some large ones, like the Robert Wood Johnson Foundation, may do so (in this case labeled Calls for Proposals, or CFPs, that define the challenges it wants to address). Others may publish requirements that are as specific as the RFP for any government grant.

Foundations

Foundations range in size from tiny family foundations with no staff (grant decisions are made by family members) and budgets under $100,000 to huge organizations that have dozens of professional staff members and give away millions each year. Foundations are an impressive and constantly growing source of funding. Between 2000 and 2015 (the latest available information), the number of foundations grew from 56,582 to 86,203, and giving increased from $27.56 billion to $62.8 billion. To tap into this resource, you must understand the differences among them. This will save you a good deal of time and energy in preparing proposals.

Family foundations. Family foundations often have narrowly focused giving patterns based on the intentions of the donor or the interests of current family members who are officers or trustees. Many do not accept unsolicited proposals, some because they are too small to review large numbers of proposals, others because their giving is earmarked for specific organizations.

Independent private foundations. This type of foundation usually has at least a small professional staff. It may have begun as a family foundation but is no longer controlled by the original donor or the donor's family. This does not mean that the donor's interests are ignored. Private foundations are ethically and, in most cases, legally bound to follow the donor's intent to the extent possible. If the terms of the original endowment or bequest said the money was to be used solely for organizations that train opera singers, that's what it is used for. The only discretion that the trustees have in making grants is, perhaps, selecting the best organizations to do the training. If the terms of the endowment are a bit broader—say, for health services for children from low-income families—many creative projects may be eligible for a grant.

Federated funds. Federated funds like the United Way were created to benefit the community by pooling donations from individuals and businesses and using those funds to support nonprofit organizations. Unlike independent and family foundations, which draw primarily on funds from a single donor or an endowment and do not seek funding from the public, federated funds maintain ongoing fundraising operations.

Corporate foundations. Corporate, or company-sponsored, foundations are independent entities created by large corporations with funds from the businesses themselves or from their founders. Most corporate foundations function like other foundations, receiving proposals and making grants, but their giving may be somewhat tied to the corporation's own goals. For example, a drug company's foundation may be established to fund medical research; a bank's foundation may fund community development.

Community foundations. In every state in the United States and in Puerto Rico, there are one or more (usually many more; the total tops 650) local foundations called community foundations, community trusts, or community funds. Community foundations have been set up to administer individual trust funds or pools of funds from individual donors who want to benefit their own city or region but don't want to create a new foundation. To determine whether there is a community foundation in your area, search "community foundation" and your city, county, or state; check with your local library; or go to a listing at the website of the Grantsmanship Center (discussed later in this lesson and in Appendix 5).

A community foundation or community trust probably includes funds set up by donors with very specific purposes in mind as well as others with more general purposes. Living donors to such foundations may be able to recommend which organizations should receive grants. Under regulations governing the establishment of donor-directed funds, the final determination must be made by the foundation, but most program officers try to accommodate the donors' wishes.

Financial institutions. Financial institutions always have administered charitable trusts set up for the donors' purposes; a trend toward this type of trust is growing. Proposals to a trust held at a financial institution often are made in the same way as proposals to foundations.

How do you find the right foundation? As noted, most foundations were established to give money to causes that were of interest to their original donors, which means that some give to very narrowly defined programs—for example, medical research on a particular disease; mental health services for teenagers affected by the Parkland, Florida, and other school shootings; or a visual arts program for senior citizens—while some give money to address a wide range of social, medical, or cultural issues. Some give primarily to support religious purposes; some will not consider giving for religious purposes. A few give to individuals; most do not. Some foundations give only within designated geographic areas; others give nationally or globally. There is a foundation for every purpose, and you have to find the right one for you.

There are two extraordinary resources for organizations seeking foundation grants: the Foundation Center and The Grantsmanship Center. Their focus differs slightly (e.g., the Foundation Center includes extensive services for foundations as well as for nonprofits while The Grantsmanship Center focuses on training and support for nonprofits), but both organizations provide a wealth of information, training, and other assistance online and on-site, some free, some for a fee. Although there is considerable overlap among the information and services you'll get from these organizations, it's worth learning what each provides; then use the one you find most useful for your needs.

- *Foundation Center.* Your first stop is the Foundation Center, the older of the two resources. Its main hub is in New York City, with regional hubs in Atlanta, Cleveland, Washington, DC, and San Francisco, and with more than 450 Funding Information Network sites in public libraries, community foundations, universities, and nonprofit organizations across the United States and in other countries.[3] There are at least two cooperating collections (usually more) in every state. These maintain Foundation Center publications and may provide free research capability even though the Foundation Center Online requires paid subscriptions for much of its content. There's a map at www.grantspace.org/Find-Us that will provide the location nearest you.

The Foundation Center provides information and other support to foundations, researchers in the field of philanthropy, and grant seekers, as well as training and tools to find resources and apply for grants. Every grant seeker should become familiar with its materials and tools. Most important are the Foundation Directory and the Foundation Directory Online (see notes in Appendix 5), but there are many other directories that describe foundations and corporations by location, program interests, size of grants given, and many other characteristics, as well as foundation annual reports. These references will let you identify grantmakers in your area, find out what kinds of activities they prefer to fund, determine the general dollar amounts of the grants they offer, define eligibility, and locate the addresses, telephone numbers, and names of appropriate contacts at the foundations. Your local library may be able to get these Foundation Center materials for you or may have other reference materials that will help you locate foundations in your city or region.

• **The Grantsmanship Center.** The other very valuable resource on grants is The Grantsmanship Center (TGCI), which provides

---

[3] The Foundation Center recently merged with Guidestar (an organization that provides potential donors with useful financial and other information about nonprofit organizations). The new nonprofit organization is called Candid, which will incorporate the functions of both. As we write, both of the original websites remain available, and we use those, but the new organization is working to create a single website incorporating information from both. Both of the original organizations and Candid now charge fees for most services.

technical assistance and training to nonprofit organizations. Most of its extensive training and subscription services now require fees that can be substantial, but at least one of the most useful sections of its website, a map that lets you search for funders by state, is still free (Appendix 5). Based in Los Angeles, TGCI offers training programs in many locations across the country, including a five-day workshop on finding and preparing grant proposals. Other two- to five-day workshops teach proposal preparation for research grants, preparing federal proposals, nonprofit management topics, and more. The center publishes materials on grants (including its own excellent *Program Planning & Proposal Writing* guide) as well as on grants administration and other topics useful to managing and supporting nonprofit organizations.

Approaching foundations. Before you submit a proposal to a foundation, you would be very wise to check its website (if there is one; many foundations are not online) or call or write for its annual report, grant application form or guidelines (if it has any), descriptions of programs it has funded recently, and any other information you can get. (Most, if not all, of this should be online through one source or another.) Your proposal is likely to be rejected automatically if it doesn't meet the recipient's guidelines. *Much* more about this later. Oh, and by the way, when you're checking out the foundation's guidelines, you would be wise to make a note of the current contact person's name, email address, and phone number, and find out whether the foundation wants you to contact it by mail, phone, or email. As you'll hear again and again from the funders we interviewed, they get annoyed when you send requests to their predecessors!

Foundations, like all 501(c)(3) organizations, are required to submit tax returns called 990s, which almost always include a list of organizations the foundation has funded during that tax year and the amounts of money given to each. Some foundations, although not all, include the particular program for which each grant was given.

The 990s are available at the Foundation Center Online; as of this writing, you can find them for free.

It is helpful to know what kinds of organizations and projects each foundation *really* funds. For instance, a foundation may say that individuals and all types of not-for-profit organizations are eligible to apply for grants, but when you read its annual reports, you notice that this foundation has funded only medical schools—not their students—for the last five years. Another foundation may indicate in its guidelines that its average grants are between $100,000 and $200,000, so if your project will cost $350,000, you shouldn't expect to get it all from this foundation. If you ask for it anyway, do expect your request to irritate the grantmaker. And if you also notice in the annual report or the 990 that in the last three years this foundation hasn't actually funded anything for more than $50,000, far less than the minimum they specified, you probably should call to find out if they've changed their guidelines.

We should mention one foundation-initiated website that may be of interest; we'll discuss it a bit more in Appendix 5. Here we'll just note that the Center for Disaster Philanthropy has a website that may have information useful to organizations working to relieve communities that are struggling with the results of fires, hurricanes, and other natural disasters.

Although some foundations are interested in brand-new organizations and may even offer some technical assistance in preparing a proposal, most want to know that you know the ropes. Let the foundation see that you are aware of its work, that you have studied the annual report, that you have looked at the organizations and individuals that it has funded, and that you are making a careful decision to apply based on all your homework. Never be shy about letting the grantmaker see why you chose it and the amount of research you have completed to ensure that there are no holes in your proposal.

Businesses

Corporations and local businesses may fulfill their civic responsibilities through grants and sponsorships to nonprofit organizations.

Keep in mind that in a bad economy, many businesses may cut back on their giving. But when they can help, there is tremendous diversity in the amount and type of support that corporations offer. National corporations may give only or predominantly to national organizations, or they may give only in the cities where they have their business offices or factories. Some give to organizations supported by their own employees. A corner drugstore may sponsor the Little League team from a three-block area—which might mean buying T-shirts with the team's name (and the drugstore's logo). Businesses may give only to major cultural institutions, universities, hospitals, or other large organizations with a strong fundraising track record, or they may be interested in supporting small local groups in a specific region. Their decisions may be made by top management, a marketing department, their own internal giving offices, corporate philanthropy or corporate responsibility departments, or independent foundations.

Although philanthropy is important for its own sake to many corporations, it is usually tied to business concerns as well. If you can show how a grant to your organization will bring broad recognition or publicity to the donor, even the most public-spirited company will be pleased.

Business donors or sponsors are often a good place for a small organization to begin seeking funding and establishing a track record in using these gifts—and your board members should be involved in this effort. Start with your local bank branch. Ask the manager if the bank provides assistance to a group like yours and what you have to do to apply for it. Call every major business located in your community to see if the company has a giving program. If you know a business leader well, ask for suggestions about where to go for help. When you are ready to go to a major corporation, you can find lists of companies near you at the Foundation Center or Grantsmanship Center website.

Local civic associations, such as the Chamber of Commerce, Lions Club, Rotary, and Kiwanis, often have giving programs or provide sponsorships for local organizations. Remember that each civic organization has its own priorities—children, seniors, people with visual impairments—and is more likely to be interested in helping you if the program you operate falls within its guidelines. If managers or board members of your organization join such civic associations, they may make important connections with business leaders in the community and promote the organization's programs. Don't expect any large gifts from businesses, at least to start, but do be prepared to use the proposal development methods that we describe in Part II.

Federal Grants

Like other grants, federal grants are made to accomplish some public purpose. The nature of the grant, the eligible recipients, the method of award, and the terms and conditions are specified in the legislation that creates each grant program and in detailed regulations that are either laid out in the statute or added by the funding agency. Some grants have relatively few restrictions while others are laden with significant limitations and extensive reporting requirements, based on the legislation. Nearly all the information you will need about the federal grants process, grant availability, and federal agencies' guidelines for applications is online at www.grants.gov, a site we'll describe briefly in Appendix 5.

Many not-for-profit organizations—and even local government agencies—are afraid of the work involved in obtaining (and reporting on) a federal grant.[4] But organizations that go to the trouble of researching and writing a winning federal proposal often find that the federal grant can offer substantial, stable, multiyear funding. Nonprofit organizations also gain credibility when applying for state, local, and foundation funding—as well as some breathing room in a multiyear grant to identify additional funding sources.

---

[4] Some years ago, one research effort demonstrated that federal proposals took more than 80 person-hours to prepare on average but that winning proposals took more than twice that amount of staff time.

We should note the federal government probably will continue a trend toward devolution that has increased in recent years: pushing funding out to state agencies, and sometimes to major cities, that it used to award directly to nonprofit organizations or local government agencies. Governments must still apply for such funding, but nonprofits will have to keep track of it and apply through their own states, cities, and school districts. Nevertheless, despite this process and despite our own concerns about the climate for federal funding in the next few years, we urge you to be alert to the possibility of appropriate federal grants in your overall fundraising plan.

It is important to get your hands on any grant information as early as possible to give you the maximum time needed to develop a proposal. Appendix 5 describes websites for the most important federal funding sources.

Elected officials. If you are pursuing federal grants, you also should visit the local office of your congressional representative and senators. Their staff have access to grant information and many will be happy to put you on a mailing or email list so they can send you this information. You also will want their support when you apply for a federal grant, so invite them to visit your organization and its programs and put them on your own mailing lists.

State and Local Government Grants

Some cities make grant information available free of charge to residents through a municipal library, government office, or other public information center. School systems may provide such grant information to staff, parents, and students. Large not-for-profit organizations are sometimes willing to share funding information with smaller ones, especially if they need to form partnerships to win grants. Not knowing what grants were available used to be a legitimate excuse for an organization or an agency that didn't seek funding. This is no longer true; the information is out there. And it is usually cost-free or close to it. It is developing the grant proposal that is now most challenging, not finding the grant opportunities.

Some states, and even some cities and counties, have an "e-grants" system in which you sign up via email and automatically receive notices in categories for which you've indicated an interest. However, in many places it may be harder to track down state and local grants information than it is for foundation or federal grants. Check with your library to see what reference sources are available, or begin to identify the state and local agencies that would be likely to fund your programs, and get in touch with the appropriate staff there (often you can be placed on a snail-mailing list for specific funding opportunities). In smaller states and municipalities this usually is fairly easy; it can take just a few phone calls. In larger states and cities, you may need to be very persistent in finding the right department.

State and local elected officials. Your local elected officials are an important resource for funding, and it's important that they know and respect your organization because they can help you find and obtain grants and because they themselves sometimes have small amounts of state or local funding to distribute at their discretion. Many elected officials have their own websites. If not, many localities publish listings of their names and addresses; again, your library will give you information on how to reach them.

Some state and local officials send out periodic grant listings. For example, the New York State Assembly leader publishes *Grants Action News* monthly, as a mailing and online (www.assembly.state .ny.us/gan); this publication describes current and recent New York State agency grants as well as some federal and foundation opportunities. Virtually all elected officials do mailings, so make sure you are on their mailing and/or email lists and read the mailings to see what committees your officials are on, what causes they are interested in, and sometimes the groups for which they have provided funding.

Funding from state and local elected officials probably will be relatively small, but every bit of funding can help, and if your local council member or state senator likes your organization, such an official can introduce you to other prospective funders. Also, if you are a new organization or program, this small amount of funding can be vital as seed money to show foundations and other funders that someone has confidence in you. As we will discuss later, funders like to give to programs that show some capacity; they want evidence that their grants will be well spent and that the organization is able to accomplish what the applicant promises.

So call and visit all your elected officials; follow them on Twitter, tweet them information on your programs, and invite them to events. Often their staff will attend, but they are the ones who will make funding recommendations so it pays to keep them informed. It may also be easier to get letters of support and/or commitment if they are already familiar with your work. In case you think we're exaggerating when we emphasize the need to call on your local elected officials for help, remember: It's their job. They care about improving the lives of their constituents. And when grant money pours into their communities, it can only be a plus for them.

Using the Internet

If you are one of the very few grant-seeking organizations that do not yet have Internet access, you'd better make this your highest priority. The cost is low and the benefits are significant to any organization, especially to the staff who need information to design programs and seek funding for them. Not only is grant information and exhaustive "best practices" information easily found online, but, increasingly, government and foundation grant applications must be submitted electronically. And there are search engines that will pay your organization (though only in pennies) to do your research on their site.

Moreover, if your organization doesn't have a website or access to social media, find a way to develop them. There are sites that allow you to create your own website and maintain it for very low monthly costs. Having your own website, Twitter account, and Facebook page puts the agency's name and work into a public space and gives you a certain level of credibility in this information age.

Appendix 5 describes some useful websites for finding grant opportunities; as noted earlier, the most important for you to explore are the Foundation Center Online (www.foundationcenter.org) and The Grantsmanship Center (https://www.tgci.com) for foundation research, and Grants.gov (http://www.grants.gov) for federal grants. Increasing numbers of state and local entities also are providing funding information online, but you often have to dig for it. The amount of information and ease of finding it varies from state to state. Some states have centralized sites that are easy to use. In others, if you dig a little deeper to specific agencies of interest (e.g., education, health, criminal justice), you will find many with their own funding sections that list their contacts and grant information. State and local agency sites also can be good sources for obtaining statistics and other information that you will need when writing your needs assessment (see Lesson 7).

Many community foundations, regional associations of grantmakers, and individual foundations have an online presence and are often rich with information that should be significant for grant seekers. For example, the Chicago Community Trust website offers "insights" into current issues in the region and nationally, and to philanthropy in general, through articles on a variety of topics and funding issues. It presents "stories" about work by its grantees and includes a listing of currently open requests for proposals by topic.

Some nonprofit "umbrella" organizations and other membership organizations that provide information and support (technical assistance) to nonprofits may conduct research on grant availability through routine daily searches. They will send out funding alerts to their members or subscribers in categories on which the recipients have expressed interest, such as youth or senior services. Ask at your library and other sources to see if a service like this is available in your area. And, of course, you can always ask google.com all sorts of questions about the availability of grants in your area—and just about anything else you want to know.

Publications and Newsletters

Many for-profit organizations sell newsletters and books providing information about federal grants. Some offer information on foundation and corporate grants as well. We have subscribed to or purchased these publications in the past but have found that our own online research produces results that are just as effective and as timely (or more so). However, some of them do discuss trends in government and foundation funding as well as current grant opportunities, so if you have a particular area of interest (such as youth funding or health care funding), you may want to try a free sample or even a year's subscription to one of these publications to see if it works for you. We prefer not to make any recommendations here, but we will say that some companies appear to do much more exhaustive research and seem to have more "insider information" about future funding prospects than others; we suggest you review them carefully before you subscribe.

You may want to check out a free publication online. *Philanthropy News Digest* (PND) is a Foundation Center newsletter (philanthropy newsdigest.org) that provides updates on trends and news in philanthropy and is searchable. PND also highlights an "RFP of the day" (and a "job of the day"), and it lets you sign up for alerts.

It's also a good idea to read the trade publications—magazines, newsletters, newspapers, professional journals, and blogs in your field of interest—so that your grant proposal reflects current trends and best practices. These publications may include lists of grant opportunities of interest to their readers.

Finding out what government and private grants are available is the easy part of the grant process. It shouldn't cost you a fortune, and it shouldn't take hours of your valuable time.

POP QUIZ

Multiple Choice

Select the best answer for each of the following questions:

1. Most requests for proposals (RFPs) include:
   a. A description of the program you must propose in order to win a grant
   b. Guidelines you must follow
   c. A due date for submission of the proposal
   d. All of the above are generally included in an RFP

2. Foundations are:
   a. Generally small
   b. Always run by an executive director and at least two staff members
   c. Unlikely to give grants of more than $15,000
   d. All shapes and sizes, with different priorities, guidelines, and purposes

3. When applying for foundation grants, you should:
   a. Know what kinds of organizations the foundation has funded, but never mention it
   b. Apply cold—without knowing anything about the foundation
   c. Know what kinds of organizations the foundation has funded and mention it when it's appropriate
   d. Ask for at least $10,000 more than the maximum amount of money a foundation says it gives, so you have room to negotiate

4. Federal government grant opportunities are:
   a. Not required to be announced anywhere
   b. Only announced on federal agency websites

    c. Always announced in the *Federal Register* or at Grants
      .gov

    d. Announced every two months in the Catalog of Federal Domestic Assistance (CFDA)

5. A good way for very small organizations to begin grant seeking is to apply for:
    a. Large federal government grants
    b. Middle-sized municipal grants
    c. Donations from local businesses
    d. Foundation grants

Essay Questions

Take 15 to 30 minutes to respond to the following essay questions, based on your answers to the essay questions at the end of Lesson 1 (you may want to write out your responses for future use). Include the following:

1. How much money do I need, realistically, to run my project?

2. What will the budget look like? Will the costs be primarily for staff, or consultants, or equipment and supplies?

3. What kind of funder (foundation, government, other) is most likely to provide the money I need?

4. Who are the three or four most likely funders for this project in this city or state?

MAKING (DOLLARS AND) SENSE OF GRANT-APPLICATION PACKAGES: WHAT GRANTMAKERS WANT

OPENING REMARKS

When I first started writing grant proposals to the federal government, I hardly paid any attention to the grant-application package. It was usually cumbersome and uninviting. The print was small, the pages packed with mysterious words in tiny print, bizarre numbering systems like (iii), and a slew of public laws that meant absolutely nothing to me. I would skim over the thing quickly and not look at the application again until I actually needed to write the proposal—weeks later.

One particular proposal I worked on was for a program for "out-of-school youth." Because I had never heard that term, I figured they were youth who were sometimes in school and sometimes not in school. Children who had chronic asthma, perhaps…or who played hooky (do they still say "hooky"?).

I wrote the proposal with my kind of out-of-school youth in mind—students who were absent a lot—and my proposal was disqualified the second it arrived at the US Department of Education headquarters. One intense month—days, nights, weekends—was wasted on a proposal for which my organization wasn't eligible. All because I did not read the dense, critically important application package that defined "out-of-school youth" in no uncertain terms: DROPOUTS. —EK

LEADING QUESTIONS

How Do I Get What I Need from the Grant Application Package?

No two application packages or proposal guidelines are the same. In previous editions of this book we analyzed a number of different sample applications from an array of federal and foundation grantmakers—most of which have changed or disappeared. These days, many things change rapidly—politics, economics, world events, unexpected calamities, and funders' priorities—and so do the availability, content, and format of grant applications that once were somewhat more predictable. So in this edition we're offering an overview of the most important things you need to know in order to get the most out of any application package you are confronted with.

Read the whole application (and all the guidelines) carefully. No matter what the funding climate is, grant applications vary wildly. Federal grant application packages are often huge—they can be 150 pages or more, with long, detailed, tables of contents. And, at the opposite end of the spectrum, at least one foundation grant notice we know of fits on a postcard. But don't be fooled by their length. Even the smallest package contains enough information to keep a proposal writer chained to the desk for days or weeks.

There is a tendency (as one of us knows well) to skim an application package, to speed-read it just as you might scan the eye-strain-inducing pamphlet that comes with your new allergy pills. With the latter, you ignore just about every other paragraph until you get to the part about your new drug causing death if taken with alcohol. *That* you read carefully. In a grant-application package, most people cut right to the chase—well, actually, three chases: the amount of money being given away, the questions that the applicant must answer in the grant proposal, and the deadline for submission. We'll get to why these items are critically important, but it is a mistake to cut to the chase. There is no chase; the whole package should be read carefully again and again. Each reading will reveal something you missed during an earlier reading. There just may be some concepts, words, or hints that, if taken to heart, will dramatically improve your chances of winning a grant.

Because application packages come in all shapes and sizes, it is obvious that they can't all contain exactly the same information organized in precisely the same way. But each package should answer a slew of important questions; you just have to know what to ask.

Common application form. This is a good place to remind you that some foundations require applicants to use a "common grant application" format (such as the Washington Regional Association of Grantmakers' Common Grant Application in Appendix 4). A common application is intended for use with every foundation in a region that accepts or requires it, but eligibility requirements are not specified and differ among the foundations that use the form. Clearly, grant seekers who plan to use a common application form still must go back to an individual foundation's website, annual report, and guidelines to be sure that they are eligible for grants from that foundation.

A Note on Using Technology

We know that most of our readers these days are very familiar with the Internet, so this won't be new to you. When we said earlier that you must become comfortable with the Internet, we were (mostly) talking about searching for grant opportunities and background information. But here's an equally important reason: More and more grantmakers are requiring that you submit your proposal online. Frequently they just want you to email the proposal and all attachments (although some attachments, such as your latest audited financials, can be mailed). But, increasingly, they provide a form for you to fill in at their websites, and usually there is a limit to the number of words the form accepts. (This can be *much* more of a challenge than keeping a proposal to a specified number of pages.) Most of these forms can be saved so you can return to finish or correct something you didn't get to when you started the process. But in a few cases, you have to finish the entire form at one sitting—or do it all over. You will need to know how to download or print the form from the website so you can fill it in by hand, then go back and fill it in online. Get familiar with the process; online applications will be even more common in coming years.

Am I Even Eligible to Apply for the Grant?

First and foremost, you must find out whether your organization is (or you are) eligible to apply for the grant described in the package. Somewhere deep in every application is a word or two—or 200— about eligibility. And even these words can be misleading!

An eligible applicant for a US Department of Education grant initiative that one of us applied for is "a local educational agency (LEA) or a consortium of LEAs that partner with their local public mental health, law enforcement, and juvenile justice agencies." The package indicated that the key to successful implementation is "partnership."

By the way, "local educational agency" was not defined until page 56 of the application in Appendix D: "A public board of education or other public authority legally constituted within a State for either administrative control or direction of, or to perform a service function for public elementary or secondary schools in a city, county, township." It is clear that if you were a small, neighborhood-based, grassroots after-school program, this would not be the grant for you— unless you worked with several much larger partners. We'll discuss how to do this in Lesson 10.

It's not unusual for foundations and corporations to establish geographic target areas, and extremely rare for them to give grants to organizations outside those boundaries.

As you read the eligibility requirements, you can look back at the exercises you completed earlier. Are you a government agency or a local educational agency—*as the package defines it*? Are you a not-for-profit organization with proof of your status? Are you located in the specified geographic area?

If you are clear about who you are but you can't make heads or tails of who you should be in order to compete for the grant (which sometimes happens with complicated requests for proposals from government agencies at all levels, but much less frequently with foundation guidelines), call the program officer whose name, telephone number, and/or email address appear in the package and ask about your eligibility. Sometimes you will have to address written questions to a fax number or email address, or leave messages in a voice mailbox. But don't get frustrated. Call again (and again) if you don't receive a response in a reasonable amount of time—say, 48 hours. Don't be shy; you have a right to know. But don't ever be rude, either. Remember, the people who develop, write, and oversee application packages and foundation guidelines take their work seriously and are likely to get offended if you call and say something like, "Why in the world would the West Kentucky Community Foundation refuse to give grants in Tennessee? It's not that far from Kentucky, right?" (This may sound silly, but, according to grantmakers, people say things like this all the time. So be forewarned.) If this foundation ever does decide to make grants in other parts of the area, your organization will find itself very low on its list of priorities!

Does My Idea for a Grant Mesh with the Grantmaker's?

This is where proposal writers can get snagged. Proposals are developed in response to a request for proposals (RFP), request for applications (RFA), or other guidelines issued by a grantmaking government agency or foundation. The RFP and RFA stipulate in no uncertain terms exactly what the grantmaker has in mind. A foundation's guidelines may be a lot less detailed and a little more flexible, but generally its priorities are equally clear. The grantmaker may not—no, almost certainly does not—care what you have in mind, unless it happens to mesh exactly with the terms of the RFP or guidelines.

You may need funding to start a chorus in a neighborhood day-care center. You may feel passionately about the importance of getting children excited about music at a very early age. Unfortunately, the RFP insists that the program this agency wants to fund in day-care centers must focus on computer technology and use of the Internet. You feel that the grantmaker is off base and would be wise to give money to the chorus. And you may be right. But don't give this grant any further thought. You may have research suggesting that little children are too young to fool around with computers—and should, instead, be singing. Don't bother. Not only will your grant be rejected, the program officer will think you are unable to read instructions, and this will put you at a serious disadvantage the next time you happen to apply.

But do bring your interests to the funders outside the grant cycle. If you want to discuss your point of view with the grantmaker, it is reasonable to call and ask whether there are plans for issuing RFPs for music anytime soon—and you can explain how excited you and your colleagues are about a children's chorus. For federal and some state and local grants, there is often a comment period during which you can express your opinion about their proposed guidelines. Furthermore, throughout the year, you (or, preferably, a coalition to which your organization belongs) are entitled to talk with elected officials and government agency representatives about needs that you see for your community or your target population.

What Projects Has the Grantmaker Funded Recently?

The Foundation Directory, among other references, generally lists the amounts of the largest grants given by a foundation in a recent year and the names of organizations that have received them. Government websites often list the winners of recent competitions. Application packages and funding guidelines also may mention past projects that have been funded by the grantmaker, especially if a foundation includes application information in its annual report. The annual report may organize grants into topics and include a brief description of the programs funded and the amount of funding. As discussed earlier, every private foundation and public charity is required to file an annual tax report (Form 990 or Form 990-PF, depending on how the organization is set up). The forms generally are just called 990s. They list the principals of the foundation, the foundation's resources, and its expenditures. Most foundations list the names of organizations or individuals that received grants and the amounts awarded; some also describe the project for which the grant was awarded and a contact person. Some include projects for which grants have been approved but not yet paid (such as the second year of a two-year grant).

Sometimes you will get lucky and an application package will not only provide useful tips but also include links to winning proposals that applicants would be wise to study carefully. It always makes sense to check out a grantmaker's website when you are thinking of applying for a grant because you never know what useful information you'll find that isn't in the application package.

Again, if you feel that the various descriptions, definitions, warnings, suggestions, and hints about what activities and purchases are allowable are unclear after several readings and discussions with colleagues, call or email the contact person listed in the application package. Don't try to guess what an "allowable activity" is—or, for that matter, what anything else is—because the likelihood is that you'll guess wrong!

How Much Money Is the Grant for, and Will It Cover My Expenses?

Proposal writers are often so excited about their projects that they lose sight of the sad truth that grantmakers do not have an unlimited amount of money to hand out, especially when there is a downturn in the economy (because income from investments drops), or when tax revenues are down and spending has been cut. Most grant announcements stipulate the approximate amount of funding that will be awarded. Some announcements just tell you what the total amount will be and approximately how many grants will be given, and let you do the math. Others give a maximum possible award or an estimate of the average award. Some, especially foundations, leave it to you to assess what a reasonable request will be.

Some foundations don't specify the maximum grant they will award, but they may describe different procedures for proposals requesting $500 and under (groups looking for small awards can use a short form); such grants may be easier to come by than if you make a larger request. Or the process may differ for those seeking, say, $50,000 and over, perhaps because the larger grants must be approved by the board of directors (and therefore also may take longer to be awarded). If a foundation has a procedure for larger awards, it gives you a clue that such grants are possible. But if you've never received a grant from this foundation before, you may want to be fairly modest in your request.

It is very tempting to ignore the amount of money that the grant-maker wants (or can afford) to give. After all, you need $50,000 and you can make a good case for why the project costs that amount. But think about it. If you told your daughter you were going to give her a generous graduation gift of a two-week trip to Venice and instead of kissing your feet she informed you that she would much prefer an eight-week African safari, how would you react?

Do I Have to Answer All Those Questions?

The short answer is yes. Many grant applications include a list of questions or topics that the applicant is expected to address in a specific number of pages—sometimes a specific number of pages for each question. Some requests for proposals even restrict the number of words per question. You may be asked to describe your program, explain the problem the program is addressing, how you will judge its impact, and how much it is expected to cost—in no more than

500 words. The proposal questions can be simple ("Tell us about your program") or complex ("Explain in detail how you will use the logic model in your program").[5]

One foundation we know requires a preliminary letter of inquiry and makes it clear that proposals are accepted only if the letter of inquiry has received a positive response (essentially a personalized request for a proposal). If the proposal is requested, the foundation's website will offer very detailed suggestions about what should be included in the seven-page narrative: a proposal summary that describes the organization, the project, the grant amount being requested, and the grant period; organizational information, including the organization's history and mission, population served, current programs, recent accomplishments, and details about staff; program and project information, including five specific items that must be described completely and in detail; information on collaborations or partnerships for the project; a description of the evaluation process; and a list of required attachments.

We'll say it one more time: You must answer every question and address every topic that is included in the application. Not only must you answer every question, you would be wise to outline your proposal with subheads that reflect each question to make it clear to the reader that you are very responsive to the funder's interests and concerns and that you have answered all the questions. In Lesson 6 we address the challenges of writing clear, well-organized responses to funders' questions.

Many government requests for proposals contain a description of the criteria the agency will use to score the proposals and often assign a specific number of points for each section of the proposal. The funding agency obviously considers a section that is assigned

---

[5] The logic model is a tool for planning and evaluating your program. We can't get into a discussion of it here, but there's plenty of information about it online. Because many funders use it, or something like it, we suggest that you take the time to learn about it.

a large number of points to be more important than a section with fewer points—but every point counts; in fact, every *fraction* of a point counts. In most government programs, grants are awarded starting with the proposals with the greatest number of points and are awarded to each successive proposal until the money runs out. So you can see that when there are hundreds or thousands of proposals for a particular grant, you want to get every fraction of a point that you can. We suggest allocating the pages in the narrative roughly in proportion to the number of points to be given for that section (unless the application package gives you different instructions). For example, if the question asking you to explain the community's need for the project is worth 10 points and you're allowed a total of 20 pages for the proposal narrative, consider allocating about two pages—10 percent—to the need section. This won't always work (there may be times when you *must* write more than just two pages to fully describe the need or when you can easily say what you need to say in half a page), but it will force you to focus on the grantmaker's priorities.

When one of us first started writing proposals, she actually thought it was fine to leave out the answer to a question asked by government funders—especially if it was only part of a two-part question or only worth a small number of points—because there were so many convoluted questions. The first request for proposals to which she ever responded asked for a complicated evaluation plan worth five points. She figured that without the five points, her excellent proposal would still get 95 percent, which was a good score. Because she didn't really know how to write an evaluation plan for a government grant proposal, she just left it out. Needless to say, she did not win that grant.

Another serious mistake is to change the order of the questions. We actually have seen a proposal with a small box at the top saying: "In order to explain my program in the best possible way, Question 1 will be moved down to become Question 7. Question number 7 will now be Question 3...." One of the authors of this book is a former teacher—and self-anointed test constructor extraordinaire. She would not have been at all pleased if one of her junior high school students had reorganized her examination. She would have tried to like the child, to find the self-confidence and proactive resourcefulness appealing. But she is nearly certain that she would have resented the student and made every effort to give the student an extremely low mark both on the test and for the class. We all have our pride. The people who write the RFPs and guidelines are proud of their documents. Keep that in mind during every minute you spend on the proposal-writing process.

What If There Are No Actual Questions in the Application Package or Guidelines?

Some funders describe what they want you to tell them without asking specific questions, or they suggest, sometimes in a seemingly casual way, what they would like to see in a proposal. In one foundation's annual report, the following paragraph constituted the grant application:

> We are interested in learning as much as possible about the applicant. This includes budget (past, current, projected), audited financial statements, an IRS letter explaining tax status, names and occupations of trustees, and examples of past accomplishments. The individual project proposal should include, in addition to the planned work, a budget, expected outcomes, plans for evaluation, background of those involved and a statement of plans for future support. The main body of the application should not exceed 15 pages. A one-page summary is required.

Take these instructions literally and include everything the funder asks for in an order that is as close as possible to the order in which the instructions are given.

Sometimes a grantmaker will indicate that a specific application form is not required but that one (like the Washington, DC,

Common Grant Application form in Appendix 4) would be accepted. It's probably a good idea to follow the outline of the "accepted" form, even if you don't have to use the form itself. It will ensure that your response touches on all of the topics that the funder expects to see.

Try a letter of inquiry. If a funder does not set forth guidelines, instructions, or specific questions, you may want to initiate contact through a letter of inquiry (LOI). Like the abstract, which we discuss in Lesson 15, an LOI is a brief summary of your organization, its mission, the need in the community that you want to address, the program you want to implement, its total cost, and the amount you are requesting from this funder. In this letter, you should explain why you are writing to this particular funder; talk about the ways in which it appears that your program fits into the funder's overall interests (which should be clear from its annual report or list of grants already awarded). Yes, all of that in one page (or a *little* more)! Follow up with a phone call.

Some grantmakers, especially foundations, require you to submit a letter of inquiry before you submit a proposal. If they accept the letter, they will request a full proposal. This process will be spelled out in the foundation's guidelines, and you must respond appropriately.

Keep in mind that the abbreviation LOI refers to both *letter of inquiry* and *letter of intent*. The latter, a statement that you plan to apply for a grant, is requested by some funders, especially federal agencies but also some other government agencies and foundations, to determine approximately how many applicants they may hear from and therefore how long the review process will take or how many reviewers they will need to hire.

What Else Is in the Application Package?

Background information. Some grant applications contain discussions of research on the topic or a historical perspective that explains why the RFP has been developed and why funds have been earmarked for a certain kind of program. An example of this was the

Safe Schools/Healthy Students application, which was first issued around the time of the 1999 deadly attack on students at Columbine High School in Colorado. The application package explained that its significant discretionary grants would provide communities "with federal funding to implement a coordinated comprehensive plan of activities, curricula, programs, and services that focus on creating safe school environments, promoting healthy childhood development, and preventing youth violence and alcohol, tobacco, and other drug use." The Department of Education grant (described in the Opening Remarks at the beginning of this lesson) clearly explained what the department meant by "out-of-school youth," as the novice grant writer would have seen if she had done more than speed-read through the application.

Answers to questions raised at a bidders' conference. Government agencies usually send a transcript of all questions raised at a bidders' conference (or technical assistance meeting or teleconference), with answers to those questions. This becomes a part of the application package, often called an *addendum*, and generally is posted online as well as sent to those who attended. If you read this addendum as carefully as the rest of the package, you will pick up a number of useful tips.

Format and other instructions. No government grant-application package—nor those from a fair number of foundations—would be complete without dire warnings about sticking to a page limit, font and margin size, deadline, number of copies that must be submitted, and instructions about where to send the proposal. One RFP we've seen actually gave examples of spacing that is *not* double spaced and fonts that are *not* 12 points—to show the applicant what would be rejected. These details do matter! When the grantmaker specifies type size and margins, it's for the good of the people who will be reading the proposal. Some reviewers may read dozens of 50-page proposals in just a few days. You do not want to irritate them by giving them eyestrain from type that is too small. Yet one of us has seen a federal proposal in which the writer tried to meet the page limitations by typing all the way to the edges of the pages (no margins at all) and using a tiny typeface that needed a magnifying glass to be read. It wasn't funded. Often there is nothing about a proposal you are submitting that is left to the proposal writer's imagination. Except, of course, the imaginative program you are submitting.

For applications that must be submitted on paper, pay attention to things like the deadline instruction that might say either "post-marked by" or "received by." If a submission must be *received by* a certain date, you have less time to prepare the proposal than you do for one that must be *postmarked* on that date.

Remember that if instructions are not followed exactly, the proposal will be disqualified from consideration. We hope we've stressed this sufficiently (but we'll say it one more time): Details matter, even if they seem trivial. We sometimes think that grantmakers are testing applicants to see if they know how to read and follow instructions—to see if potential grantees can be trusted with vast sums of money. You can't blame the funders for that, can you?

POP QUIZ

True or False?

1. Grant-application packages may come in all shapes and sizes, but they all contain the same basic information.

2. Don't ever call a program officer to ask a question about the application package. The officer is not permitted to provide any information to grant seekers.

3. Most grant applications will have at least one question that will not pertain to you or your organization. You are not expected to answer every question.

4. When a grant-application package lists eligible applicants, it is just a suggestion. This is America: all organizations are eligible to apply for all grants.

5. If you need more money than a foundation or government grantmaker is providing, it makes good sense to try to persuade the program officer (in your grant proposal) to give you what you need. You'll never know unless you try.

Just for Fun

Just for fun (yes, we call this fun!): Write a three-page proposal to a foundation about the project you identified earlier, using all the elements that we have indicated should be included. You're on your own for this one. There's no right answer.

GETTING READY TO WRITE A GRANT PROPOSAL

ALTHOUGH GRANT SEEKING IS a process that is similar in many ways for nonprofit organizations, local government agencies, and individuals, as we worked on this lesson we came to realize that differences can mandate somewhat different kinds of preparation. For example, nonprofits are less likely than government agencies to have unionized employees (although some do). Civil service regulations involve procedural requirements for hiring or transferring staff, whereas nonprofits have greater flexibility. These differences are addressed by dividing this lesson into three sections: one for nonprofit organizations, one for local government agencies and schools, and one for individual grant seekers. Keep in mind that this division is somewhat arbitrary. For example, the complaint about having no time to pull information together for a proposal is heard no less in government agencies than in nonprofits, no less in large organizations than in small ones, and certainly no less from busy individuals who may be faced with application packages several inches thick. Also keep in mind that many proposals from universities or hospitals for grants to conduct research may reflect overlapping requirements for foundation and government proposals, so if you are submitting such a proposal, you may want to read both sections.

Different grantmakers require different documentation. Some of the items we mention in this lesson may have to be submitted with the application; some must be available by the time a grant is awarded; some may not be part of the application itself but will be important in preparing a narrative. Whether you are a not-for-profit, a government entity, or a local education agency, you should have the relevant and most up-to-date version of these documents on hand before a funding opportunity becomes available. For example, all incorporated not-for-profit organizations have a board of directors or board of trustees. If you haven't updated the list of board members recently, do this during one of those quiet periods we discuss below. All types of organizations will need updated job descriptions of key staff and the most current résumés. You also will need local, citywide, and school district demographics and other data that are as up to date as possible. We'll talk about this in Lesson 7.

IF YOU'RE A NOT-FOR-PROFIT ORGANIZATION...

OPENING REMARKS

As I did so often when I was a consultant for nonprofit organizations, I told the director of a teen pregnancy prevention program that it would cost her agency a lot less if her secretary pulled together all the documents I would need for the federal grant proposal that I was writing for the organization. But it turned out that the director didn't have a secretary. As in so many nonprofits, it was a small office, and everyone working there did everything. Staff members were getting ready for a board meeting. Nobody had the time to pull together the materials I needed, so I had to charge them for the time I spent going through their files and setting up a separate folder with copies of these materials. They could have saved that money with a little prior planning. —ASF

LEADING QUESTION

There's Always a Crisis to Deal with in This Place. Who Has Time to Put Together a Proposal?

The answer is that everyone has time to do what it takes to write a proposal, although you may not realize it. Every organization or program has its own rhythm. Every single one has times when staff feel they never get to go home; every single one has times when everyone can sit back and take a deep breath. Some organizations are busiest during the summer, when they run their day camps. Some are busiest in September, when school and after-school programs start. Some are busiest around the holidays, when staff organize special meals for homeless people or when clients are feeling especially lonely or depressed. But for other organizations, holidays can be slow times because clients, or their families, are away, or just too busy to come in.

DISCUSSION

It's a good bet that any slow time your organization may have will not occur during the few weeks before the proposal is due. That's why you feel as if you never have time to deal with a proposal, and that's why we recommend so strongly that you begin *now* to prepare for that perfect funding opportunity that is bound to come along when you are busiest and most overwhelmed.

In Lesson 14 we talk about demonstrating your organization's capability to handle a grant if you get one. Many of the same suggestions apply to preparing for a grant proposal—and preparation now will make it easier to demonstrate your capability then. Here's how to start: On one of those slower days, when you're not racing around putting out fires, assemble a folder—preferably on your computer—with subfolders for materials about your organization, its financial status, and its staff. For most of the items we mention below, you probably will just need to rummage through your file cabinet and online files. For others, you may need to do a bit of writing.

We're not saying you will need to use all of the documents described here for any particular proposal—almost certainly you won't—but it will save you a lot of time if you have them available to draw from and submit as you need them. If you keep as much of this information as possible in digital form, you can just copy or cut and paste when a proposal is due. For example, when you get a résumé by email and hire an applicant, just save the résumé to a staffing folder. That way it can be updated quickly when you need to submit it. And keep every proposal and every budget spreadsheet for possible use in the future. Thank goodness for computers! When we first started writing grant proposals, it was much more difficult to keep track of all the paper material we needed for each new grant application.

Among the documents that may be required or useful for an application are the following (if you need a definition, see the Glossary, Appendix 3):

- **Agency mission statement.** Some foundations will be puzzled if you don't have one, and many application forms usually ask for it. If you don't have one, get your board to start writing it. (You may need to draft a few versions for their review.)
- **Certificate of incorporation** as a not-for-profit organization. Almost every grantmaker requires that you submit this with an application or proposal.
- **Most recent 501(c)(3) letter** or other proof of tax-exempt status. This is another document that almost always has to be submitted with a proposal.
- **Employer identification number** (EIN).
- **DUNS number.** Dun & Bradstreet assigns a number (a Data Universal Numbering System, or DUNS, number) to every organization that applies for this identification. This is required for

all federal applications and increasingly requested by other government funders. You can apply online at http://fedgov.dnb.com/webform for an expedited response. You should allow plenty of time for the application process (although they say it will take only one business day if expedited). If you have difficulties with the application or are working against a deadline and need the number immediately, call 844.241.1775. You will be asked for several pieces of information, including the organization's legal name, address, web address, name and title of the individual authorized to sign legal documents, purpose of the organization, and so on.

- *List of board members*, including name and home address, place of employment, and position. Many grantmakers ask for this basic board list. For some funding opportunities it is also necessary to indicate board members' race/ethnicity and gender or some demonstration that they reflect the community; for some, you may need to show other organizational affiliations.

- *Annual record of board contributions.* Foundations expect to see that 100 percent of board members make a financial contribution. If your board includes individuals who were asked to participate because of special expertise—say, a deep knowledge of best practices in youth services or home care—and are not expected to make financial contributions, you need to explain this to the funder. But also explain to these board members that even a small contribution from every member signals a commitment that grantmakers want to see.

- *Organization chart*, showing the overall organization structure, reporting arrangements, and so on. Larger organizations may need a chart for each major department.

- *Job descriptions for all positions.* Create and save job descriptions for all programs; do this for each new program, whether you plan to fill these positions with current staff or hire new people. Don't forget to have up-to-date job descriptions for your executive director, directors of finance and human resources, and other administrative managers.

- *Number of full-time and part-time staff members, seasonal workers, and regular volunteers.* Sometimes these numbers do not change much from year to year, but be sure there is someone in your organization who updates the information regularly.
- *Current résumés of managers and key staff.* "Key staff" means anyone who has responsibility for a program. For most funders this includes managers and supervisors, but occasionally includes all staff members involved with the program. You receive the résumés anyway when someone applies for a job; you may as well keep them on file. But be sure the résumés are updated to reflect experience at your organization as well as what they did before they came; ask all staff to submit new résumés each year or each time they are promoted or change positions.
- *Brief "biographies" of key staff.* In addition to résumés, it is worthwhile to have a document in your files that gives a one-paragraph summary of the background and experience of the executive director and heads of all departments. This is requested instead of résumés by some grantmakers, and should be updated regularly.
- *Most recent (current and previous year) overall organization budget and individual program budgets.* If you don't develop budgets like this each year, you should.
- *Auditor's report* for the most recent and previous fiscal years. Again, if you don't have a yearly audit, you should. We know it costs money and time you don't feel you have. And you may have received minor grants without going to this trouble. But if you want a funder to take your organization seriously, it's absolutely critical.
- *Annual report*, if you publish one.
- *List of all current funding sources, and potential sources of matching funds.* It may help to have a two- or three-year chart or spreadsheet showing how much you've received each year from each source. You also should indicate planned submissions, showing funders, amounts, and dates.

- *Floor plan* showing access for people with disabilities, or a description of plans to accommodate people with disabilities if the facility is not readily accessible. It is rare that you will actually have to submit this document, but you may be asked to describe the facilities available for a program and to show that you have the ability to accommodate people with disabilities. If you cannot do this, you should be able to describe other locations you will use or other programs in the community that do. For example, if your school isn't accessible to children with physical disabilities, you may explain that a newer school, designed to be barrier free, accepts all children in the district with this need.

- *Personnel policies and procedures* demonstrating compliance with Equal Employment Opportunity Commission requirements, Americans with Disabilities Act, Drug-Free Workplace, and so on. If you do not have such policies and procedures in place now, you will need them as your organization grows. Borrow and modify examples from similar organizations to make it easier and less time-consuming to put these in place. A board member may be willing to help with this. And have an attorney look over the document to ensure that all current regulations are addressed.

- *Disaster plan.* Although such a plan is not required by most funding sources, there may well be occasions when describing it in a proposal will enhance your reputation as a reliable and well-prepared organization. And some funders do require this when you work with children or frail adults.

- *Boilerplate.* In addition to specific documents, lists, and charts, it is useful to put together some "boilerplate" materials in the form of brief narratives (paragraphs that can be used repeatedly for most purposes, with small modifications to suit the interests of a particular grantmaker). Among these items, include:

    Your organization's history. A paragraph or two about when and how the organization started and significant milestones in its history. This "boilerplate" can be used over and over, with modifications to emphasize different elements of your growth (when you started programs for seniors, when you initiated youth programs) for different funders.

Current programs. A paragraph or two about each program you operate, including a description of the population it serves, objectives, and any demonstrated successes.

The community. We'll address a lot of the kinds of information that might go into a description of the community when we get to Lesson 7, describing the need for a program. The point here is that a lot of this information can be collected during those few quiet moments and developed as a set of paragraphs on the population, the schools, existing services and institutions such as teen centers or hospitals, health issues and data, crime statistics, and other topics so that you can pull them out as you need them for a proposal. Remember that this information must be updated regularly; it can become obsolete in no time.

- **List of existing formal linkages** with organizations in the community, area, or city, and **letters of agreement** or **memorandums of understanding** specifying how each organization participates or will participate in collaborative work with the others. In Lesson 10 we discuss funders' interest in giving grants to partnerships rather than to individual organizations, and you need to begin thinking about these things long before a funding opportunity appears. The letters of agreement may need to be updated periodically, but you can establish a basic agreement—for example, that a program for children and parents will refer to a counseling organization when a need is identified; or that a school will provide space and custodial services for an after-school program and that the program will provide snacks as well as activities; or that a church will provide a meeting room for the senior center, and the center will make its programs available to church members. You might keep a chart showing all the existing relationships with other organizations in your community.

- **Any recent needs assessments, program evaluation reports, and examples of forms or procedures** you use. As we explain in Lesson

11, grantmakers want to know that you're using their money effectively and that you are committed to evaluation. Most organizations do not have the resources to hire outside professionals for needs assessments or formal evaluations, but if you've ever been able to do this, be sure the documents are on file. Refer to them in any proposal when it's appropriate (that is, almost every one!). If you don't have any external evaluation documents like this to show, be sure you do have some indicators that you use to inform you about how well your programs are working. You should collect data and report at least once a year on every program you operate; many excellent organizations expect programs to report monthly. We'll talk more about this in Lesson 11 on evaluation.

- *Recent publicity* (news clippings) and a *list of awards* to the organization, its programs, and its staff members.

IF YOU'RE A GOVERNMENT AGENCY OR SCHOOL DISTRICT...

OPENING REMARKS

When I started working for city government, an agency program manager told me that she wasn't allowed to write grants, except to apply for formula funds or certain entitlements. Her boss felt that if she had time to fool around with "pie in the sky" proposals, he wasn't giving her nearly enough to do to keep busy. —EK

LEADING QUESTION

We Get Plenty of Formula Grants. Why Should We Bother Applying for Federal Grants That Take So Much Time?

Hey, come on. Every little bit of extra money helps the residents of every town, city, and state. And wouldn't (and shouldn't) the public be outraged to learn that a city agency didn't bother to pursue a competitive grant that would provide a sweeping rodent abatement program in a neighborhood overrun with rats because no one had the time—or the inclination—to write the proposal? And wouldn't (and shouldn't) the public be outraged if a county decided not to take the trouble to apply for a competitive grant that provided drug abuse prevention programs in schools or housing projects? Such grants provide funding that absolutely would not come to a locality in any other way. Yet unlike not-for-profit organizations, which understand the importance of grants to keep them and their programs afloat, municipalities, school districts, and other government entities too often view competitive grants as optional. Local government managers and staff are supposed to think about these grants only when they have nothing better or more pressing to do with their time.

It's easy to forget that states, municipalities, counties, and school districts are (or should be) major grant seekers. Many, many interesting and important competitive grants actually require a government agency to be the applicant, specifically excluding not-for-profit organizations or universities, for instance. Everyone knows that the business of government and schools is to provide services to citizens of all ages, dealing with emergencies that rear their heads (such as acts of terrorism, mass shootings, hurricanes, blizzards, fires, epidemics, or floods). And they must defend themselves to the public and the press when children can't read, garbage isn't collected, roads or levees buckle, murder rates soar, or traffic is congested. But many local governments are constrained by the difficulty of bringing in enough tax revenues to provide the needed services and constantly raising taxes to meet new demands. This is never popular, if it's even possible. Grants can help.

Income Streams for Local Government

There are essentially four types of income that come to states, counties, municipalities, and school districts. Everyone knows about *tax-levy funds*; these come from income taxes, property taxes, sales taxes, and so on. Money for *capital expenses* such as school construction usually is raised by issuing bonds that a government entity has to pay off over many years out of its tax-levy income. Other funds come from higher levels of government—state or federal. *Entitlement funding* is written into law, usually at the federal level. It must be spent on behalf of any individual (for instance, a person with the HIV virus) who has qualifications specified in the authorizing legislation. The amount of money that the locality gets is based on the number of residents who qualify (thus this kind of funding also is called a *formula grant*). The formula for the grant might include, for example, the number of people with family incomes below a specified amount, the number of children in a school district whose parents' income is below a certain level, the number of elderly people living in poverty, or the number of people with disabilities. Examples are Medicare, Medicaid, and Social Security.

Discretionary grants, the focus of the present section, are available through a competitive process from a higher level of government at its discretion, depending on available funds. At the federal level, as the general public is learning, discretionary funding covers all government spending other than debt service and entitlements—including the military, the FBI, emergency management, early childhood programs, housing, education, transportation (including air traffic controllers), and health.

Discretionary grants of all kinds from higher levels of government can support state and local entities in providing services. These agencies may in turn hire—meaning subcontract or issue grants to—not-for-profits or for-profit businesses to run hospitals, conduct arts programs, provide technology instruction in schools, beautify parks and open spaces, develop housing for senior citizens, run after-school programs, and many other services. For successful grant seeking, local governments and schools have to plan ahead—just as not-for-profits do.

Competition for grants pits the Los Angeles Police Department against the New York City Police Department and the Indianapolis

Police Department; it pits the Des Moines Health Department against the Boston Health Department. At the present writing, as we've discussed, federal funding cuts are feared, while demands for infrastructure replacement and disaster recovery (from catastrophic hurricanes and wildfires) are soaring. This means that federal grants to states and localities will become even more competitive than they have been for all kinds of discretionary funding. And because these grants are competitive—not entitlements, not based on formulas—they require a tremendous amount of the kind of work and homework we are stressing in this book. And sometimes a culture change is required as well. Winning competitive grants—not just relying on formula funding—must become a major priority of school districts, cities, and states.

BUT REALLY—WE'RE NOT KIDDING. WHEN YOU WORK FOR THE GOVERNMENT OR THE SCHOOLS, THERE JUST ISN'T TIME!

Sure, there are commissioners, superintendents, and other leaders in government and education who claim that if their staff members have time to be thinking about grants, they probably don't have enough to do. This is silly, of course. Every time a worker recognizes a need or gap in services that isn't covered by the budget, that person should be thinking about programs and grants to address the problem; it is, or should be, part of the job description. And the more time staff members spend thinking about and getting ready to write a grant proposal, the more likely they are to win the grant to supplement other local money.

One important way to make sure there is time for a grant proposal is to use slow periods to develop boilerplates (material that can be used again and again) for much of the text and supplementary material that a proposal will require. In order to spend precious time developing the program for a grant, you should collect and organize the following information and update it regularly:

- *Overview of your locality*, including the number of residents, methods of governance, descriptions of who the local elected officials are, crime and health statistics, immigrant information, unemployment rates, number of city workers, unions, and accomplishments.

When one of us submitted a grant proposal for the city of New York to a large national foundation, she was shocked to learn (too late, unfortunately) that although the foundation was located only 90 miles from New York City, the lead reviewer was a consultant from the Northwest who did not know that the city is divided into five boroughs and that the mayor and the borough presidents don't necessarily see eye to eye. All the reviewers were so confused about who was in charge of what that they couldn't appreciate the enormous effort that had gone into building a workable partnership among normally warring parties. They kept asking questions such as, "Who's responsible for garbage collection—the mayor or the borough president?" "Where does the sanitation commissioner fit into the mix?" As a result, we developed a concise, two-page description of the political, geographic, and ethnic characteristics of the city that could be used for every major proposal.

- *Information about the various neighborhoods or sections of the locality*—for example, the number of residents, age and family composition, ethnicity, crime and health statistics, and needs.
- *Overview of the school system* including, for example, form of governance, number of schools, number of students, structure of the system, number of children eligible for free or reduced-cost meals, school and district performance, number of children receiving special education services, and the types of services they receive.
- *Specific neighborhood/district/school information*—for example, reading scores, math scores, dropout rates, children with language problems, attendance data, and incident reports.

- *Overview of the particular agency* you work for—and for which you will write proposals (e.g., police, transportation, health). Include the agency structure and mission, overall budget, staffing and "lines," leadership, responsibilities, achievements or existing grants, gaps in services, and awards.
- *Résumés of key staff members*, consistently updated.
- *Organization chart* for your agency. For each proposal you write, it is easy to plug the proposed program into the existing organization chart showing just where and how it will fit into the organization. Show to whom the grant-funded staff (if there is any) will report and how the program will be an integral part of the agency's business.
- *Hiring and procurement issues.* Unlike not-for-profit organizations, government agencies and school districts are required to follow very stringent procurement and hiring regulations. While most not-for-profit organizations can hire whoever they feel is the best qualified or the best fit for a grant-funded program (subject, of course, to equal employment laws), governments also must be sensitive to accusations of favoritism, union issues, seniority issues, and other concerns that should be addressed before applying for a grant. If an agency wants to collaborate with a particular not-for-profit on a grant, it may still have to go through some kind of formal bidding or other procurement process. This means that timing and communication are important, and tricky. In order to be ready to write a proposal, the agency will have had to qualify potential partners first; these organizations will have to go through the qualification process knowing that funding may not in fact be forthcoming.

Many cities have been working on streamlining the procurement and hiring processes so they will be able to implement grants quickly and efficiently. New York City, for instance, has developed a negotiated acquisition process that speeds up contracting. There is nothing worse, as we've said before, than winning a whopping competitive grant from the federal government and not being able to spend the money because of bureaucratic roadblocks.

IF YOU'RE AN INDIVIDUAL GRANT SEEKER...

OPENING REMARKS

Two friends wanted to make a documentary about a 75-year-old woman—an animation filmmaker who had succeeded against very long odds in a "man's world" after her husband died. Neither friend was a documentary filmmaker, neither had ever written a grant proposal before, and neither was independently wealthy. But they had this dream of making a one-hour documentary. And somehow they did it... and had it shown at film festivals...and it won prizes! And on the way to making their movie, they found themselves engaged in a smaller project that won them an Emmy. Talk about building a track record! —EK

LEADING QUESTIONS

But I Don't Have All Those Documents That Nonprofits and Government Agencies Have; How Do I Prepare in Advance?

You may not think you have much in the way of documentation to keep in a file, but there are items you can prepare in advance for a proposal.

- *Résumé, curriculum vitae, or professional biography.* You probably have something like this if you've been around for a while; just make sure it's up to date. If you don't have one, prepare one immediately, and get help—and samples—from people in your field whom you respect.
- A *portfolio.* If you're an artist in any field, you probably have a lot of samples of your work—whether they're paintings, drawings,

poetry, photographs, essays, videos, or any other representative materials. If you haven't done so, select the very best of these to put into a suitable presentation format. And review and update your selections frequently.

- **Reviews.** You should keep absolutely every scrap of press coverage that you've received—but sort these scraps regularly so you can always show the best ones.
- **List of clients or partners.** If you've worked on projects with or for individuals or organizations, maintain an up-to-date list of the projects and the contact persons. They can serve as references, be considered as possible fiscal conduits for a grant you may receive, or just demonstrate a track record.

You Said Your Friends Got the Film Made? And It Ended Up in Film Festivals? *Please Tell Us How...*

Basically, they followed the steps we discuss when we talk about non-profit organizations and government entities. They developed a clear project proposal, describing whom and what their film would be about, who the target audience was, what the point of view would be, and why they felt a film like the one they were proposing should be made. In addition, they had to produce a fundraising trailer, and because they had no money even for this, they were lucky to find people who were willing to give them in-kind contributions—of their skills, time, and materials—so the trailer could be made without the two of them going broke. They found that the funders weren't concerned about the quality of the images. They wanted to know if the film was about a compelling subject and whether the filmmakers knew how to put images together to tell a compelling story.

Then they did their homework on funding sources. They paid many visits to the Foundation Center library and searched for potential funders, using the library's reference materials. (Today they might use the center's Internet site; see Lesson 2 and Appendix 5.)

They realized immediately that most foundations do not give grants to individuals, so they found a 501(c)(3) organization called Women Make Movies, which agreed, after seeing the fundraising trailer, to act as their fiscal conduit. The filmmakers refined their search for funders by reading annual reports to see if foundations ever funded documentary films, movies about women, or anything else related to their work. They read industry publications to see if available grants were mentioned. They also found government funding sources such as the National Endowment for the Arts and National Endowment for the Humanities (which had a daunting application process), and the New York State Council on the Arts. Then they applied for everything and anything they could. And they got rejected everywhere...because they didn't have a track record.

But because of all their efforts and the contacts they made along the way, they got help from an unlikely source. Four filmmakers—including the subject of the film they wanted to make—had received grants to make very short animated films. Our friends proposed incorporating each of these four animated shorts in its entirety into individual half-hour programs in a two-hour series about the process of making animated films and the filmmakers' lives as artists. The result was an Emmy-Award-winning series, *Animated Women*, which featured the four filmmakers and was first shown on PBS.

Now they had a track record...and now they started getting grants for their documentary. They told us that personal contact was extremely important. In each case when they received a grant, they had spoken directly to a program officer at that foundation.

You Can Do It Too

Artists and scholars who need grant funds to write, study, or paint must do the same type of homework that these filmmakers did. Sadly, no one can do it for you. The funding sources and the types of application you will need to submit depend on the nature of the work you plan to do. Most scholars wonder about applying for a Fulbright or Guggenheim Fellowship, but universities can assist in finding less-well-known sources of funding for study.

Similarly, artists, filmmakers, and teachers can learn about grants, scholarships, fellowships, and awards in professional journals and newspapers—even in labor union publications—that they routinely read (or should be reading). Writers can apply for grant funding from the National Endowment for the Arts, which offers creative writing fellowships in fiction, poetry, and creative nonfiction. Filmmakers might want to join AIVF, the Association of Individual Video and Filmmakers. Once again, as much as we wish this weren't so, no one can do it for you. As much as we'd like to tell all painters to contact the So-and-So Foundation to get a grant that will pay for you to work on your canvas, we can't. What we can tell you is this: Look at our friends the filmmakers. Think creatively. Be resourceful. Hang on to your vision at all costs. Beg friends and relatives to help when necessary. Don't give up without a fight. Link up with a 501(c)(3) if possible. Read everything. (Most publications are available online, so there is no excuse for not keeping informed.) Talk to everyone (nicely). And finally, prepare the best-developed and best-written proposal that is humanly possible using all the information we provide in these lessons.

POP QUIZ

True or False?

1. If my organization is a not-for-profit and I apply for a grant that's directed only to not-for-profit organizations, there's nothing special I have to do to prove we're eligible.

2. The process of applying for a grant for individuals is completely different from the process of applying for a grant for a nonprofit or a government agency.

3. Not-for-profit organizations only get foundation grants, never government grants.

4. Individual artists only get foundation grants, never government grants.

5. School districts should stick to the three Rs and leave grants to the not-for-profits.

6. In order to get a grant, an individual must have a 501(c)(3).

Essay Question

Whether you are a not-for-profit, a government entity, or an individual grant seeker, describe the three best ways to prepare yourself for a proposal in advance of a funding announcement.

INTANGIBLES: THINGS THEY NEVER TELL YOU (ABOUT PROPOSAL WRITING)

OPENING REMARKS

I have a friend who recently started writing grant proposals for her smallish nonprofit. Although she is an excellent writer—and a whiz at all the things we cover in the rest of this book—there is one recurring problem she faces that would drive her to drink if she weren't a tee-totaler. She can never seem to get people to give her the material she needs to write the proposal! She has to beg—sometimes right up to the deadline—for demographic, financial, or program infor-mation. She loves writing grant proposals, but she hates feeling like a stalker. —EK

LEADING QUESTIONS

What's Up with Intangibles?

Over the years, many people have asked us what it takes to be a grant writer and what secrets successful grant writers seem to know and not-so-successful ones…don't. Some who ask tell us they are thinking of switching careers or changing their job descriptions within their current organizations, like the friend in the Opening Remarks. And others are currently writing grant proposals but feel they're missing something in all the "how to write a winning proposal" road maps. So for this lesson we interviewed funders and people who write (successful) proposals themselves or who hire and supervise proposal writers. The advice that follows—perhaps obvious when you think about it, but usually not part of a "grantsmanship" discussion—is gleaned from their responses and from our own hard-earned experience.

Who Actually Writes the Grant Proposal?

In Lesson 1 we described all the different types and sizes of government agencies and nonprofit organizations that could be seeking grants. Even within those different categories, organizations differ widely in the ways they handle grant proposals, usually but not always based on resources, and often changing over time. The person who writes proposals may be a founder of the organization, an executive director, an assistant commissioner, a teacher, a scientist, a professor, a program director or program staff member, a board member, a development director or development associate, a designated grant writer on staff, a consultant, or a volunteer. Or—you name it—someone in almost any other job title you can think of can end up doing the writing if the circumstances require it.

Some organizations and agencies use a team approach to writing grant proposals, pulling together program and financial leadership and staff to work with the writer, who may (or may not) serve as the team leader. Other organizations use this "all hands on deck" approach only for major government or national foundation proposals.

But whoever is responsible for writing a grant proposal (and submitting it on time and in excellent shape) needs to be aware of the "intangibles"—the not-so-obvious secrets of success—we cover in this lesson. From our own experience and what we've heard during interviews, the job descriptions don't come close to the reality of the position. This really is where the intangibles come in.

Writing a Grant Proposal Is Challenging Enough—How Can I Make Things a Little Easier on Myself?

Writing a proposal is never easy—and it shouldn't be, given the amount of money at stake—but we've come up with a few hints that might help you out.

Beware of internal politics! Politics—internal and otherwise—seem to play a part in most jobs, including the position of grant writer. Here are questions to ask at the beginning of the proposal process to protect yourself from unexpected political landmines.

- Is everyone—from the organization's leadership to the program and budget staff to the people who will participate in the proposed grant-funded program—100 percent on board? Does someone in authority think it's a waste of time? Do some staff members think the proposal should be for *their* program rather than the planned program? If there's significant disagreement on any issues, all doubts had better be hashed out and resolved—or the project should be scrapped.
- Is it clear that you are the one who will write the proposal? If someone else claims the honor, have a friendly discussion, draw straws, or get the boss involved.
- Has it been decided which staff members in the organization will develop the program—and who will take the lead? (If not, let whoever's in charge know it needs to be resolved *now*.)
- Who will be responsible for providing you with all the material you need to write a winning proposal? What staff input is needed, and what managers will follow up? If this isn't spelled out, good luck in getting the proposal written.
- Does everyone involved know the due dates and deadlines so the grant application can be completed on time? (Put it in writing.)

You may wonder why these questions appear in a section on internal politics, or it may be completely obvious to those proposal writers who have ever had to beg for statistics from program staff or who found out close to the deadline that the executive director didn't really want the program. We don't mean to be cynical—but we are. We don't want your efforts to be undermined by confusion, hostility, competition, or anything else that has nothing to do with the actual grant proposal.

(Try to) be a friendly, smiling "people person"—even when people don't do what they promised. As we've mentioned before—but it's worth reminding you again—a big part of the grant writer's job is enlisting support from others in the organization. You need buy-in and active participation, not to mention lots of information, from program managers and staff. As the executive director of a large nonprofit told us, "The most important strategy for a successful grant writer is to get inside the program staff's heads."

Even if they understand what you need and when you need it, *you must respect the fact that staff have their own, very necessary, jobs to do*, leaving them limited time to help you even when they are excited about the proposal and have promised to do their share. Sometimes you do have to be a bit of a stalker (we're trying to think of a friendlier term) to get the information you need from the people who have it. You may need to schedule and reschedule meetings to accommodate staff; you may need to make multiple phone calls for information when staff don't have time to call for themselves; you may need to offer to go through files and records yourself to find crucial information that you really wish the program staff would give you. And you should (somehow) do all this with a smile on your face! It's not surprising that some of our respondents said that being flexible is a key to success. One suggested, "You'd better leave excess baggage at home...and you'd better not be overly sensitive."

Finally, you need to know when (and whom) to call after you've tried everything else and still don't have everything you need to write an excellent proposal.

What's the Best Way to Get Off on the Right Foot?

Ask for files. Before you do anything else, locate anything that's ever been written about the program for which you'll be writing— past proposals if there are any, proposals for related programs, letters, memos, and so forth. This is especially true if you are new to the organization and/or unfamiliar with the program; otherwise ransack your own files to find materials you can use. Review these carefully before you proceed so you know what questions you need to ask.

Have a kickoff meeting. It is our experience that for any proposal that is significant to the organization in terms of money or prestige, you must have what we think of as a kickoff meeting, which may get you much of the information you need and resolve some of the issues we mentioned in the last section.

Normally, you, the proposal writer, should be chairing the meeting. The kickoff meeting should be carefully planned to elicit this information and engage the participants in the proposal process while respecting the limited time available to most participants. As the facilitator of the meeting, everyone will be looking to you for answers. Don't be caught off guard: Plan this meeting within an inch of your life.

Have an agenda. Remember that many people are meeting-phobic (we've made up the name for this phobia, but we're certain it exists). The only thing that can reduce the fear that the meeting will never end (or will be a waste of time) is a very specific agenda, which you should create and distribute in advance. You may want to specify how much time will be spent on each agenda item. Here's a sample of items for inclusion:

- Provide a description of the proposal guidelines and requirements (no more than 10 minutes).
- Discuss the problem the grant-funded program will address (10 minutes).

- Brainstorm how the proposed program will address that problem (30 to 40 minutes).
- Are there other programs similar to ours in the neighborhood? The community? The city? If so, how are they working and how does our program fit?
- What goals and objectives do we hope to achieve with the program?
- Do any obstacles immediately come to mind? How do we address them?
- How will we evaluate the program's success?
- Will we be able to sustain this program after the grant money runs out? How?
- Do we have the organizational capacity to efficiently implement the program? What do we need?
- Set a timeline and the assignment of responsibilities for follow-up (5 to 10 minutes).

Take attendance. Some funders like to see who is involved in the preparation of the grant proposal, especially if the grant is large or targeted to a collaborative effort. It is a good idea to make sure all participants fill out a sign-in sheet for each meeting in case you decide to include names and titles of participants as an attachment to the proposal. We talk a lot about "buy-in" throughout this book; attendance sheets can show commitment to the project in ways that support letters may not.

Intangibles That Don't Appear in the Application Package and Why They Are Left Out—Could It Be That They Seem Too Obvious?

Sure, the application may explain the program guidelines, legislation, other relevant information and research, selection criteria, eligibility requirements, deadline, page limit, font and margin size, and many other important and helpful facts until you're sick of seeing them. But it does not explain underlying assumptions about the entire grant process. You are expected to understand certain truths, which are different from tips and helpful hints. There are a few other things that people rarely discuss when they talk about grant proposals. These other intangibles may seem too obvious to mention—but ignoring them can hurt your proposal's and your organization's odds of winning a grant.

Know the grantmaker. First and foremost, as we've said often and will say again, before designing a program or writing a word, it is important to know as much about the grantmaker—whether it is a tiny family foundation or a huge federal government agency—as possible. It is just common sense. You are rarely asked to show explicitly how the proposal will serve both your organization's mission and that of the grantmaker, but this is one of those intangibles that underlies everything else you say in your proposal.

Know the field. Remember that although application packages do not generally say anything about "knowing the field," often you must demonstrate exactly that—especially for larger grants. Your organization really needs to make sure that it is up to date not only about the kinds of programs that have been shown to work successfully but about local and state policies as well. The grant application must reflect this wisdom.

Be honest! Nowhere does the application warn you not to fib, embellish, or lay out unrealistic plans or outcomes—which you can be sure the reader of your proposal will recognize immediately.

This is a good time to mention again that you shouldn't seek a grant to solve a problem that you don't have or that is not a high priority for your organization. Too many not-for-profits are so desperate for money that they may try to get any funding that's available, even if it's not directly related to what they really want to do. A child care agency in dire need of money might apply for funds to provide homemaker services. An arts organization in serious financial trouble might apply for a grant to provide substance use intervention.

Even if such organizations genuinely believed they could offer these services effectively—and even if by some remote chance they won a grant—this fundraising approach could endanger their organization's mission by moving into areas that are outside its experience and fundamental concern. But what is more likely to happen is that the grantmaker will see this as a ploy to get money, not an honest attempt to solve a compelling problem. The need for support may be very, very real and very, very compelling. And the grantmaker may understand this and sympathize. But an honest request for funding from sources that are appropriate is a far better approach than scattershot applications to anyone and everyone who offers grants.

Don't be greedy! Among the intangibles that "everybody (supposedly) knows," is that you shouldn't ask for excessive amounts of money. Nowhere does any application package or set of guidelines remind you not to be greedy. You will never see any indication that $200,000 a year is too much to pay a grant-funded project director of a tiny community youth program, or that the executive director's entire salary or an expensive new color printer won't be paid out of a grant to treat substance abusers at a community clinic. And if you ask a funder how much is appropriate, you probably will be told it depends on the program, or the organization, or the skills of the executive director; you need to exercise some judgment, based on what you know or learn about the real costs.

But be fair and realistic about salaries (and other costs). The application guidelines also won't tell you to treat your employees fairly and pay a reasonable salary for the responsibilities they are entrusted with. Nowhere does an application indicate what type or caliber of staff should be hired for a particular program or how much they should be paid. Rarely will it tell you what proportion of a grant—if any—can be allocated for project supervision or for support services such as bookkeeping or a security guard. The application or guidelines won't tell you how to design your program or formulate your budget or your evaluation plan. As we discuss in Lesson 12, you always have to decide what's reasonable and make the case for each item in your proposal.

Include in-kind contributions. Unless legislation or regulations require it, you will rarely see any suggestion that your grant proposal should show your organization's commitment to the project (e.g., by contributing in-kind personnel and resources to supplement the grant funds). But you may be providing such resources anyway (space for the project, volunteers, management oversight, bookkeeping). Doing this, and saying so in the proposal, demonstrates your commitment to the project.

Show you're diversifying funding. Some grantmakers are specific about wanting to know what your other sources of funding are and how you will sustain the program after the grant runs out, but many others won't ask. If space allows, tell them about other grants you're seeking or have received for the program. Tell them about board contributions to the organization and the board's other fundraising initiatives. And if you are engaged in entrepreneurial initiatives to raise money for the program or for the organization as a whole (see Lesson 18), by all means tell them about that.

Enhance the organization's reputation. Nowhere does any guideline say that an organization's reputation can help or hurt your chances to get a grant (although it is often implied in a question on organization capacity; see Lesson 14). If your programs are known, if your staff members are recognized experts in their field, if you generate model programs that others replicate—all of these things speak to your organization's capability to manage a grant. So publicize the good things you're doing and awards you receive, and—if there's room—talk about them (and the publicity) in your proposals. Send out cheerful newsletters describing your organization and programs, and include them in a proposal package (if it's appropriate; check the guidelines or ask the funder about this). Speak, and encourage staff to speak, at conferences; host conferences; become known as experts in the field.

Consider the reader. Nowhere does any application tell you to write in a clear, reader-friendly manner. Nowhere in any instructions does it state that you should not include drawings or cartoons to make the case (although the funder may tell you not to send videos, or to limit illustrative materials like news articles to a certain number). It probably doesn't tell you to provide a table of contents (Lesson 14) to let the reader skip back and forth to be sure you've covered everything. And although a grant-application package may give precise instructions on the size of margins or font (also for the benefit of the reader), nowhere does the package say that one abbreviation or acronym after another strewn throughout the pages of a proposal only confuses reviewers.

Watch your language! Nobody ever tells you to watch your language. As we discuss in Lesson 6, it is very important to be aware of the way you describe your target population, partners, and everyone and everything else. Sometimes you may think that avoiding certain terms is just too "politically correct." But you never know. One of us was planning a capital campaign and developed an "adopt-a-room" initiative, only to learn that some parents of adopted children hate to see the term applied to anything else because they feel it cheapens the adoption process. If we had used the term in a proposal, we might have offended the very program officer we were trying to impress.

Build relationships with funders well before you apply for grants. You will see this approach put forward by grantmakers throughout the roundtables, and executive directors give this advice as well. "Relationships matter," warned one of the executive directors we spoke to. "Putting business cards into the hands of grantmakers you meet at meetings or conferences is silly. People who give grants need to trust your organization, not stare at your business card." Inviting funders to visit your programs or sending news articles or brief newsletters is a much better way to build the kind of relationships that can lead to trust and, eventually, to grant funds.

Keep up with the news. Every person we interviewed for this book insisted that the best grant writers are "just" smart and savvy. Executive directors and development directors certainly don't give IQ tests or look at applicants' college grades when they make their hiring decisions (although some give writing assignments), so we assume they recognize smarts some other way. One likely strategy that will help you to be one of those smart grant writers is to make sure you know what's going on politically and economically in your community, your town or city and state, and in the country. Even if it's subtle—a sentence here, a sentence there—winning grant proposals reflect the climate in which they are developed and written. You are not writing proposals in a vacuum. It is not acceptable to say, "Gee— I work so hard that I don't get much of a chance to read newspapers or watch the news on TV or online."

You also need to be up to date on research related to your organization's mission. You should be aware of the trends and the current thinking. Just think—you'll not only increase your chances of winning grants (and having your boss call you smart), you'll also be a terrific conversationalist at parties!

But Wait, There's More!

Some of the most important intangibles you will bring to this job involve your own personal skills and characteristics. You'll probably be under a lot of pressure to get things done, so consider the following intangibles essential.

Don't dawdle. Successful grant writers need concrete skills— obviously, you must write well—but also, as some executive directors have explained, you must do a clear, concise job "to pace," or "to meet the deadlines," even when many proposals are due in a short time frame. You usually don't have the luxury of writing multiple drafts; you're lucky if you have time to circulate a first draft and get responses before the proposal is due. So writing well is, of course, crucial to your success as a grant writer. But writing quickly is important too. And as one executive director warned, "You not only need to write fast, you'd better write meaty and not fluffy!"

Be organized. Most job descriptions for people who write grant proposals (and for most other jobs as well) call for "good organizational skills." Executive directors have told us that it's one of the things they ask about in interviews—but what does it mean? For one thing, you probably are the person in an organization who researches or oversees research on grant opportunities and keeps a calendar of all upcoming proposals. You (and your boss) will be very upset if a planned proposal for a critical program slips past a deadline. You also may be the person who keeps track of grants received and reports that are due to the funders. And while you're in the process of developing and writing a grant proposal, you will have endless deadlines for other proposals, meetings, research, telephone calls, and quite a few other things to keep straight. Being scattered is not an option for a grant writer!

Be technologically savvy. On the surface, it seems that word processing, and maybe a spreadsheet, are the only computer skills you need to use if you write proposals. But many of the people we interviewed mentioned the importance of technology. "Top grant writers these days have to be 'digital natives' rather than 'digital immigrants,'" one said. Another added the importance of doing graphics. In small and medium-size organizations, grant writers may wear many hats: you may handle the website, the Facebook page, the Twitter account, the newsletter, the annual report. Even if your only job is writing proposals, you will have to submit proposals online (see Lesson 3), conduct comprehensive Internet searches for funding sources and research materials for your proposals, and create charts and graphs for your proposals (when they are permitted).

Focus on the big picture. Remember: Whatever your job title, *you are one of the few people in an organization who must look beyond a specific program to consider the good of the entire organization.* There's a world of grants you *could* be seeking (and program staff will be imploring you to find more), but it's not only constraints on your time that should limit which ones you pursue. We've talked elsewhere about mission creep. You have to look at each grant opportunity in light of the organization's mission, its long-term needs, and its sustainability, not only in light of the immediate need to get money to keep a program alive. You also must encourage and help managers and staff to be creative in pursuing alternative means of funding beyond grants (see Lesson 18). In other words, you need to be a planner, considering how each grant and each program serves the agency's mission and fits into its other operations.

Of course you can't make these decisions alone, so, unless you're the mayor or commissioner or executive director (and probably even if you are), you should be prepared to advocate for the appropriate grants internally and maybe externally, and to explain why others are not appropriate. In some organizations this just may mean holding out for a grant for general operating funds from a particular funder (remembering that general operating funds are true gold for an organization) instead of one for a program that staff members are pleading for from that same funder. It may mean you are constantly looking at the long-term strategic plan or arguing for a new planning process that identifies funding priorities along with service priorities—and lays out conditions for closing a program if necessary. And again, you need to know when you *must* enlist the proper authorities in these efforts.

IN CLOSING

We hope this lesson has convinced you that grant proposals aren't lottery tickets. And the people who develop and write proposals aren't just good writers who can follow directions. Far from it! You don't win grants (for the most part) because it just happens to be your lucky day. There are no right answers on a grant application, but there are plenty of wrong ones. Put yourself in the shoes of the people reading your proposals—the people representing the interests of the grantmakers—and think about what would make sense to them.

As you read the following chapters and as you develop your own proposals, keep these important (but unmentioned) intangibles in mind.

POP QUIZ

True or False?

1. In most ways, writing a grant proposal is as straightforward as filling out an application for a credit card.

2. Let's be honest about it—winning a grant takes luck, just like winning the lottery.

3. An executive director never writes a grant proposal—it's not appropriate.

4. Grant writers should ignore internal politics—it's none of your business.

5. People who give grants expect grant seekers to ask for more than they need—it's part of the process.

6. If a grant application doesn't say, "No abbreviations," use them as often as you want; they save space.

7. Rarely does a grant application tell you the specific qualifications of staff you must hire with grant funds.

8. Grant writers should take as much time as they need to write an excellent proposal.

THE "GUIDELINES" ROUNDTABLE

IT MIGHT SURPRISE YOU that in a grant-writing book we don't talk about writing a grant proposal until Part II, Lesson 6. Obviously we are true believers that a lot—a lot—of preparation is necessary before you can begin developing your proposal. For each edition of this book, we asked the people who give grants to suggest ways that organizations could increase their chances of getting funded. Their responses are as diverse as their organizations. There are certain things that every funder cares about and certain things that are unique to an individual. And there are certain things that continue to be emphasized each time we ask the questions.

LAYING THE GROUNDWORK FOR GRANTS

This Funders Roundtable includes suggestions from our panelists about why and how grant seekers should do some homework (mainly, finding the funders who are the right fit for your organization and your project) before even thinking about writing the proposals. We call it the "Guidelines" Roundtable because we learned that grantmakers too often find that applicants haven't read a word about the foundation that receives their grant proposals—not the guidelines, not the biography of the original donor that often appears on the foundation's website (and whose intentions guide the program officers even generations later), not the annual report, the names and projects of current and former grantees, or the composition of the board of directors. Some applicants don't even know the name of the current program officer (let alone how it is spelled). So most of the funders suggested a few ways *not* to get ready:

"Less than 10 percent of the proposals my foundation receives fit our guidelines—and the ones that don't fit are rejected," said one funder. "Believe it or not," said another, "some proposals that come my way have cover letters addressed to the program officer who was here 10 years ago!" She said she tried not to let this fact affect her perception of the applicant but acknowledged that it did call into question the competence of the writer. "I've been in this job for more than two years and still get letters addressed to my predecessor," yet another funder said. "Doesn't it make sense to check the website or call the foundation and ask for the name—and correct spelling—of the foundation staff? It sure would save me a lot of aggravation and save the applicants from a subconscious blot against them." And a funder recently warned us not to "formalize up." If it says the program officer's name is Joe Smith, don't write to Joseph Smith—his real name might be Joe, or Jonathan, or Sam. If it says Joe, write Joe—or ask!

Not surprisingly, every foundation grantmaker we spoke to emphasized the importance of knowing the foundation's guidelines before applying for a grant. This used to be a much more difficult task before the Internet came into wide use, although many foundations do not have websites. "There's nothing worse a grant applicant can do than come out of left field, which means not being strategic," explained one of our panelists. "The way to make sure that our foundation is one that you can create a partnership with is by reading the guidelines."

Can We Talk? Are Grantmakers Willing (and Able) to Talk to Grant Seekers?

Some foundation program officers are willing to discuss their guidelines (and other matters) on the telephone or in email correspondence with prospective grantees, and some emphatically are not. Government grantmakers, on the other hand, have procedures established for contact with applicants who request it. They almost always will talk with you, but what they can say is carefully circumscribed. They are required to operate in such a way that no group gets a leg up on any other group because of personal contact. We'll talk a little later about how they handle this.

We asked our panel of funders where they stand when it comes to chatting on the telephone, which can seem a little old fashioned in this era of emailing and texting. Here's what the foundation representatives had to say.

Some said, "sure...give us a call." "Since we only fund projects that fit our guidelines," explained one program officer, "grant writers should do their homework, know the intricacies of the foundation, and give us a call—with a short verbal pitch. Ask, 'Can I take five or 10 minutes of your time to find out if your foundation might be able to fund my project?'" (To us, 10 minutes seems a little lengthy. We'd stick to five minutes at the most.)

Another funder agreed. She takes calls from prospective grantees who have read the guidelines. "When someone calls and asks for five minutes of my time, I give it. I personally believe that program officers should be like guidance counselors."

"The telephone rings incessantly," another grantmaker explained, "but frankly, I'd rather that a group call to get clarification than waste its time—and my time—later on." But keep this in mind: "If prospective applicants call first to make sure we are the right foundation for their projects (which is fine), their letters of intent should reflect what we talked about beforehand."

If you call and find out that a foundation is unlikely to fund your project or organization, don't send in a proposal anyway on the off chance the program officer or board or executive director will have a change of heart. The funder will surely wonder what part of "no" confused you. And that's not a good thing for your reputation in the funding community.

Be considerate of the person you're calling. "Speaking on the telephone is a bit of a workload issue. I get about five calls a day from people who want to pitch projects—and each call lasts at least five minutes. Sometimes I wonder if my time could be put to better use reading the proposals. But we are responsive to callers," said a member of the panel. "With all those calls, though, I don't usually retain much information about the caller."

And others said, "write…don't call." Most funders are not amenable to—well, that's not fair: simply don't have time for—phone contact. One panelist said, "We don't encourage personal contact. We just don't have time. We suggest that if you have something that looks like it will fit, send either a letter of inquiry or, better yet, a proposal."

Going back to one of our favorite themes, the panelists all agreed that grant seekers must do their homework (the word that nearly every funder used) before any contact and learn as much as possible about the foundation. "I don't take calls," said one of our panelists, "unless I have a piece of paper—a proposal or a letter of inquiry—in front of me that tells me there's room for additional discussion."

And when it comes to emailing, all we can say is that it is getting harder and harder to find email addresses for grantmakers. Obviously, having inboxes bursting with queries that run the gamut from the ridiculous to the reasonable is unappealing to funders. Often all you will be able to find is a central email address for a foundation. If you're desperate, use it.

With government funders, it's a (bit of a) different story when it comes to human contact. Government grantmakers generally have a great deal of contact with potential applicants, although much of it is systematic. One government funder explained that his agency has five or six bidders' conferences in all sections of the country. (More recently, many of these conferences are being held online or by teleconference.) "These sessions give the public a chance to get to a senior staff member. And as a follow-up to bidders' conferences, questions and answers from all the sessions are compiled and made available on the Internet." But he added, "You can still call a program officer, and we are inclined to add new questions and answers online as they arise."

Another government grantmaker said, "We want people to call if they have questions. We prefer that they talk with us and not waste their time giving us something that we won't fund or that won't work. We won't help them write, but we're always happy to talk." This funder explained that her agency has a process that differs from most government agencies. Instead of a single deadline each year, her agency uses a less common "rolling" deadline two or three times a year for the same grant program. This gives applicants time to develop a proposal, send a draft, and get feedback before the next deadline. But, the panelist said, "It has to be understood that just because you receive feedback, there's still no guarantee of success. The program staff are separate from the review process for a purpose: to ensure fairness."

One government panelist admitted that he doesn't have much time to talk to prospective grant seekers. "But I list my bartenders just in case someone is desperate to get in touch with me." (We *think* he was kidding—so we decided not to list the names of the bars he frequents after work and on weekends! But we know for a fact that he answers emails from home.)

Yet another government funder suggests, "When in doubt, ask. You have absolutely nothing to lose." She reiterates that for government funders, "What you tell one [applicant] you must tell all. We'll give generic information freely—questions like, 'Is there a cash match or can we use xyz to make a match?' But more elaborate questions are harder to generalize about." She added an important bit of advice: "Check the agency website constantly. Agencies may create sub-websites for certain grants—and they can be a wealth of useful information."

But don't bother calling after the closing deadline for proposals. The review process is considered confidential, and no information is given. This is to protect the process and to protect the reviewers from harassment. There's no point in calling because nobody will tell you anything. Of course you may call "if, after several weeks you haven't received a postcard or email saying that your proposal was received."

And still another government grantmaker offered a hint that applies to any funding phone call, whether to a foundation or government program officer: "Get your questions together, don't keep repeating yourself, and try to find a friendly person when you call. The truth is, though, there is a trend toward putting questions in writing these days. It seems like a more consistent way to get the information out to everyone."

Final thoughts on calling. Before we leave the question of whether to call, it might be useful to look at the reason for your call. Clearly, the only telephone calls that are appreciated are those that ask intelligent, carefully thought-out questions that reflect a good knowledge of the foundation's or government agency's guidelines and mission. Calling just to say something equivalent to "Hi, would you give us a grant?" is not a smart strategy.

If you have methodically done all your homework and still have a question about your eligibility, or about something that you didn't understand in the guidelines or request for proposals that may affect whether you submit an application, then by all means call. But if you are calling to chat up the funder to make an impression, it's probably not a smart move. Better to let your proposal or letter of inquiry or whatever else the funder wants to see do the talking for you. Sure, many funders will take your calls (and many won't), but they're busy people, just as you are.

And finally, a foundation grantmaker has this reminder: "We all talk to each other. So don't tell something to one funder and something different to another."

SO JUST HOW IMPORTANT ARE THE GRANT GUIDELINES? (DON'T MINCE WORDS.)

In Lesson 2 we talked about the constraints grantmakers are under because of the way in which the donor set up a foundation or because of the language of the law establishing a government grant. The grantmakers recognize those constraints and find it difficult to understand why applicants don't. We kind of understand the applicants' problem. In some locations, grant seekers are familiar with one or two foundations. They may be aware that their projects don't fill the bill for these foundations, but they don't know of any others. They may have an impulse to try to fit a round peg into a square hole because they can't think what else to do. But as you'll see in the panelists' comments, the better impulse is to do the research. If you've done the research and haven't come up with anything, let the program officers know you're aware you don't fit their guidelines and ask if they know of any foundations that would be appropriate. Take the time. Don't send a proposal to a foundation just because you know it's there or because you know that its director is a nice person. Our panelists were very clear about this.

"I don't want to reward people who don't read the guidelines," explained one foundation funder. Another added, "So many applicants are so damned sure that they're the perfect partners for us...but they have no idea because they haven't read the guidelines. They're out in left field."

"I like to see evidence that grant seekers read the guidelines versus getting a very bad sense that they sent shotgun applications to everyone in the world. Show some thinking! It shouldn't just be about asking everyone for money," warned a panelist. "And another thing: Check out our application format on the Web instead of using any format you can get your hands on." Another grantmaker had this advice: "Do homework. Get annual reports. See which groups have gotten funded. Look at the board members; you may find that the board chair is your uncle's best friend." In fact, "learn about our board," suggested another panelist. "We send the whole proposal to the board, so it makes sense for an applicant to know something about the members."

"There's nothing that bothers me more than a proposal that has no business being sent to us," added a panel member. "We say that we fund in two counties—so why would someone send us a proposal from another part of the state?" Also, he suggested, "Do research to see who we've funded. Don't just look at the guidelines, which could be broad—saying we support 'education,' for example. We do support education, but only middle schools these days."

"I'm a believer in relationship building. Get to know what my foundation does and work with the people we work with," one funder said. "I like to see evidence that applicants have a grasp of the focus of the foundation—and even looked at who our grantees are and paid them a visit."

Finally, one grantmaker managed to give us a bit of a shock. "Grant seekers should read the guidelines and if they don't see anything in the material that is similar to their project, don't send a proposal," she said. "Believe it or not," she added, "one applicant actually called and scolded us, 'You've made an oversight. You're not funding what our organization does!'"

Do You Ever...Well...Not Follow the Guidelines?

"We've funded groups that don't fit our guidelines," said a foundation grantmaker, "if their work is addressing a clear, poignant, immediate need." A foundation funder pointed out that "there are exceptions to eligibility—where the applicant has a relationship with a board member, perhaps; but, in general, eligibility is about empowering certain groups—which is why we have an eligibility requirement in the first place."

"It is possible," said a member of our panel, "for the program officer to send a quirky idea to the foundation's board, as long as it is in the guidelines' ballpark." She described a grant to an individual, which normally is not within foundation guidelines. This individual's project, however, was connected to an interest of one of the board members and did relate directly to the foundation's interest in historic preservation, so she brought it to the board—and it was approved.

"It is possible—once in a blue moon—that you meet a person who is so smart that you make the program fit the guidelines," explained another funder. But one foundation grantmaker offered this wise reminder: "There is great diversity in the foundation world—so find the right fit."

A reminder. While talking with the grantmakers about the importance of reading—and studying—guidelines, it became clear that there is no such thing as going overboard. Grantmakers mentioned everything from simply reading the guidelines, to visiting groups that already received grants from the foundation, to talking to people who know about and are known to the foundation. One moral of this story is that when it comes to doing guidelines homework, less is not more. A second moral is: Don't ever—not even if you think the program officer is kind and compassionate—suggest that the foundation change its guidelines in order to give your organization a grant.

What About Government and Large Foundation Grants... Aren't Your Guidelines a Little Different?

As we said in Lesson 3, most government agencies and large foundations announce funding opportunities through a request for proposals (RFP) process that includes a detailed description of who is eligible to apply and what is required in the proposal. RFPs also include a detailed description of the scoring criteria for each section of the application. Reading, understanding, and adhering to the eligibility requirements and the scoring criteria are exactly the same as understanding and following the guidelines for a foundation—only more so. One federal funder explained, "We may see an incredible, creative proposal that we can't even review. We evaluate on the criteria in the application.... The message is, develop the proposal in response to the requirements of the announcement. If you don't, it could very well earn you a very poor score or even get the application tossed out before it's even read." Furthermore, "eligibility is nonnegotiable once the RFP is out."

One panelist commented, "In a 'call for comments' [which can be found in the *Federal Register* by searching the relevant agencies— e.g., Health and Human Services, Education] before the issuance of the RFP, you can put anything on the table," but once the RFP is issued, you must follow its instructions to the letter. Another government funder explained, "People applying for grants from the government have to be aware of authorizing language [the language given in the legislation creating the grant]. It's not our call who is or isn't eligible."

If you forget "the required certifications and licensures, the signature of the CEO—it seems minor, but it's required," noted one program officer, "then we have to exclude the proposal before it's reviewed."

Are Big Cities and Small Towns Equally Eligible for a Grant?

"Although all cities and states may be eligible for a government or national foundation grant," one federal funder said, "large cities and states sometimes score higher because they know how things get done. Small places are often a little unsophisticated. One grant proposal I saw, for example, suggested that a clergyman and a secretary could run a million-dollar program alone." She offered a suggestion for smaller groups or smaller cities: "When applying for grants, don't be afraid of things that seem out of your realm—like doing an evaluation plan. Someone can help you, even if there is only a small junior college not too far away that has a graduate instructor who will work on your evaluation plan with you. There are always resources out there."

Another federal program officer explained that review committees are established specifically to reduce bias against any particular area, offset the lack of sophistication smaller locations may demonstrate, or overcome a lack of awareness by reviewers in some parts of the country about conditions elsewhere: "We pull together review committees from the types of areas the proposals come from. For example, reviewers from Chicago would review applications from New York City."

How Do the Really Little Guys—Grassroots Organizations— Get on the Grant Funding Map?

Many small grassroots organizations are anxious to break into the grants process to start raising more money than they can get from membership dues and bake sales. We asked panelists to suggest how the grassroots groups can begin the process of successful grant seeking. All the funders we spoke to acknowledged that small organizations are generally at a disadvantage when it comes to grants, especially, of course, if there is an economic downturn. But one funder commented, "Certain foundations are willing to fund grassroots organizations—but the organizations need at least some fundraising track record." She suggested some strategies: "Figure out a way to show community support, recruit volunteers, document in-kind contributions to your organization [things other than money that are donated, such as meeting space and supplies], even develop a relationship with your local bank branch."

Here again, finding the right grantmaker can make all the difference. One foundation officer told us, "We fund 'emerging' organizations for up to five years. We hope these groups will graduate to larger funders who will be able to give larger grants. This foundation also offers hands-on guidance and support to help small groups grow."

Another funder also looks for a track record: "I ask, 'What are they thinking, what is their leadership like, what kind of groundwork have these brand-new groups done? How well do they know their community? Are they open to talking to existing, established groups that are doing a really good job?" I check to see whether a new group actually follows up by contacting existing groups that I recommended. But, with all that, we don't fund a lot of start-ups."

Yet another grantmaking colleague agreed. "We suggest that grassroots organizations—especially small immigrant groups—talk to other groups to see what they are doing. We will give start-up grants (but the applicants should ask for a small amount of funding at the beginning) to do concrete projects, for instance, instead of for operating expenses."

A government grantmaker agreed that "small and new programs are disadvantaged. They often have a lack of sophistication about how to get things done. Occasionally there are start-ups funded, though," she added. "You just have to keep your eyes open for the announcements."

"We've given authentic grassroots organizations their first grants," said a foundation grantmaker. "But we give in a modest way to new and grassroots groups. For new groups we try to find and talk to contacts who know about them. It's risky. I wouldn't take a big financial risk but I would take a small one."

"If it's a start-up," said another funder, "it's hard to get in the door. But if we decide the organization is pretty good, we'll try to market it to other foundations. Then we'll suggest that they work with an organization that helps small groups get their 501(c)(3)s and do board development with them. If they show effort, we'll provide funding for these types of technical assistance activities."

Another added, "We love to help small groups. They deserve a push. We're sympathetic about their size. Their proposals don't have to be glossy—they just have to tell a compelling story."

A final hint for grassroots groups. A member of our panel offered a good hint: "Foundations may not say directly that they fund grassroots organizations, but they may indicate that they fund 'seed grants' [grants, usually small, intended to get a project started], which may be a subtle message that grassroots organizations should apply."

AND A FEW MORE HINTS...

The Guidelines Say That This Grantmaker Doesn't Accept Unsolicited Proposals. Is There Anything I Can Do?

Lots of small foundations (and a few larger ones) say they do not accept proposals; their trustees usually allocate money to preselected organizations working in the donor's areas of interest. Funders were asked to give some advice about whether (and how) a frustrated proposal writer who has read the guidelines carefully and thinks that her program would be a perfect match might approach such a foundation. Keep in mind that there seems to be a lot of effort by foundations to find the organizations from which to solicit proposals. One funder noted that, even though her foundation does accept proposals, and has clear guidelines for them, "90 percent of the proposals we fund are solicited by asking around. Who's doing good work in the area we're looking to support?" Another said, "Part of our job is to go out looking for people doing the kind of work we like to support."

Although in most cases there's not much you can do to persuade a foundation to fund you if it has its own pet causes, another panelist told us, "People fund people. Get the attention of a staff member or a board member. Send newsletters and other information about your work. Savvy individuals can make connections with people who can swing the door open for them."

"If foundations don't accept unsolicited proposals," said another grantmaker, "then a board member of your organization can call a board member of the foundation. If your board members don't know people on the foundation's board, you can send a letter just to say that we'd like to tell you what kind of work we're doing (acknowledging that you know the foundation doesn't accept proposals, of course, because you always want to show your deep understanding of those guidelines!)."

And When I Do Submit an Application, Do I Need to Know Someone?

Many grant seekers worry that they'll be shut out of grant funding if they aren't lucky enough to know a board member, a program officer—or someone—at the foundation. We asked funders whether grant seekers need to know someone to have a shot at getting their proposals funded.

The answer is, absolutely not.

Both government and foundation funders are clear that when there is an application process, it's completely open. "No, you don't have to know anyone to get funded," promised one of our panel members. Even more encouraging, "One hundred percent of the grants we give are to groups we don't know," said another. "We accept unsolicited applications. That's where I live. I want to hear the idea I haven't heard before—like, 'I'm going to climb Mt. McKinley on my hands.' Every great organization or idea starts small...everyone starts with less capacity and less visibility."

Another foundation grantmaker said, "We get a lot of proposals sent in cold. People think you have to know someone, but you don't." She does talk to other funders who know an applicant organization. "Or we'll talk to our grantees to ask them about an organization that has applied to us for funding. We actually rely on grantees to help us keep up with what is going on in the field."

And in case your uncle knows a board member and you think this will help you get a grant, one of our panelists had this observation: "At staffed foundations, it's not a good idea to make an end run around the program officer directly to the trustees. If you happen to know someone, 'cc' him or her. Strategic philanthropy is not supposed to be about who you know."

For Government Grants, Do We Need a Letter from Our Elected Officials to Give Us a Chance?

We asked government funders whether a letter of support from an elected official would help or hurt. (We asked about the "hurt" part because we wondered if reviewers saw input from local political officials as pressure rather than simply as support.) A panelist from the federal government said, "Every unit of government has protections of the procurement process, but we're all human and it can't hurt you. There are several levels of review. But the secretary has complete discretion on what grants are made. We have to maintain objectivity, but we have to maintain [geographic] balance as well. We had 160 applications [for a particular grant opportunity]. Even if all the best proposals had come from one state, we couldn't make all the grants there."

Another government funder agreed that such a letter wouldn't hurt but said it wouldn't help much, either: "It's nice but doesn't do a lot of good." He offered this very technical analysis of the grants process for his program to show how objective it is and why support from a politician may not be particularly helpful: "The applications are read by a panel of three peers. The average panelist reads 15 applications over a four-day period. Eight sites, 2,780 applications received. Scores are fed into a computer, standardized to account for reader bias (the national standard deviation is 16)—too lenient, too severe—then rank-ordered, 1 to 2,780. We fund down the slate until the money runs out. There were 308 grants last year."

So it's not who you know. Whether you win or lose, a grant is not about "who you know." Although other factors (such as the resources available to a foundation or government agency) affect grantmaking decisions, the quality and substance of your proposal and your program make the difference. Our panelists told us that if you do good work and manage to develop a good reputation in your field, among your clients, and in your community, local grantmakers will know and respond. They said over and over again that they want to fund organizations and individuals doing excellent and important work.

One other thing to keep in mind: Grantmakers may not want you to throw names at them, but they are interested in which other funders support you. Tell them. And encourage them to speak with those other funders about you. They will anyway!

Are There "Intangibles" That Nobody Thinks to Tell Grant Seekers?

As we said in Lesson 5, there are a number of things nobody ever really talks about—things that grantmakers and experienced grant seekers do or say almost instinctively. Before we left the preparation phase of the grants process, we asked our panelists to think about some intangibles—things that aren't mentioned (or even hinted at) in grant-application packages or in any guidelines—that might help you get ready to develop and write your proposals.

Know the field. Several panelists talked about their interest in improving the field, or making an impact on communities through their grants. For this reason, they expected applicants to be aware of bigger issues, although they rarely said so in application guidelines. For example, one funder suggested that proposal writers put their programs in a "current political, economic, and environmental context." She wants to make sure that applicants "know exactly what the city is doing" when their program relates to urban issues. Another agreed: "Groups need to have a big picture about trends. Living for the day is good, but be strategic. And know the field—because the funders certainly do."

Make sure funders understand your community. A government panelist suggested, "Large cities need to make their structure clear. Reviewers see New York, for example, as a monolith, and don't realize it's a bunch of little cities." She suggested that you try to use the language in your proposal to help the grantmakers visualize the neighborhoods. "Show funders around, take them to the neighborhoods, show them that the city and the nonprofits all sit at the same tables."

Avoid "guns for hire." Some funders had specific, personal advice for proposal writers, sometimes not so complimentary to those of us who are not program staff: "I see development people—grant writers—as 'guns for hire.' I think of them as 'turnstile people'— this week they're writing grants for a youth organization, next week they've moved on to the arts, then to AIDS. Their proposals have a mechanical feel. They lack passion. The grant writer should convey a sense of commitment rather than a sense that a person is moving up a career ladder." Ouch! But the point is extremely important. If the person writing the proposal is not a staff member who is passionate about the program to be funded, that person should be committed to your program or working closely with someone who is. It shows.

Make it easy to read. And although the proposal should be presentable in terms of format, spelling, grammar, and—above all—clarity, don't feel you have to spend money packaging it or putting on a show with it. A funder said, "Make it easier to use, with headings, bullets, and so on; visuals put the reader in a good frame of mind....But at the other extreme, sometimes proposals can be so glossy you feel the applicants are spending too much money and fitting you into their pattern. This happens with the big organizations like think tanks." In other words, your proposal shouldn't look like a corporate marketing package that's been attached to a few pages in which you respond to the request for proposals.

Any Other Suggestions for Preparing to Write a Proposal?

"Thoroughly understand what you are writing," suggested a government grantmaker. "Have a clear idea about what you want to do. Don't start thinking about it as you write...think things through before you write." Another government panelist said, "Don't assume anything. Reviewers don't know about your programs, and even if they did have knowledge, they couldn't consider it. Like a jury. They can't consider anything but what's in the application, the words printed on the page." She also commented, "There is a skill, an art, to writing a proposal. Put yourself in the reviewer's chair." This was heartily seconded by other funders: "Try to write your proposal imagining yourself as the reader."

"I like an application that's tight and clear and has a logic I can follow, from exactly what the need is to how they're going to respond to it, what they'll do, who'll be included," said a government panelist. "That clarity tells me they've really thought it through and that they're able to pull off what they say they're going to do."

"Our job is to look for good ideas, good things. We are actually looking for things to fund," said one panelist. Another added, encouragingly, "To make a credible 'ask' shouldn't be hard."

Several funders offered final thoughts and suggestions like these: "It's like dating—you're not going to meet your wife at the first party you go to" (so don't worry if you don't get a particular grant). "Find a way to make yourself known and appreciated through the written word. There are so many flat proposals—like white bread."

PART II

IT'S FINALLY TIME TO WRITE THE PROPOSAL

SO NOW YOU KNOW HOW TO FIND FUNDING OPPORTUNITIES, how to read requests for proposals and funders' guidelines, and how to match funders' needs with those of your organization. You have pulled together files of information about your organization and all the other materials you will need for proposals. And you understand all the unsaid and sometimes intangible elements that are involved in the process of writing a good proposal. You realize that preparing a grant proposal is a process, not just a simple matter of responding to a series of detailed questions and attaching a batch of forms and adding columns of dollar amounts. You know that to be a successful proposal writer, you have to put your grant in perspective; you have to understand the mood of the country at the time you are submitting your proposal because this affects how a reader will respond. You know you have to understand the issues facing your city or town, and the concerns of philanthropy. You have taken pains to know the particular grantmaker you're approaching, whether it is a government or private funding source. You know that getting the funder to believe in your organization, to trust it, and to feel sure that its leaders know what they're doing is essential to winning a grant, as is getting the funder to recognize that you've thought things out, that you're not greedy, that you're honest.

And, of course, you know your organization well and are able to place your program in the context not only of your organization's mission but also in the context of what the community—and the grantmaker—needs and wants. And you've engaged the key staff in the process. Now you need to put your proposal into a document, and the lessons in this part of the book will help you do it.

Lesson 6 focuses on writing style. Because bad writing can undo all your hard work in preparing for a proposal, we lay out some of our own admittedly idiosyncratic dos and don'ts to ensure that the words you put on the page will communicate what you want to communicate to grantmakers and not offend them.

In the succeeding chapters we go into more detail about the separate sections of the typical grant proposal. Lesson 7 focuses on identifying and describing the need for your proposed program. Lesson 8 helps you figure out something that often stumps all of us: how to describe the goals and objectives of your project. Lesson 9 continues with a discussion of how you can develop and describe the program in light of the objectives—and communicate all of this to the grantmaker. Lesson 10 addresses a topic of interest to many of our Funders Roundtable panelists: Collaboration as a way to strengthen the program. Lesson 11 focuses on evaluation, another concept that is hard for many organizations to master, and provides a few alternative ways of dealing with this issue. Lesson 12 explains what it takes to convince a funder that your budget makes sense, and Lesson 13 addresses an increasing concern of grantmakers: how you will sustain a program once a grant runs out. Lesson 14 tells you how to persuade the funder that your organization is amply capable of managing a grant if you get it. Lesson 15, the last lesson in this part, pulls together all the bits and pieces of a proposal that should accompany it—or not: the cover letter, the abstract, the table of contents, and the appendices (attachments).

Closing this part, we present our next Funders Roundtable, giving you a chance to hear the panelists discuss the importance and value of each part of the proposal.

WRITING (PROPOSALS) WITH STYLE: 12 BASIC RULES

OPENING REMARKS

A friend of mine, an experienced and successful proposal writer, told me (with some embarrassment) that every time she starts to write a grant proposal, she cuts and pastes words, phrases, paragraphs, and pages from old proposals she has written, even when they have no relation to the current proposal and make absolutely no sense.

"Why?" I asked, surprised that such an expert would resort to this.

"Because I panic—and freeze—when I'm confronted with the blank page," she admitted. —EK

LEADING QUESTIONS

Shouldn't It Be Pretty Easy Just to Tell a Reader About My Great Program in My Own Words?

If you believe that, we have a swell bridge to sell you. Many important elements separate winning grant proposals from those that are turned down. One element that often is neglected is the actual writing style. Some proposal writers don't think enough about stylish writing because they are too busy trying to make sense of the application and attempting to flesh out the program...with an immovable deadline that is just around the corner. They cross their fingers, hoping that their responses to all the questions the grantmaker asks will glide—error-free and in appropriate language—onto the blank computer screen (in 12-point type, with adequate margins, and in the required number of words and pages).

No such luck. Although grantmakers don't usually comment about the quality of the writing unless it's so bad that they can't make heads or tails of the proposal, they notice it, so you've got some work ahead.

DISCUSSION

There has been a lot of hand-wringing about the sorry state of writing lately, with people lamenting that "no one can write a decent sentence anymore" (and those who write grant proposals aren't immune from this charge). Teachers, employers, grantmakers, and just plain folks like us attribute this to all that screen time—Facebook, Instagram, Twitter, text messaging, computer game playing, movie streaming—that not only keeps people from reading books but gives them too much practice writing in the kind of casual shorthand that just doesn't fly in grant proposals (LOL, IMHO).

News flash: Those who write grant proposals must be effective writers no matter how sound their programs are or how highly regarded their organizations happen to be. It's just common sense. If a proposal is a mess, grantmakers will tend to think the organization may be equally sloppy.

THE BASICS

Good proposal writing follows the principles of good writing in general, but there are some rules that we urge you to observe that would not necessarily apply to essayists, fiction writers, journalists, biographers, or poets. Sure, proposals can—and should—be enjoyable to read (and so should books about how to write them). But the reason for writing grant proposals is not to entertain. They are written to convince grantmakers to hand over money to you; that's their unique and specific objective. In this lesson, we lay out 12 "rules" describing our strong preferences and pet peeves about proposal writing. Although there are exceptions to each of these rules (and we sometimes break them ourselves), we have found that you can't go wrong by following them most of the time. If you break any of these rules, you should have a very good reason to do it.

Rule 1: Before You Write One Word, Make an Outline

Whether you are writing a letter to your aunt or a story or a grant proposal, your first order of business when confronted with the blank screen or page is to write an outline. (If the friend in the Opening Remarks had done this, she wouldn't have had to cut, paste, and panic each time she started a new proposal.) This is a technique you probably learned in fifth grade and probably forgot soon after. Your outline, which you will fill in later, should exactly follow the funder's guidelines, questions, or selection criteria for the proposal. A good outline not only will demonstrate to the grantmaker that you have read and understood what she is looking for (and in what order) but it also will let you get something down on paper quickly.

We should mention that if you are required to submit the proposal online, the outline may be done for you in an online form you must fill out. Although generally you will develop the proposal and submit it by email or at the funder's website, in some situations you are required to fill in boxes that may even constrain the length of your responses.

We've said this before and will say it again: Follow the funder's outline to a T. If the first question on the application asks how you plan to evaluate the program (even if you haven't been asked yet to describe the program), then, as strange as that may be, it will be the first item on your outline. As we said in Lesson 3, don't omit questions or portions of questions on the outline, even if you think they're irrelevant to your program, and don't change the order of the topics because you think the funder asked them in an illogical sequence.

Each topic in the outline becomes a subhead to make sure you don't lose your way. This sounds obvious, but it's important because a poorly organized proposal will make even good writing seem incomprehensible. You may not use all the outline's subheads in the final proposal; often space is just too limited to include subheads in the shorter proposals. But subheads—the more the merrier—are useful when you're trying to get started, and they keep you focused as you write. They also ensure that you don't inadvertently omit important information.

Before you start filling in the outline, organize the material you have available. As we said in Lesson 4, you should have on hand all sorts of information about your organization, programs, and target population, including census data, historical facts, program descriptions and performance statistics, demographics and other statistics on participants, staff résumés, articles, newsletters, and much more. All of this material should be organized in files in your computer—all résumés together, all crime or health statistics and other research together, all budget and funding source data together—before you even think about starting to write. (If you haven't done this already, do it *now*.)

Of course, some of the information you have on hand will be left out of some proposals and featured prominently in others. For example, bios for key staff of your senior center will have no relevance in a proposal for a new youth program; job descriptions of your organization's staff members may be inserted in an appendix (if appendices are permitted), or left out completely if the grantmaker doesn't want them. Often you will struggle with what to include and what to leave out. The funder's guidelines and the way each question in the grant application is framed will tell you what to cover in the narrative, what to add to the appendix, and what to save for another proposal. Below is one sample of an outline that we borrowed from a funder's grant application. Remember, this is just an example; again, you will develop the outline to reflect what the grantmaker wants.

Once you have the outline done, writing the proposal will be a lot easier.

Sample Outline

- Program Title
- Executive Summary
- Description and Background of the Organization
- Problem Statement/Need for the Program
- Program Description
    - Goals and Objectives
    - Program activities
    - Timeline
    - Staff
- Evaluation Plan
- Budget/Budget Narrative

Rule 2: Write as You Speak (or as You Should Speak)

You are not speaking, or writing, as a Shakespearean actor speaks… or as your awesome 14-year-old nephew speaks… or as those you follow on Twitter "speak." You should not be overly formal, pretentious, or ponderous in a proposal. Nor should you be so casual that the grantmakers are left scratching their heads in confusion. Compare the three statements below:

- The executive director of the Meridian Mews Center, the delightful Ms. Jane Manning, is erudite, learned, and has never been known to bloviate when she addresses her comrades at worldwide conferences.
- The executive director of the Meridian Mews Center, Jane Manning, is lit and all the kids at the center think she's hot. (Okay,

maybe no self-respecting proposal writer would ever sink this low, but you get the idea.)

- In April 2019, Jane Manning, the executive director of the Meridian Mews Center, was voted Most Popular Executive Director and one of the 50 Most Respected Leaders of Nonprofit Organizations by the 3,000-member National Association of Children's Programming at their annual conference.

The first two statements obviously break this rule; the third one is direct, to the point, and actually sounds as though an adult wrote it!

Don't grantmakers have 14-year-old nephews also? Don't they know exactly what the proposal writer means by "people enjoy chillaxin' at the Meridian Mews Center"? They may know what it means to "chillax" and to be a "hottie," but that kind of lazy writing by adults suggests lazily, casually run programs. Some grantmakers feel it is disrespectful for the proposal writer to assume that they are comfortable with that level of casualness. Many grantmakers feel that adults should not talk the way teenagers do but act as well-spoken role models. Besides, isn't it more meaningful to the reader to learn that the executive director of the Meridian Mews Center has won recognition from respected professional organizations rather than to hear that she is "hot"? So, dudes, stick to conventional words and phrases. The best strategy for writing about your executive director is to let the facts about her speak for themselves. Even if she is gorgeous, it is not appropriate to mention that tidbit in the proposal.

Rule 3: Double (and Triple) Think Your Choice of Words

Never, accidentally or on purpose, fall back on slang or on imprecise or insensitive terminology. We aren't going to get into a discussion here about good slang and bad slang or the merits of political correctness—we may be opinionated, but we aren't lexicographers! We recognize that some slang expressions are used by people of all ages while others usually are restricted to the vocabularies of preteens and teenagers—and yes, we realize that many slang words even make it into the dictionary. But we don't think they belong in a grant proposal. We also believe you must take great care in describing, precisely, the traits and attributes of the people who participate in your program or who live in your community or city. Compare the statements below:

- The cops think the Meridian Mews Center has helped the kids in the 'hood stay out of the slammer.
- The girl who runs the youth program has a master's degree in psychology and has worked with the retarded at the Meridian Mews Center for ages.
- Kids in the program are really messed up.
- Children between the ages of 7 and 10 who have learning disabilities will be recruited by staff members to participate in all the activities at the Meridian Mews Center.

The first three are loaded with slang as well as imprecise and insensitive terminology. The fourth statement uses appropriate terms and sticks to the facts. What's the big deal about saying cops instead of police? And everyone knows what the 'hood and the slammer are. No big deal. But why not play it safe and use the correct words? The reader's father may be a policeman who complains about the disrespect he encounters on the street. You have to admit that there are some people who are really adamant about referring to young ones as *children* and not *kids*. And many groups prefer or resent being referred to in certain ways. It used to be perfectly acceptable to say "retarded children" or "the retarded." Now it is much more sensitive to say "children with intellectual disabilities." It's up to proposal writers to keep on top of changing trends in language. If you think this is petty, just check with a parent of a child with special needs and you may very well get an earful.

Rule 4: Don't Exaggerate

No, your organization is probably *not* running the most cutting-edge, innovative, earth-shattering computer instruction on the planet—and grantmakers often just laugh and shake their heads when they see this kind of grandiose claim.

Is there a proposal writer around who isn't constantly searching for words that convey the extraordinary attributes of the program? (Hint: Terms like "cutting edge" have become clichés.) Let the organization, the neighborhood, the program, the staff—and the facts—speak for themselves. (Who likes to eat in a restaurant just because it advertises fine dining? You choose the place because you're in the mood for the type of food or the specific menu. After you finish your meal, you'll decide whether the dining was fine.) So do use a few appropriate facts, statistics, or examples of program outcomes. Compare the following pairs of statements and decide which of each pair is strongest:

- The Meridian Mews Center offers cutting-edge basketball instruction to the children who participate in the program.
- The Meridian Mews Center offers basketball instruction to the children who participate in the program. The instructor is a basketball coach at Meridian University who received a grant from the Basketball Institute to teach the art and science of basketball to children. (Now that is an innovative, cutting-edge program—but you don't have to use the words!)

- The executive director of the Meridian Mews Center, Jane Manning, is a most brilliant scholar.
- The executive director of the Meridian Mews Center, Jane Manning, received her master's degree in psychology with high honors from Metropolis City University. Her articles about children have appeared in *Family and Youth*, among many other journals.

- The extraordinarily innovative basketball program at the Meridian Mews Center helps teenagers succeed in life.
- One of the teenagers who participated in the Meridian Mews Center's basketball program during the 2018–2019 season

received a full scholarship to Metropolis City University and will be a student coach for the college's intramural basketball teams.

- The Meridian Mews Center is located in the poorest section of America.
- The Meridian Mews Center is located in a Metropolis neighborhood where 80 percent of the residents are on public assistance and 60 percent of the children under 16 live in single-parent families.

In each of the pairs of statements, the second statement doesn't need to exaggerate to make a point. The proposal writer takes the trouble to explain why the program is extraordinary, a staff member is brilliant, and a neighborhood is considered disadvantaged.

Rule 5: Buy a Grammar Book—and Use It When in Doubt (and Even When You're Not in Doubt)

Nothing is more disheartening to a grantmaker than poor grammar. Right or wrong, it suggests either that you are poorly educated or don't care enough about the proposal to proofread and rewrite. What funder wants to give money to an organization that allows a proposal to be sent out with grammatical errors? We aren't going to give you grammar instructions; you know the rules, or you know where to find them. A couple of hints: If you work in a professional field, say, education, youth services, or social work, use a grammar book or guide published or approved by a journal or professional organization in that field. And use your word processor's grammar check—but don't depend on it! It's only as good as the programmers who wrote it.

Rule 6: ...and a Dictionary and Thesaurus While You're at It

Your computer has a spelling checker and many other tools that can help you. No excuses for misspellings and no reason to discuss this any further. But, again, we realize that spelling software isn't foolproof (the computer often doesn't distinguish among *two*, *too*, and *to*, for example), so you should also proofread carefully, ask friends and colleagues to read and edit your proposals, and use a dictionary to double-check when you are the least bit unsure.

Rule 7: Stick to the Active Voice

This is a more straightforward way to write, and it is the only way to keep from getting tripped up—or tripping up your reader—in a grant proposal. All sorts of people (not just proposal writers) rely on the passive voice—saying things like "You are loved" rather than the active but often terrifying "I love you." And how often have we heard politicians say, "Mistakes have been made," rather than the more earth-shattering "I blew it!" In grant proposals, the active voice keeps you honest and clear. In the following paired statements, decide which is more straightforward, giving the reader the most detailed information:

- Students will be recruited to participate in the Meridian Mews Center's activities.
- The Meridian Mews Center's outreach workers will recruit children to participate in the center's activities.

- Parenting workshops will be conducted for parents of the children who participate in the Meridian Mews Center's programs.
- Nurse-practitioners will conduct parenting workshops for parents of the children who participate in the Meridian Mews Center's programs.

- A project director for the grant-funded program will be hired.
- Jane Manning, executive director of the Meridian Mews Center, will hire a project director for the grant-funded program.

After reading the first item of each pair, the funder is left wondering exactly who will do what to whom. The second statement of the pair uses the active voice and leaves nothing to the imagination.

What if we don't know who will recruit students, conduct workshops, hire staff, evaluate the staff, and so on at the time that we are writing our grant proposal? Wouldn't it be misleading to give the funder inaccurate information? Aren't we better off using the passive voice? No! Funders want to be sure that you understand how these tasks will get done; they don't necessarily expect to know the names of the individuals who will be doing them. And in any case, you still don't need to use the passive voice. You can say, "The program director (or executive director, or whoever is responsible) will hire the appropriate workers" or "The program manager will develop a contract with a professional evaluator."

Rule 8: Keep Your Own Voice Out of It

Keep your value judgments, controversial ideas, political views, and sense of humor out, out, OUT of the grant proposal. Proposal writers often mistakenly think that everyone reading their proposals agrees with them about the state of the world, politics, and educational philosophy, and that their idea of a good joke will make the people reading the proposal fall over laughing. Consider the statements below (we'll help you along on these):

- The Meridian Mews Center was created to counter the federal government's shocking lack of interest in children. (This is a political point of view and a value judgment.)
- The Meridian Mews Center staff think "children should be seen and not heard" and we often punish them for talking if they haven't been spoken to. (There may be people who agree with this, but it is a very controversial idea.)
- The Meridian Mews Center is only for good little lads and lassies in the neighborhood, not for little ones with problems of any kind. Just kidding. (This is the kind of joke that beginning proposal writers think livens things up.)
- The Meridian Mews Center's entire staff voted Republican in the last election. (Political point of view—and even if every politician in the district is a Republican, the reader may not be.)

- The Meridian Mews Center posts rules that explain to children how they are expected to behave when they participate in the program. (Whew! No controversy and no humor.)

Rule 9: Limit the (Yawn) Adjectives

When too many modifiers are tacked on to a noun, verb, or phrase, the reader is likely to see them as just the opinion of the proposal writer rather than documented facts. Overusing adjectives can seem to be a shortcut for the proposal writer—saving the time and trouble of explaining what is meant by the adjectives. Excessive use of adjectives smacks of desperation. As Mark Twain said, "When you catch an adjective, kill it." Look at the following statements:

- The Meridian Mews Center runs high-quality, exhilarating, well-regarded programs for poor, disadvantaged, disabled children.
- The Meridian Mews Center runs four programs that have been cited for excellence by the National After-School and Weekend Program Society. Attendance at all four programs is over 90 percent. During the last year, parents have written more than 50 letters to the executive director praising the programs.

The first statement is just...words. It doesn't really say anything that has meaning. The second statement is meaty and informative.

Won't the grant proposal be dry and drab—okay, boring—without some juicy adjectives perking it up? Adjectives *can* be effective if you can flesh them out and explain exactly why you have selected them. For example, "This innovative program is among the earliest in the city of Metropolis to pair college students and preschool children for basketball lessons." Otherwise, adjectives like "innovative" are meaningless—and annoying.

Rule 10: It's Not Personal

A grant proposal is neither a personal essay nor an autobiography. Save "I," "we," and "our" for your memoirs. Whether you are writing on behalf of a not-for-profit organization, a school or school district, a college, a consortium of groups, a faith-based organization, or a government agency, it is not a good idea to get personal when talking about the organization and the project that you hope to get funded. Compare the pairs of responses below and decide which is perfectly clear, leaving nothing to the imagination:

- We are located at 12 North Meridian Street in downtown Metropolis, Indiana.
- The Meridian Mews Center is located at 12 North Meridian Street in downtown Metropolis, Indiana.

- We will conduct workshops for members of our community.
- Staff psychologists will conduct workshops for parents who live in the North Meridian Mews community.

- Our executive director is Jane Manning.
- Jane Manning is the executive director of the Meridian Mews Center.

- Our partners include local schools, churches, and businesses.
- The Meridian Mews Center's partners include local schools, churches, and businesses.

In each pair, the example that specifically mentions the Meridian Mews Center, the staff, or the executive director is crisper and less confusing.

Don't you think you're being a little rigid with this rule? Yes, it's rigid, because so many people either overuse the first person or use it inappropriately. It's much easier to tell you to avoid it altogether than to tell you when to use it and when not to. One of the authors agrees with this rule in principle, but in practice she finds that there are times when the less formal use of the first-person plural is more effective. This choice depends on her familiarity with the prospective reader or the feeling she is trying to convey about a proposed program or the organization. The point is that if you break this rule, you should do it consciously and for a reason.

Moreover, if you're not careful about using the first person, you may confuse the grantmaker. If you say, for example, "We will run workshops for our parents," the reader may have to stop to figure out if you're talking about your own parents, the parents of the children in your program, or any parents in the community. Every time the grantmaker has to stop to think about what you mean, you lose a little momentum in what otherwise may be an excellent proposal.

Rule 11: Brevity Isn't Always the Soul of Wit

Unless you are trying to confuse the grantmaker, abbreviations and acronyms have no place in a grant proposal. Believe it or not, even the most commonly used acronyms are bound to confuse someone—and that someone may be a potential funder. PTA, NFL, NYC, and probably a few others shouldn't stymie even the most insulated grantmaker, but as a general rule, the term represented by an acronym should be spelled out over and over again—or not used at all—unless you've just explained it in the same paragraph (or at least on the same page). Even talking about acronyms gets confusing. Compare the following:

- The Department of Health (DOH) has a branch at Meridian University, with a staff of 450 physicians, nurses, and nonmedical personnel. Starting on January 4, 2020, DOH will begin offering free tuberculosis screening for children at the Meridian Mews Center.
- The Meridian Mews Center has collaborated for the last eight years with professors from the PE Department at MU. DOH has a branch at MU and also works closely with the IT Department and the local Y.

In the first example, the Department of Health is spelled out first—then the acronym is used again quickly. The second statement is filled with enough acronyms to make your head hurt.

Rule 12: Prove It!

Very little of what you write is common knowledge, even if it seems obvious to you. Grantmakers want to see backup information, proof that what you say is true. Certain statements express universally agreed-on knowledge that you don't have to prove: The sky is blue (at least once or twice a year), grass is green (if there is any), winter is cold. But the unproved, unexplained statements that are thrown into grant proposals can drive reviewers up the wall. Compare the following pairs of statements:

- Everyone in the community thinks the Meridian Mews Center runs educational and enjoyable programs.
- According to surveys that were conducted in two community churches and two schools, 60 percent of residents of Meridian Hills Mews think the programs offered at the Meridian Mews Center are educational and enjoyable.

- The police are excited about the Meridian Mews Center's activities.
- According to interviews conducted by program staff with police officers in the Meridian Mews precinct, 20 of the 25 officers questioned feel that the center's programs encourage children to stay out of trouble.

In both cases, the second statement of the pair takes nothing for granted and offers proof for every proclamation.

IN CLOSING

Following the rules that we've highlighted in this chapter will not guarantee that your grant proposal will receive funding, but you can be certain the grantmaker won't be too confused, too frustrated, too offended, too angry, or too shocked by your writing to fund your project.

POP QUIZ

True or False?

1. Don't be a stickler for political correctness. The PC police went out of style years ago.

2. Being too organized in your grant-proposal writing puts you at risk of seeming stiff or stilted.

3. It is a good idea to show funders that you relate to your clients and program participants by using the words and phrases they use as much as possible throughout your proposal.

4. If you are a published poet, it is perfectly acceptable to include some poetry in your grant proposal as long as it answers the question.

5. It is not enough to say that you are conducting a "reading program." Make sure that you let the funder know it is a cutting-edge reading program.

6. Make sure your grant proposal contains every statistic you have available or you will be disqualified.

Short Answer

In this lesson, we described 12 rules that you should follow as you write your grant proposal. Which rules are broken in the statements below? (Hint: Some of these statements have more than one broken rule, and some may have grammatical or spelling errors.) For each, write a sentence that complies with the rules.

1. The Meridian Mews Center is known all over the world.

2. Everyone in the neighborhood respect the executive director of the Meridian Mews Center, Ms. Jane Manning.

3. Volunteers will be recruited for the Meridian Mews Centers programs.

4. The Meridian Mews Center has the smartest, best-educated, most experienced staff in the city of Metropolis.

5. The Meridian Mews Center uses neighborhood schools and churches for it's activities.

6. After-school and weekend programs, such as the ones offered at the Meridian Mews Center, help children improve there grades in school and there behavior at home.

7. The Meridian Mews Center receives grants from HHS, DOJ, and DOE.

8. The mural that was recently painted on the wall of the Meridian Mews Center's activity room is awesome.

9. The Meridian Mews Center's Geezer program is an intergenerational program for old folks and young kids.

10. We are requesting funding for the Meridian Mews Center's cutting-edge basketball program and its innovative intergenerational program.

IDENTIFYING AND DOCUMENTING THE NEED: WHAT PROBLEM WILL A GRANT FIX?

OPENING REMARKS

A group of three well-dressed women, looking perplexed, asked if they could speak with me after a meeting. They explained that they had to give up their health club memberships because they could no longer afford them. Their companies had downsized, their salaries had been slashed, and their positions were in jeopardy. "I know this might sound farfetched," one of the women said, "but would it be possible for us to get a grant for our local YMCA so it can put in a state-of-the-art gym? Then we can work out just like we used to. We can't do this now because the facilities at the Y are decrepit and the equipment is ancient."

"Well," I pointed out, "you're identifying a compelling problem that affects you, but you aren't framing the problem in a manner that would be likely to entice a foundation that is dealing with one major problem or need after another. But maybe you could…with a little thought and by thinking of others as well as yourselves." —EK

Why Would a Grantmaker Give Money to My Organization?

Most foundations and government funders prefer to give grants to address problems where the need is greatest. So how could a dilapidated YMCA make the case that it needed funding for a state-of-the-art gym in what is presumably a middle-class neighborhood? In this example, the organization would have to think about a broader issue than the few women who want to keep fit.

If you were the Y, some questions you might want to raise and answer in a proposal could involve the relationship of exercise to health, the alarming increase in obesity and diabetes nationally, and the lack of exercise facilities in the community—not just for adults, but for children, teenagers, and older people as well. Information could be presented showing how many children are sedentary and overweight or how many older people in a cold or rainy climate fail to get regular exercise. Data that support a need for exercise could be just as relevant to a senior center that wants to get funding for an exercise program for its participants or to an evening teen program that currently offers only boys' basketball and wants to engage young women (and young men who may not be great basketball players but do want to be in shape!).

Although the Y may be located in a community that appears to be affluent, that can be deceptive. Forest Hills, a community in New York City once famed for its annual tennis tournament, is perceived as a wealthy suburban area and has its share of affluent residents. But it also has a significant number of lower-income residents with needs that can be documented, and a community-based organization in that area has won many grants to address these needs. Whatever the community's demographics, you must know them in detail, and you must use facts to demonstrate the need or problem you have identified.

DISCUSSION

Because grants generally are earmarked for specific purposes, almost anything (notice we said *almost* anything) a grant will fund is a *solution to a problem* or a *strategy for addressing a need* that you've identified. If you're a fifth-grade teacher and you want to start an intergenerational program with a neighborhood senior center, it's probably because you've identified a problem that you are anxious to solve. Something is bothering you. Maybe you're concerned that your students aren't getting enough nurturing because their parents are working long hours, or they're from single-parent households. Maybe you've seen some of the school's elderly neighbors sitting on their porches or in front of the senior center looking very bored. Maybe you feel your students are too self-involved and uninterested in the community. Whatever the problem is that you've noticed and that concerns you, the idea for developing a program with the senior center is your way of addressing it. It's your idea for solving a demonstrable, compelling problem.

Even if you're not always sure where in the world your ideas come from, you can be certain that, most of the time, ideas for grant programs don't come out of the blue. You can bet that they're creative, thoughtful responses to identified and compelling problems that are worrying you. But the funder is going to want something concrete to go on, and here's where research—a little or a lot—comes in.

How Do I Prove There's a Compelling Problem That Deserves a Grant?

First, don't think that submitting a fabulous program idea to the grantmaker will be enough to win the money. Think about all the fabulous ideas there are. Soothing programs for rambunctious children. Helpful services for harried parents. Technology centers for the whole family in inner-city neighborhoods. Drug-abuse prevention programs for middle-school girls. Or how about a comprehensive (understatement!) program for children, including middle-school girls and their harried parents, that addresses both technology and drug prevention? So what will persuade a grantmaker that your cover-all-bases intergenerational program—or the Y's new gym—fills a critical need or addresses a compelling problem?

Too many proposal writers assume that the existence of the problem (and, for that matter, the wisdom of the solution) is obvious. Who could dispute that parents of rambunctious children are harried? Who would argue that drug-abuse prevention programs are not needed for middle-school girls? Who could imagine that an intergenerational program for fifth graders and nearby seniors is not a great idea? But common sense doesn't always persuade. You can be certain that, no matter how much or how little money you are requesting from a grantmaker, you'll be competing with organizations that have carefully documented their need by using (formally or informally) one or more of the following:

- A variety of economic and demographic statistics about the community, including the latest census data
- Relevant and up-to-date research, trends, and literature
- Anecdotal information from participants, staff, and community residents
- Waiting lists for their programs (or for those of other community organizations)
- Focus group results
- Assessments of needs and evaluations of past programs
- Newspaper reports
- Police precinct data
- Health department data
- School report cards, test scores, attendance figures, demographic data, and incident reports

A few websites listed in Appendix 5 tell you where you can get statistical information that can help in formulating your statement of need. Examples include the National Center for Education Statistics and the US Census Bureau.

Does Every Grant Application Include a Question About Need?

Certain funders, such as the National Endowment for the Arts, do not require an applicant to demonstrate need. Instead, the funder assesses the artist's portfolio and track record. Some fellowships are awarded because of educational achievement. Certain award programs (MacArthur Foundation "Genius Awards," for example) do not select grantees based on need but rather on creativity, talent, and brilliance.

Many foundations' grant applications and guidelines don't say a word about a need or problem. They simply ask you to describe your proposed program in no more than five pages. But it doesn't matter. Whether the funder uses the word "need" or the application package stipulates that a problem must be solved, it is smart to address the need even if you have to condense it into a couple of paragraphs. In fact, if the foundation grantmakers are local, they may already know the demographics and problems but want to hear, briefly, which issues have a specific impact on your community or program—and to be sure that you know about them.

What Are the Components of a Strong Needs Section or Problem Statement?

If you're like many other proposal writers—especially if you work for a small grassroots or even medium-size organization—you wear many hats. You have a lot of duties besides looking for grants. The idea of developing a high-quality proposal that everyone is counting on to receive funding is difficult enough; finding data for the need or problem section may send you into panic mode. But it doesn't have to.

First, for more reasons than we've yet described, it is important to put yourself in the grantmaker's place. Instead of seeing the program officer of a foundation or government agency as a nasty professor assigning a research paper to an overworked student, look at the officer as someone who has to make an informed decision and persuade others to come to the same conclusion. Foundation program officers must justify grants to a board of directors or trustees. Government agencies are responsible to legislators, who in turn must account to the taxpayers who are footing the bills. So if you were the grant-maker, how important would need be to you?

With a finite amount of money to spend and two delightful arts programs requesting that money, would you give it to the applicant who writes, "All children need exposure to artists and the opportunity to paint on weekends to keep them out of trouble," or the one that says,

> Children in the Wishbone Housing Project have the highest school-dropout rate in the city of Rosemont. Their family income is the lowest of any Rosemont housing project. According to their parents and teachers, as well as police officers, clergy, and local business owners, children who will participate in this weekend arts project have no other activities to occupy them. The proposed arts program has been shown in other cities (e.g., Memphis and Sacramento) to provide children with an outlet that increases reading scores, reduces their participation in vandalism, and encourages them to stay in school.

If you have space, you might insert a chart here, documenting the facts you are presenting. No contest, right?

Target population. As the example above indicates, you need to describe a target population, the group that has the need and to whom your program will be directed. In this case, the population is low-income children living in public housing in Rosemont, but it could be elderly immigrants in Milwaukee or incarcerated mothers in Poughkeepsie. You need to show that those living in the target area are needier than those in other areas, using key indicators such as income, age, education, employment status, crime, and many other statistics that we will describe later in this lesson. You would collect data for the target area, for the city as a whole, and perhaps for the state as well. The table that follows (with invented numbers for an invented housing project, city, and state) shows how you might analyze this information. You may decide not to include a chart like this in the proposal, but organizing the data will help you explain clearly how your target population differs from the rest of your city, town, or state.

Sample Population Statistics

Indicator	Wishbone	Rosemont	Statewide
Average family income	$16,000	$32,000	$36,000
Percentage of single-parent households	67%	25%	22%
School dropout rates	44%	22%	18%

Context. The best way to approach the need section is to put your particular problem in a context. If it's relevant, you may want to start with a national context. The teacher who is concerned that her students don't get enough nurturing would probably find a great deal written on the topic, and the information should not necessarily be disregarded because it reflects a research study that was done in California when her school is in Maine. What are the national trends? What kinds of research have been done and with what findings? Once a national perspective has been addressed, move in closer to your own city, town, or neighborhood. Often a simple search online will bring you a wealth of relevant information.

Are Need Statements Different for the Federal Government and National Foundations?

The need or problem statement for a proposal to a federal agency or a national foundation usually requires some extra work. Just like other grantmakers, these funders look for a detailed description of the population to be served and strong justification of the need for the proposed project (the funding agency may call this a *needs assessment*, a *problem statement*, or something similar). Unlike private funders in your state, however, who probably are fully aware of conditions in your community, the people who read and score federal applications may be from anywhere in the country, and those who read for national foundations may be consultants hired to develop and judge specific grant programs. Although they are experts in their own fields, they are likely to be unfamiliar with the physical, political, and social conditions in your area. They know nothing about your experience and qualifications in the field (although a separate section of the proposal will document this), and usually they are giving very substantial grants for which they expect clear results. So for these proposals it is doubly important to include:

- Proof that the target population in the community is in fact eligible to receive services under the federal or foundation guidelines
- Data that demonstrate the existence and extent of the problem in the community, including specific gaps in service that the proposal will address
- Full understanding of the theories and practices that have been put forward to attempt to solve the problem in your community and elsewhere
- Knowledge of relevant solutions that have worked in your community and elsewhere, especially when some elements of these efforts are incorporated into the proposed program plan
- Explanation of why there is still a need for a new program if successful solutions already exist

Example. Here's one way of moving from a sweeping national perspective to a local one. (The problem, context, and references are pure fiction, by the way.)

Many researchers have identified a lack of parental nurturing as a problem for children in today's economic and social environment. The absence of nurturing is, according to Ames (2019), Reese (2018), Bolger (2018), Uncles (2016), and others, the primary cause of student alienation and disenfranchisement, which can lead to violence, suicide, and other dangerous behaviors.[6]

In studies in Texas (Jones, 2016) and California (Smith, 2018), researchers have found that 75 percent of teachers report that their students "practically seem to be raising themselves." Piazza (2019) indicates that 56 percent of fourth graders in his Pennsylvania research study don't see their parents until after dinner, and Wilson (2016), in Wisconsin, suggests that more than half of the state's seven-year-olds go to day-care centers for at least three hours after school.

The lack of nurturing is both a national and a local problem in Indiana. For example, in Metropolis, Richardson (2018) found that more than 60 percent of elementary school children studied in a citywide project were "latchkey children" at least three days a week. In North Metropolis, the problem is even greater. A citywide study of what children do after school and on weekends (Johnson, 2019) indicated that more than 80 percent either go to crowded day-care centers or sit in front of their television sets watching programs in an unsupervised manner. And in the target neighborhood of Meridian Mews, Johnson found the situation even worse. Ninety percent of the children under 16 who live in the neighborhood served by the Meridian Mews Elementary School do not see their parents until after 9:00 P.M.

Warning. There is a temptation to throw research data, statistics, and other documentation of need into a grant proposal haphazardly. Proposal writers can be so ecstatic over finding usable information

---

[6] The form of documenting sources used here—just authors' names and publication date in parentheses—is from the American Psychological Association, and we use it because it doesn't clutter the text or take up room for footnotes at the bottom of the page. We would put an alphabetized reference list at the end of the grant proposal, giving the authors' names, title of book or journal and article, date of publication, city of publication, publisher's name, and page of a quotation, if any. But any other reference system can be used (e.g., putting all of the reference information into a footnote) as long as it is consistent throughout the proposal.

that they may neglect organizing the material to make their case for the need. But this portion of the proposal is not too different from a research paper. The variable is how much research—and what kinds—makes the most sense for a specific grant proposal. You almost certainly wouldn't do the kind of work involved in the example above for a $5,000 grant. But even if you are requesting only $5,000 and the proposal is only three pages long, it is a good policy to show you are informed about the problem and include some documentation, even if only in a footnote or parentheses. Again, put yourself in the program officer's shoes. Wouldn't a presentation of pertinent information encourage you to think highly of an applicant's seriousness—and appreciate her respect for you as a grantmaker?

But I'm a Nonprofit Staffer, Not a Doctoral Candidate at Harvard...

Stay calm. A closer look at the components will reassure you that the grant proposal is not the equivalent of a doctoral dissertation—well, not exactly. The information you need should be readily available if you've done the prep work we described in Lesson 4. Much of this information can be pulled from your files and just updated. Let's talk about these other kinds of information, and then go back to "the literature."

Community demographics. Most government grants (and many foundation grants) are targeted to communities with predominantly low-income populations. Many are targeted to specific members of a low-income community, such as children, AIDS patients, unemployed or underemployed individuals, a particular immigrant group, and so on. Your first stop for this kind of information is the website of the municipal or county agency that deals with the population of interest to you—a child welfare agency, a housing agency, the health department, a board of education or school district office (the local education agency), a department of employment, and so on. Localities maintain a gold mine of statistics on issues like homelessness, poverty, income, race/ethnicity, public assistance, foster care, substance use, schools, recreational facilities, hospital admissions, vital statistics, vandalism—you name it.

Another excellent place to start is the local census office, if there is one, or your city or county planning department (which probably has staff who work with census data). This should be easily accessed online, but it may be worthwhile to get to know your local planning officials and call on them for advice when you get bogged down in data.

You often will find important data in city or county management reports, and at municipal, state, and federal government websites. Local United Ways and other large not-for-profit organizations collect all sorts of statistical information and may publish it online or make it available at their offices. Get on every mailing and emailing list, and send for free newsletters and other documents that may be useful. The school district or central board of education will have information on students on its website as well as the names of contact people or division heads, if you are working on grants that will help youngsters. The department of health's website should have useful information for health-related proposals. Of course, if you are a nonprofit developing a grant proposal that includes schoolchildren, you should be working closely with the schools and school district on program planning. The same principle holds true for proposals that affect the health department or any other local government agencies.

Organization records. Remember that your own organization's records also provide important data. Whenever possible, your programs should have an entry or registration form that summarizes as much information as the participant will stand for—and as much as your ability to protect the participant's privacy will support. Sometimes this isn't feasible, of course; a jumpy out-of-school youth population, for example, may resist providing you with any information, and in order to retain their trust you may not want to try.

Participant surveys. Surveys of participants can help too. A survey of parents of the children in one after-school program we know showed that 92 percent of the parents were born outside the United States. Talk about a gold nugget of support for an agency that seeks funding to serve immigrants! And keep records of individuals who want to participate in your program but have to be turned away. From Meals on Wheels to sixth-grade karate, if your program can't meet the demand, you can show a need.

Anecdotal information. Many proposal writers shy away from anecdotal information, fearing that it is too casual. But anecdotal information can be very powerful when used in the right way. It can put a human face on otherwise cold statistical reports. And sometimes there just isn't any hard "proof" that a problem really exists—although "everyone knows" that it does. There may not be actual data on whether the residents of a senior center are bored, but formal or informal interviews with senior center staff, participants, and family members may indicate universal agreement. People may be willing to say things in response to oral questions that they wouldn't say in a written questionnaire.

When using anecdotal information in a grant proposal, be careful not to insert it haphazardly so it seems fabricated. A good approach is to cite the individuals you've spoken to—if not by name, then by title or relationship to the community. For example:

> The director of the Starview Teen Center has tried for the last two years to get teenagers to join clubs such as chess and current events, and take trips to places like museums and sporting events. But he has found that they are apathetic and unwilling to do anything but play basketball. Two mothers of teenagers here say that their sons seem lethargic; another mother says…

Although these data are "soft," the problem is very real. It is hard (although possible) to measure "tried to get teenagers to join the chess club," but efforts to get the teenagers involved can be described. Interviewing the Teen Center director is a good way to glean poignant stories that add human interest to a proposal.

Focus groups. Information gathered from focus groups reflects the participants' dialogue, interaction, and safety-in-numbers venting about a problem. A focus group is just a gathering of people with opinions on or a vested interest in a particular issue who respond to a set of questions prepared by a neutral facilitator to collect those opinions. The discussion can be recorded on audio or videotape, by a cell-phone app, or, more formally, by a stenographer; the object is to have a usable record of what is said for inclusion in a proposal, report, or advocacy document (or all of these). A single focus group can include a few individuals; a more elaborate effort can include hundreds of people who represent one side or many sides of an issue, randomly assigned to discussion groups. Focus groups can help you clarify the problem and craft a solution that is likely to work. Because of the importance of "community buy-in" or "stakeholder buy-in" to the success of any program, focus groups are becoming more and more common. This is especially true for large-scale government or foundation grants.

Grant seekers sometimes make the mistake of expecting the community—the stakeholders—to come to focus group meetings at locations convenient for everyone except the stakeholders. Don't hold such meetings at the university or a hall outside the community, even if someone gives you the space for free. It is crucial to have the meetings in the communities where the problem exists and where the solution will be implemented. To get the maximum amount of information from the greatest number of participants, you should expect to hold more than one focus group meeting, scheduled at different times of the day, on different days of the week, translated into different languages depending on the target population, and to offer the services of a sign language interpreter.

Needs assessments. Needs assessments generally are used to document conditions in a community or population that show gaps in service that you intend to fill. Normally, a community needs assessment is a fairly major project that will be used for many purposes for several years. Ideally, a needs assessment report will include statistical data, anecdotal information, and results of interviews and focus groups (as well as any of the other sources described here).

The needs assessment can be as formal as a major research project using validated survey instruments to collect information from a random sample of community residents or target populations; such an approach generally requires consulting assistance—at least—from a university research program and can be very costly. Before you plunge into such a study, check with your city or county planning office, mayor's or city manager's office, state or local elected officials, or other community organizations to see if this has been done already.

On the other hand, a needs assessment can be as informal as your own staff members collecting questionnaire responses from your current program participants. The important thing to remember here is what you need the information for: systematic documentation of a gap in services. If you find a community needs assessment that gives you information on all services and needs except health but you are considering developing a women's health clinic, then it is worthless to you and you had better find a way to conduct your own.

Newspaper reports. Newspapers are convenient sources for all kinds of powerful material that can be included in the needs section of a grant proposal, either alone or supplementing other statistics. Newspapers from all over the world can be read online, either free or for a fee, so if you want to know whether the problems you are addressing are more than local, you can see what's happening in other cities or countries. Online newspaper sites also give you easy access to archived articles that could come in handy.

If you want to provide seniors in your community with information about and help in applying for government assistance to heat their homes in winter, an article in the local paper about the problem, with photographs of elderly people wearing coats, scarves, and gloves indoors, will be as compelling as health department statistics about illnesses and deaths attributable to the cold (use *both* for the most compelling argument). When other data are unavailable (e.g., if your health department doesn't keep such statistics), newspaper articles still can serve as support for your position. If you have the time or staff (or interns or volunteers), review the local papers daily and save articles that may become relevant to your proposals and your reports to the funders. Sometimes you can use these in an appendix too.

One (very topical) caveat about newspapers: You should be aware of the point of view of the newspaper's publisher if the published data can be, for any reason, controversial, open to interpretation, or possibly taken out of context. It used to be that we didn't question anything we read in a newspaper. Times have changed!

Police precinct data. If your program is intended to serve youth at risk of substance use, vandalism, gang participation, or crime; if you want to show the need for an alternative sentencing program for youth or adults; if your focus is on neighborhood crime prevention efforts; or if you want to show a need for any similar crime prevention or intervention program, your first stop is the local police department or precinct. All police departments are required to maintain data on a variety of types of crime, and they usually compile it by geographic area and age of the offender. How it is summarized or released to the public may differ by state or locality. You should find out whether you must apply to the local police station, the central police department offices, or some other department to obtain statistics. You may be required to submit a formal written request, stating how you will use the information, or you may be encouraged to visit the officer in charge of maintaining the data. You may be allowed to photocopy the police statistics or summaries, or you may have to sit in the office and take notes.

Be sure you know what the requirements are well in advance of your need for information—and be sure you leave plenty of time for the precinct (or yourself) to collect and organize the information.

School reading and math scores, attendance figures, dropout rates, and violent-incident reports. Similarly, if you plan to run a program meant to help children or teenagers improve their academic achievement, stay in school, go on to college, or any other education-related initiative, you should be able to show the need through data from the school in question, the school district, the local education agency, or state department of education. If you don't already know which standardized tests are used in your community, or at what grade levels they're given, you should. Show that your target school (or schools) has a greater proportion of children scoring below grade level on these tests than other schools in the district; show that the school (or schools) has a higher dropout rate or more incidents of violence than others in the community. You also may be able to demonstrate from school records that your school has a higher proportion of children in poverty (e.g., a greater percentage of children eligible for free or reduced-cost meals) than elsewhere.

Hospital and health department statistics. If your program is intended to address domestic violence; teen pregnancy prevention; alcohol, tobacco, and other drug use; children's asthma; gunshot wounds; or any other health-related issue, your local hospital and state and local health departments will be good places to start. If the particular institution does not keep data on a particular problem, staff there will be able to refer you to appropriate sources.

"The literature." Yes, relevant and up-to-date research, trends, and literature are the types of information included in college and graduate-school research papers, but you are generally not expected to scour every esoteric journal or conduct far-flung searches for your proposal. But it helps your cause if you know what the trends and issues are in your area of interest. And why wouldn't you want to know this?

Let's say, for instance, that the literature on nurturing is controversial (some may think there is a subtle "family values" message that encourages parents to stay at home). It would be important to know this and cite it. Suppose that recent trends in the attitudes toward latchkey children indicated that, rather than being disenfranchised and at risk, these children developed strength, character, and resiliency. You would acknowledge this in the proposal, and offer other reasons why it's still important to run a program for these children.

Most important, being familiar with the literature—which is another way of saying the prevailing or conventional wisdom, the accepted thinking—will help you design, refine, and enrich your program. It will afford you the opportunity to study best practices and see what kinds of program elements have been more or less successful. This component of your needs section leads you into describing your program idea. What, if anything, has been tried in your community to address the problem that you have identified? Why do you think these efforts have failed? Why will your program not repeat past mistakes? Why do you expect the "stakeholders" to "buy in"? Even a brief review of the literature can help you address these questions in your program and proposal.

Here again, a search engine such as Google can help you get this information. Thanks to the Internet, there is no longer any good excuse for ignoring trends and research on a full range of issues.

Stop for a Minute: Do I Have to Identify a Need or a Problem If I'm Looking for a Grant to Study Abroad or to Make a Movie?

No. Individual grants are different. They may be research, study, or travel grants connected to a foundation or a university. Research grants certainly will require you to be familiar with the literature and best practices in your field, but "need" may not be relevant. And, as we discussed earlier, other grantmaking decisions may rely on your portfolio of work, your experience, and other documentation.

What If the Grantmaker Has Identified the Problems for Me?

Although foundations tend to provide funding in certain topic areas (such as youth, parks and open spaces, animal rights, the arts) that are spelled out in their annual reports, they generally don't tell you how to identify or solve problems within the areas that they fund. You could apply either to a "youth" or an "aging" funder with your intergenerational program for fifth graders and senior citizens. You know the types of projects the funder supports because you have read the annual report. You know the topic areas the funder supports. It's up to you to describe the problem and explain why the program you've developed will more than likely solve it. It's also up to you to describe the need for your program in a way that clearly shows how it fits the funder's priorities.

Unlike most foundations, federal and other government agencies and large national foundations spend a good deal of time spelling out a problem in the application package, usually citing research on a problem of national importance that they expect the grant seeker to solve locally. Such compelling problems might include the increase in school shootings, opioid addiction among people of all ages, elder abuse, and many others. You may be expected to allude to the data in the RFP or provide additional information relevant to your particular community or problem.

IN CLOSING

As you can see, there are plenty of ways to describe and support the need for your program. You just need to select the best approach to convince the prospective funder that you're fully aware of the need and that your program can address it. Your next step will be to show that you have indeed set out the goals, objectives, and action plan to address it.

POP QUIZ

Multiple Choice

Select the best conclusion to each of the following statements:

1. Grants are usually given to organizations that can demonstrate:
    a. Longevity of five years or more
    b. Continuity of leadership (same leader for no less than two years)
    c. Creativity in juggling their mission statements
    d. Compelling need

2. Which of the following is *not* a good example of the kind of data you might include in a grant proposal?
   a. Police precinct data
   b. Anecdotal information (e.g., stories about a client's need)
   c. Focus groups
   d. Your own intuition

3. The best example of a needs statement is:
   a. According to police precinct data, 50 percent of youth between 15 and 19 in the Bayside neighborhood have been arrested
   b. According to the Area Agency on Aging, 75 percent of senior citizens in the South Senior Center are immigrants who don't know if they can receive any benefits
   c. Three clergymen in Bayside expressed their concern about the drug problem
   d. All of the above are good examples

4. How many footnotes should there be in a typical needs section of a grant proposal?
   a. No more than 5
   b. No fewer than 10
   c. At least 1
   d. As many as you need to make your case

GOALS AND OBJECTIVES: WHAT DO YOU HOPE TO ACHIEVE IF YOU GET THE MONEY?

OPENING REMARKS

I can't tell you how many conversations I've had with managers, program planners, proposal writers, and others about goals and objectives. Over and over, even from the most experienced individuals, I hear the same questions. What is a goal? How does it differ from a mission? What is an objective? How does it differ from a task? And how do I figure out what mine should be? They know what they want to achieve, but they're intimidated by this formal way of expressing it. No wonder the goals and objectives section of a grant proposal is the one that proposal writers often are inclined just to gloss over. —ASF

LEADING QUESTIONS

So—What Are Goals and Objectives?

Go back for a minute to Roundtable I on the Funding Environment and you'll realize that goals and objectives are more important than ever to funders. They want to know their grants will have an impact. What follows may help you show that it will.

Goals normally refer to broad, long-term intentions. Although a goal can seem similar to a *mission statement*, the mission statement usually summarizes the overall purpose for an organization's existence—for example, to work to improve the lives of children. Goals normally pertain to more specific issues you want to address—for example, to improve the education system in this community.

Because goals are broad statements of intention, a particular goal probably won't be met within the time period of a proposed grant project and probably can't be met through the project alone, if at all. Everyone, proposal writer, staff, and grantmaker alike, is aware of this. For example, eliminating youth violence is a goal that, realistically, may never be achieved completely, and certainly not by a single organization or program within a year or two, because it is affected by factors that are numerous, complex, and to a large extent outside the control of most single interventions. A proposed program—say, a youth mediation program—may be only one of many possible steps toward reaching the ultimate goal of eliminating youth violence.

Objectives should be thought of as outcomes that *can* be expected from the project itself. Whereas the accomplishment of goals may or may not be subject to measurement, objectives must be concrete and specific, measurable, realistic, attainable, and time bound. We'll show you how to do this a little later in the lesson. Creation of such clear, measurable objectives is necessary to the development of an appropriate evaluation plan, which we'll discuss in Lesson 11. (As you can see, each section of a proposal is connected to the other sections. Although it's important to engage all the key personnel in proposal preparation, one person shouldn't write the goals and objectives, another the evaluation plan, and another the budget. There has to be a logical progression and a consistent "voice.")

Everybody Says I've Got a Great Program Here. So Why Do I Need to Talk About Goals and Objectives? Why Can't I Just Talk About the Great Program?

A good program speaks for itself, doesn't it? Let's be blunt: As great as the program seems, if you haven't thought through what it's really supposed to do, you may be wasting your time and money (and your funder's)—or you may in fact be doing more than you think, only in the wrong arena. Too often people design a program that has little to do with a problem they've identified and nothing to do with solving the problem. Maybe this is because the program is what their staff members are good at; maybe it's because clients are asking for it; or maybe it does address a problem, just not the one they think they're addressing. But they won't really know that unless they do some systematic assessment. And when they seek funding for this program, or when they have to report on it to get a renewal grant, they'll have a hard time making the case that it has accomplished anything substantive.

DISCUSSION

Because so many proposal writers take a "let's get a grant to pay for our excellent programs" approach—and may have succeeded to some extent in the past—it is not surprising that the idea of methodically moving from a well-documented problem through measurable objectives to a well-designed program seems like a lot of needless work. But what is a good program if it doesn't achieve desired outcomes? What is the impact of your good program on the participants—and on the community? If your first grader spent three hours each week in a delightful Saturday reading program, would that delightfulness be enough for you if the program didn't actually improve her reading ability? And what if you were paying $5,000 a year for the program? Would you even use the word "delightful"?

Come to think of it, what does "delightful" actually mean when placed next to the words "reading program"? That the classroom is colorful and festively decorated? That the instructor has a winning smile? That the children are adorable and well behaved? Remember the rule in Lesson 6 about meaningless adjectives? "Delightfulness" may have a place in a reading program, along with many other important elements, but it has no place in a grant application. "Delightfulness" of a program cannot be measured—but scores on reading tests and attitudes toward books and reading can. Let's look at some examples of concrete objectives.

- One obvious measurable objective for a weekend reading program would be an improvement in reading scores by the end of the year. Because reading scores are affected by many variables—everything from the child's physical and mental health to things going on in the home—a weekly program cannot be expected to magically raise individual scores, say, by a full grade level. But it should be expected to raise the average scores for all the children by at least a small, measurable amount.

- A second objective for the reading program might be any measurable improvement in children's expressed enjoyment of reading (attitudes toward reading) on a standardized, validated attitudinal survey.

- Objectives for a mediation program for at-risk youth might include a positive change among program participants, by the end of the first six months or year, on a standardized measure of attitudes toward nonviolent conflict resolution; a reduction of 50 percent in violent incidents among the participants by the end of the project; and a 60 percent increase in school attendance in that population during the same period. (Notice that we said "objectives." There are three different objectives mentioned here—and each is measurable, although possibly a little optimistic.)

Keep in mind that you will need to develop activities to address each objective (Lesson 9); if your program is intended to be a small, simple program that serves only a few participants, you will want to keep your objectives short and simple as well.

WHAT ABOUT THE GRANTMAKER'S GOALS AND OBJECTIVES?

There are two layers of goals and objectives to think about, and each layer is significant: First, the goals and objectives of the funder, whether stated or unstated, must be understood. Second, the goals and objectives of the grant applicant must fit cozily into the context of the funder's requirements.

What outcomes does the grantmaker want? Many foundations approve funding for a range of programs within their areas of interest, letting the prospective grantees decide what specific goals and objectives they hope to achieve. But government agencies, and many larger foundations, usually have stated or unstated sets of goals and objectives that they expect the applicant to address. If the program announcement or guidelines spell out the goals and objectives for a federal grant program (say, to reduce incidents of domestic violence in an immigrant community), or if the goals and objectives are stated or implied in the background or legislative history of the program (e.g., the Violence Against Women Act, which, at the time of this writing, has lapsed), the proposal that is submitted should incorporate those goals and objectives into the applicant's own plan. For example, depending on their perspective, goals, and target populations, some grantmakers expect to see an *increase* in arrests by the time a funded program is over (because of more police vigilance in a certain community); conversely, some might call for a *decrease* in arrests at the end of the program (because of a reduction in crime). Some funders expect to see that program participants apply to college in significantly higher numbers than nonparticipants. It is important not to lose sight of the goals and objectives of the grantmaker, because the money will be allocated to achieving them.

Sometimes these goals and objectives are the result of extensive research in a field previously funded by a government agency; often, too, they are part of a political agenda. If a presidential, congressional, gubernatorial, or mayoral candidate runs on a platform to do away with illegal immigration, or as the "education guru" or the "crime buster," campaign promises may be fulfilled through grants to programs intended to fix the problems the candidate complained about during the campaign.

How do your goals and objectives fit the grantmakers'? Even if proposal writers are working with the goals and objectives stipulated by a funding agency, the organization's own goals and objectives should emerge clearly as a logical response to the proposal's statement of need, not as a rote response to a funder's demand for specific goals and objectives. If you lose your own goals and objectives in trying to meet the funders', or if you have to twist them out of recognition, this grant probably is not for you.

But language can make it work. You may describe your goals and objectives in one way while the grantmaker describes them another way, but in a careful reading of the RFP or guidelines you may realize that in fact the goals and objectives are not so different; just the descriptions are. This is when using the grantmaker's language matters. We are completely in favor of doing this as often as possible in a proposal (in the text and in the subheads), but it must be used within your own specific context, or the proposal will fail.

With all this talk of using the grantmaker's own language, it might be a good time to revisit something we said in Lesson 3: Foundation and government program officers generally have worked long and hard on the research and policymaking that goes into crafting a program announcement, application, proposal guidelines, or requests for proposals. There is nothing pandering about reflecting the grantmaker's language, research, or perspective in your grant proposal, if you agree with the approach. If you disagree with the funder's premises or priorities—either politically or philosophically—then don't apply for the grant!

BUT HOW DO I MAKE MY PROGRAM'S OBJECTIVES FIT WITH THOSE OF THE FUNDER WITHOUT LOSING THE WHOLE PURPOSE OF THE PROGRAM?

You don't! Remember, you are not going to do anything different from what you believe is needed to solve the problem you have identified. You are just going to think about how you may describe your program and your intended outcomes to make it clear that they will meet the funder's own objectives too. Before writing your objectives, carefully check what the application package says about the program requirements. Have specific objectives been identified that you are expected to address and achieve? What is the problem that the program has been designed to fix? And finally, what elements of your program are likely to alleviate the problem?

In a federal grant competition one of us applied for, applicants were expected to "develop performance indicators that link to proposed goals and objectives, and include levels of performance for each indicator, time frames for achieving levels of performance for each indicator, and source of data for measuring progress." Again, your intention is to understand what the funder is getting at, which is sometimes not easy. If you are confused by the language, this is the time to reach out to the contact person named in the application package for clarification. Why has the money been allocated? What does the funder hope and expect will happen by the conclusion of the project period?

So what DO I do? Sometimes proposal writers are so anxious to win grants that they overlook the funder's goals and objectives in expressing their own. If, for instance, a grant from a local foundation is earmarked for programs that will decrease the number of students who drop out of high school before graduating, you certainly would approve of a reduction in the dropout rate. But you're concerned right now with getting money to pay for a collaborative after-school basketball project. If you only give lip service to the dropout problem, you may be missing the ways in which you can make this basketball project into one that can successfully address the escalating dropout rate in your community. If you think about the design of the after-school basketball project as a solution to the dropout problem rather than merely as "an excellent program," you certainly will come up with a number of worthy measurable objectives that the program should be expected to achieve, and you may want to add some programmatic elements to achieve them.

We can think of three objectives for a collaborative after-school basketball project for at-risk youth, including a reduced dropout rate for participants (there are many more).

- *Objective 1: Improved behavior.* By the end of the first six months of the project, participants in the after-school basketball project will demonstrate improved behavior in school as a result of project requirements and activities, as measured by incident reports and teacher observations before the league starts and six months later.
- *Objective 2: Reduction in violent incidents.* By the end of the basketball project, participants will demonstrate a 50 percent decrease in violent incidents, as measured by school incident reports.
- *Objective 3: Improved school attendance.* By the end of the basketball project, participants will have a 40 percent better school attendance record than classmates who did not participate in project activities.

These measurable objectives may seem surprising. Maybe when you started thinking about the basketball project you imagined teenagers coming to the gym, changing their clothes, getting out on the court, and starting the game. But if you receive funding to reduce the dropout rate and you hope to achieve that objective, then, while the teenagers are "just" having a good time playing ball, you can add some elements to that basic scenario to do just that. And the popularity of the activity—basketball—could help you introduce these elements without losing participants.

For example, if you require the ballplayers to arrive by 3:15 P.M. or be benched for that day, you are teaching them promptness and responsibility without necessarily saying so. Before the games begin, you may feature a discussion period (with light refreshments), led by a popular "coach" who is actually a social worker with experience working with at-risk teenagers. The coach might ask the students to talk about their day in school and any problems that they experienced, and use peer counseling techniques to help them resolve these problems. Discussions on sportsmanship, fair play, and following rules could be emphasized during the games, with team penalties enforced for roughhousing and offensive language. On some occasions the games could be followed by a potluck supper, with the families of the ballplayers included. Or, instead of discussions before the games, you might run a homework help program with tutors from a nearby college who are studying to be teachers (and who also might serve as coaches), as a condition of playing.

As you can see, what started out as a simple after-school basketball project has evolved into a program with a very outcome-directed twist that aims to make a real impact on the teenagers' lives. Every activity associated with the basketball project is part of a master plan that expects to solve a compelling problem and achieve measurable objectives. And it in no way detracts from the teenagers' fun.

Once the objectives are decided on—with the participation of program staff who have the required expertise to help you assess whether the objectives are realistic and optimistic—it is much easier to design a comprehensive program. If you try to design a program without objectives guiding you... well, forget about it. It just makes no sense.

POP QUIZ

Multiple Choice

Which activity would be most likely to achieve each of the objectives listed below?

1. To increase school attendance for teenagers who are truant:
   a. Send warnings home to the parents each time the student is absent
   b. Provide student stipends based on good attendance records
   c. Require regular attendance as a condition of participating in a popular activity
   d. All of the above

2. To decrease feelings of loneliness and depression among older adults at a senior center:
   a. Offer a creative writing program that promotes discussion among participants
   b. Assign a staff member to introduce new members and engage them with existing groups
   c. Bring young children to the senior center to join seniors in an intergenerational arts program
   d. All of the above

3. To make the streets in your community safer:
   a. Bring the community together to advocate for more frequent police patrols
   b. Start a block watch committee
   c. Both of the above

Realistic or Unrealistic?

Which of the following objectives are realistic for a one-year career education course for unemployed adults?

1. Sixty percent of the participants will remain employed for three years after the program ends.

2. Participants will show improved attitudes toward work after completing the yearlong course.

3. Participants in the program will attend an average of 85 percent of the sessions.

4. Ninety percent of the participants will have created a résumé by the end of the year.

DEVELOPING AND PRESENTING A WINNING PROGRAM

OPENING REMARKS

I was working with the director of a youth program who wanted a federal grant for educational support for young women. Because he didn't have time to work on the proposal with me (he would be on vacation), we met briefly to discuss his plans. Then I constructed what seemed like a responsible program to meet his objectives for the young women as well as the objectives set out in the request for proposals. But I made some assumptions that we had not discussed directly. Never assume!

The RFP required intensive work with participants, but the grants would be small. I designed a small program addressed to the age group we had agreed on, showed how it would fit into an existing program, and specified that a small number of new staff would be hired to work with the small group of young women who were identified as most needing the help. It turned out that the director had assumed that the federal grant could be larger than the announcement specified, and envisioned it supporting a much larger number of *existing* staff, working with all of the young women in that program. Obviously, I hadn't communicated the RFP guidelines clearly. When he finally had time to read the draft, it became clear that we had to start over or scrap the proposal entirely. Unfortunately, because of the limited time left to revise the plan, and the requirements in the RFP, we missed this opportunity. —ASF

LEADING QUESTIONS

Okay, I've Identified a Need and Set Out Some Goals and Objectives for a Program I Think Will Meet That Need. Now What?

It's finally time for the meat, the heart, of the grant proposal. The program description, or program plan, should show that you have a thoughtful, workable solution to the problem that you described in the need statement. A clear and detailed description of the proposed program must be strongly supported in several ways. And, as we discussed in Lesson 5, and as the opening example demonstrates, these details must be worked out (and sometimes argued out) in an ongoing, close partnership between the proposal writer, who understands the scope and limitations of the request for proposals, and the program supervisor and project staff, who understand the population to be served, the needs to be met, and their own objectives for the funding.

The program description must match the funder's priorities. The program description should explain what you intend to do and clearly address what you know about the funder's priorities. As we've said before, whenever possible use language from the grantmaker's guidelines to describe your own program to show readers that the proposal focuses on the grantmaker's concerns as much as your own.

Note again that this is not—indeed, must not be—a matter of changing the way your program operates in order to meet the guidelines. When organizations change their programs to chase funding rather than because they see the need or because they have thought of a better way to do things, they can lose touch with what they're working for. Rather, describe your program in a way that lets the reader see how it fits into the funder's priorities.

The program description must address your problem. Next, your program description must show exactly and realistically how the program will solve the problem you have identified. You need to include enough details to demonstrate that the planned activities, the number and type of staff, the number and type of persons who are to receive services, and the time frames for accomplishing your objectives are realistic, and that the program you have designed has a good chance of succeeding in achieving those objectives and making a positive impact.

The program description must be consistent with other parts of the proposal (not to mention clear and well organized). Consistency across all components of the proposal is extremely important. If one of your objectives is to deliver 80 additional meals a day to homebound individuals, you must be able to show exactly how you plan to accomplish this. How will you route deliveries to accommodate your full roster of current and new recipients, and still deliver the meals while they're hot? Will you use an existing van for one or more additional routes? Will you purchase an additional van, and if so, is that part of the current proposal, or do you have other funding sources for it? Will you hire additional staff to prepare and deliver the meals, or will you use existing staff and volunteers? How many of each, how do you arrive at that number, and how will you rearrange the time of existing staff to squeeze in any additional meals that they need to prepare and deliver? Who will supervise them? How will you train any new workers to serve your target population?

In later lessons we discuss additional elements of your proposal that must be consistent with the objectives and the program, including evaluation and budget. For the moment, remember that you also need to know how much the extra 80 meals a day will cost, how much of that expense you are asking for in this grant proposal, and where the rest of the money is coming from.

The program description must show how the proposed program will fit into the organization. You may not just be adding 80 additional meals but rather creating an entirely new program, which cannot be "added on," no matter how needed, but instead must be fully integrated into the organization. If the Meals on Wheels program is new, you also must discuss issues such as who will manage it, where it fits in the overall organization structure, what other programs should be linked to it, and for what purposes.

Whether the funding agency requires it or not, system-wide changes may be an outgrowth of many grants, especially very large ones, and you need to describe what changes you might anticipate and how they would be managed under the proposed program. Grant-funded programs, services, and staff members cannot be suddenly slapped onto a nonprofit, school district, municipal agency, or university structure like a sloppy coat of paint. The programs must become an integral part of the organization, linked to all the other diverse activities being conducted. You will need to show in your grant proposal exactly how you plan to achieve this.

The program narrative should describe how you will handle obstacles, including unanticipated disasters. Some of these obstacles may be simply programmatic: What will you do if you can't recruit enough participants, or if you have too many? What will you do if your program space is not accessible to individuals with limited mobility?

Other obstacles may become more relevant during crises, and this is where a disaster plan comes into play. This has become a much greater concern lately. For example, if the proposal is for a school or after-school program, how will you protect the children in a disaster or even a shooting, and how will you ensure that the children are reunited with their parents as quickly as possible? What will you do if the parents can't get there for some reason? If you run a home care program, how will you ensure that your clients continue to receive life-preserving services during and after a hurricane or an earthquake? How will you work with other nonprofits or government agencies in your community to address residents' needs? If you're a hospital or a nursing home, do you need an emergency generator to keep life-support systems going? (If you have one, where is it located? We learned from recent catastrophic hurricanes that such a generator needs to be in a place where it cannot be damaged by flood water—and that you need to have plenty of fuel on hand to keep it going.) What will you do if you have to evacuate staff or clients? What will you do if transportation is *not* available? Many of these issues may never come to the fore, but now, even for proposals that are not requesting a large sum of money, you should be able to demonstrate that you've thought about them.

It Seems Like a Waste of Time to Do All This Planning When We Don't Know If We'll Even Get a Grant. Why Can't I Figure Out My Plans Once I Win the Grant?

Writing a proposal that doesn't include a detailed, specific plan of operation is like a builder trying to build a house without blueprints. Program plans are the blueprint of the program and the proposal. Without this blueprint, you won't get funded; grantmakers must see exactly what you plan to do with the grant money before they fork it over. If they don't like what they see, they'll go elsewhere. The reason that proposals generally follow a path that begins with a compelling, documented problem to be solved, followed by measurable objectives, is to make sure that the activities—the plan of operation, the blueprint—are designed to increase the chances of achieving the objectives. Besides, if the program is important to your participants, you may very well use this proposal to seek grants from other sources.

How Do Objectives Fit into a Program Plan?

A person who wants to start literacy classes for immigrants probably recognizes a need or problem that confronts immigrants in her community. She sees a literacy program as a good solution to the problem. We hope that she also recognizes the need to spell out measurable objectives that can be achieved through the program. Maybe she wants 60 Spanish-speaking immigrants to learn to read newspapers and be able to fill out forms written in English. Maybe she wants the participants to be able to apply for and get jobs or prepare for the citizenship examination. Maybe she hopes they'll learn how to read labels on the food they buy for their families at local supermarkets. The objectives frame the way that activities will be designed to achieve them.

Without linking activities directly to objectives, staff members and proposal writers can get carried away. Suddenly they may find themselves proposing to take participants in their programs to the theater as a way to learn English. If you don't look carefully and repeatedly at the objectives as the activities are being planned and developed, the program elements are likely to be haphazard and random. They may be fun, like going to the theater, but what outcomes are they achieving, what impact are they having? (And if you think the theater outings really will achieve your objectives, why would a funder give you money for the theater without knowing why you are going?)

How Can I Know Whether Certain Activities Will Achieve Objectives?

This should be the easy part. As we indicated in Lesson 5, you, the organization's only proposal writer, may have absolutely no background in literacy programs, no knowledge of immigrant cultures. Or you, the program person *and* writer, may have a lot of knowledge about literacy or about immigrants and their cultures; this may be your area of expertise. But no matter what the programmatic expertise of the person writing the proposal, individuals with experience, background information, and commitment to the community certainly must be deeply involved in the development of the program and the fleshing out of activities. They're the ones who know what activities are likely to work to meet the objectives—and they're the ones who will have to run the program and who will be responsible for the results.

What's in a Program Plan?

Don't scrimp on the program development phase of the proposal process. Use kickoff and planning meetings (described in Lesson 5) to flesh out the program elements and address potential obstacles to achieving your objectives. The program plan must address everything that will occur from the time a grant award is announced to the time the money is received, and to the end of the funding period (and beyond).

Timeline and staff responsibilities. Construct a timeline, whether the application requires one or not. The timeline should include absolutely every activity that you must undertake to establish, implement, and evaluate the program. What will you do in Month 1? Who will do it? Can you do more than one thing in the first month, or will you be spreading yourself too thin? Here is a sample timeline for the literacy program for Spanish-speaking immigrants (by the way, notice our use of the active voice, as discussed in Lesson 6):

- *Upon notice of a grant award:* The agency director recruits a project director through advertising on the Internet and in local newspapers, notices to relevant organizations, flyers in local schools. If appropriate (and if not completed before the proposal was submitted), the agency director begins to form an advisory board for the project.
- *Month 1:* If not completed before proposal was submitted, advisory board initiates community literacy needs assessment, using focus groups, surveys, and questionnaires. With input from the advisory board, the agency director hires the project director.
- *Month 1 to Month 2:* The project director takes the lead in working with the advisory board; begins recruiting project staff. The project director and advisory board collect relevant curricula from appropriate sources, then review and adapt to serve the needs of the program. If necessary, staff members develop a new curriculum.
- *Month 2:* The project director, with advice from the advisory board, completes hiring project staff. The project director sets the schedule for classes and ensures that space is available.
- *Month 2 to Month 3:* Project director, advisory board, and program staff begin to recruit participants and develop or modify evaluation materials. Staff members prepare materials for classes.

- *Month 3*: Project director, advisory board, and staff recruit 60 participants to join the program. All participants take pretests of English literacy skills and are placed in groups with comparable skill level.
- *Months 4 to 11*: Program staff teach literacy curriculum to groups of 15 students in a class, each class meeting two evenings a week at the Fifth Street YMCA. Staff serve refreshments before class. Project director reviews students' work monthly to assess participants' progress.
- *Month 12*: All participants complete posttests of English literacy skills. Project director and advisory board will analyze changes in test results to measure program effectiveness, and project director prepares a final report to the funder.

The timeline need not be described in a list like the one above; it may be in paragraph form, with one or two sentences for each activity. Or all of these activities may be summarized simply in a chart like the following, either in the text, if there is space, or in an attachment. But don't omit the narrative description of when things will occur and who will do them.

Sample Timeline for Literacy Program

Month:

Activity	Prep	1	2	3	4	5	6	7	8	9	10	11	12
Prepare ads for staff	▓												
Develop advisory board	▓												
Recruit/hire director	▓	▓											
Recruit/hire staff		▓	▓	▓									
Recruit participants				▓									
Complete skills testing				▓									
Implement curriculum					▓	▓	▓	▓	▓	▓	▓	▓	
Final test of skills													▓
Report to funder													▓

Job descriptions. You may or may not need to submit job descriptions with every proposal, but your plan should include detailed descriptions for each type of staff member who will be hired through the grant. In the example above, who are the necessary staff members and what are the necessary experience, qualifications, and responsibilities of each? If there will be workers other than the project director and teachers of English for speakers of other languages (say, a clerical worker to maintain student records), what are the necessary experience, qualifications, and responsibilities?

Staff recruitment plan. This plan should define how and where job postings will be distributed. (Nationwide or local? Internet sites or newspapers? Which outlets? College placement offices, newspaper advertisements, flyers distributed throughout the community? Are trade union contract issues involved in hiring?) It should include everything you will need to do to get started once you know the grant funds will be available. Some grants require a lengthy contract process, so if you don't start addressing recruitment until the money becomes available, you'll be so delayed in implementing the program that you may have a difficult time conducting all the activities you mention in your proposal and spending the money on schedule. This is especially true for local governments, where the hiring process can take considerable time (see the discussion below on government recruitment and hiring).

Advisory board recruitment. If you need an advisory board but don't have established relationships with people you think should be members, now—before you start to implement the program—is the time to call or write emails or letters, describe the project to them, and invite them to join the advisory board if the grant receives funding. If the project is a collaborative one, the advisory board may simply be members of the various organizations you're working with who have assisted in the development of the program. But the role should be formalized.

Government agency recruitment and hiring. If you are writing a proposal on behalf of a city, school district, county, or state government agency, you may need to start the procurement and hiring process as early as the time the proposal has been submitted, even before you know you've won a grant—maybe even before you finish the proposal. Many cities have rigorous and complex procedures for subcontracting with not-for-profit organizations and for hiring staff; these procedures may be completely different from procedures for not-for-profits, which are relatively simple. The best way to plan ahead is to decide while you are developing your grant proposal what staff members you need and which agency personnel lines are appropriate. Check with your budget or contracting office to see how you can hire staff most expeditiously and receive contracted services so that grant funds can be spent quickly. Do this *now*, before you even apply for a grant. We mean it. You don't want to get all tangled up in bureaucratic red tape as you're trying to get your exciting grant-funded program off the ground.

Participant recruitment. Don't take participant recruitment for granted. Some grant recipients are surprised to find that offering a great new program to a target population with a clearly demonstrated need doesn't always bring the participants flocking to the door when the program opens. You need to explain in your program plan what methods you will use to recruit participants, how you will ensure that the program will grab and hold their interest, and how you will keep them coming back. Will you conduct extensive outreach in the media? Will you ask professionals in your field (physicians, schoolteachers or counselors, social workers, youth workers, senior center staff) to make referrals to your program? Is a proposed activity so popular in your community that it will keep every participant engaged for the entire time? If you're not sure whether it's that popular (even if sorely needed), will you pay stipends? Provide child care? Give a gift certificate or a pizza party or a job to everyone who completes the program successfully?

Marketing plan. While working on your proposal, think about how you will sell your program to the community—not just to those who will directly participate and benefit. Will you invite reporters from community newspapers and local radio and television stations to visit? Will you send out short press releases describing the program or announcing an existing program's expansion? Funders often ask about community buy-in or stakeholder buy-in. Although they sound like clichés or buzzwords, these terms spell out exactly what you want to achieve. You want the community to take ownership of your program—to brag about it—to feel secure knowing it's up and running. We've mentioned buy-in often; it's important.

How Do I Make Sure That the Plan of Operation Covers Everything?

If you view your grant proposal as a marketing tool—to sell the seriousness of your problem and the wisdom of your solution—then the activities are the key to your sales pitch. For each of your objectives, you should have one or more activities that are clearly designed to accomplish that objective. Let's say one of your objectives for that "delightful" weekend reading program discussed in the previous lesson is to improve attitudes toward reading as a result of the program. What, exactly, will happen during the program that will improve attitudes toward reading? Maybe some famous people can visit and discuss their own attitudes toward reading. Maybe a well-known local author would agree to discuss her reading history. You might take the children to visit the library, or to a place where books are bound. Popular athletes may promote reading. None of these activities are necessarily likely to improve reading scores, but they very well may improve attitudes toward reading, which may be a good first step toward improving the scores.

No matter how many objectives you propose to achieve, specific activities must be described for each one. Be as detailed as possible. Instead of saying "athletes will read to children," say "football players from John F. Kennedy High School have agreed to read to the children; the football players will receive community service credit for their participation." If possible—and that depends on space and other limitations—a letter from the high school principal should be included in the proposal package, describing the football players' involvement in the program. The more details, and the more partners who have signed on (like the principal and football players of John F. Kennedy High School), the more likely the program is to receive funding.

POP QUIZ

True or False?

1. Activities are the least important part of the grant proposal.

2. Too much detail in describing your program distracts the reviewer.

3. Use terms you know the grantmaker will understand and appreciate in describing the program.

4. Funders prefer that you propose only about half of the activities you expect to conduct so there's room for change.

5. Try to write in generalities just in case you change your mind.

6. Make sure you list specific activities for each of your objectives.

7. Write the activities first, then frame the objectives based on what you plan to do.

8. Timelines are baloney; they waste precious space in a proposal.

9. Funders understand that the person who writes the proposal may not know too much about activities; they'll be sympathetic if you're vague.

10. It is a good idea to do some grant-related work as soon as you know that you've won the money.

FINDING PARTNERS AND BUILDING COALITIONS (THE MOUS THAT ROARED)

OPENING REMARKS

A woman asked me where she could get a grant to fund her "fabulous" idea. "I want to start a summer program that takes at-risk kindergarteners and high-achieving inner-city teenagers to camp in the Catskill Mountains for three weeks," she explained. "The teenagers will be camp counselors and work on reading skills and social skills with the young children, along with sports and arts and crafts. In return, the high school students will get a stipend and community service credit, along with three weeks of fresh air. Participation in this camp will look great on their college applications and we may get some good students interested in teaching or social work."

A great program, right? But when I asked her if she had gotten support from the local schools, community groups, churches, parent associations, or anyone at all, she gave me a quizzical look as if to say, "Why would I do that? I simply need a grant to pay for the idea." —EK

LEADING QUESTIONS

No matter how well designed you think your program is, you must have at the table the right people with the right attitudes and the right expertise and knowledge representing the right organizations before it can evolve into a winning proposal. "At the table" is sometimes a polite (but inaccurate) way of saying that a lot of different organizations support your idea but are doing nothing to demonstrate that support. To turn a good idea into a winning program, the right partners really have to be actively involved. At a real table. And they have to be there willingly and maybe for a number of weeks or even months. Designing a high-quality program is not something that can be done quickly by someone like the woman with a fabulous idea described in the Opening Remarks.

Is This Where Collaboration Comes In?

We have mentioned collaboration throughout this book, and we'll continue to mention it in the next lessons. Collaboration is one of those words that everyone throws around, assuming that it's simple to do, as natural as breathing. In truth, collaboration does not come naturally to most people because it goes against everything we have learned and believe. In *No More Teams!* Michael Schrage[7] reminds us that although most Americans say they want to be team players, they'll grab their bats and balls and head for home unless each of them can be team captain.

Americans usually respect rugged individualism, often viewing people who believe in working together as wimpy idealists or non-self-starters who don't have an original bone in their dreary, bureaucratic bodies. Yet whether it is in the operating room, the boardroom, the basketball court, Congress, or just about anywhere else, people who have a genuine problem and a limited amount of

---

[7] Michael Schrage, *No More Teams! Mastering the Dynamics of Creative Collaboration* (New York: Broadway Books, 1995).

time to address it need to work together to come up with a solution. Schrage says:

> The act of collaboration is an act of shared creation or shared discovery. James Watson, who won a Nobel Prize with Francis Crick for their discovery of the double helix, put it simply: "Nothing new that is really interesting comes without collaboration."

Because collaboration is a lot easier to say than to do, most people have no training in how to be a valuable partner, occasionally leading critics to complain that someone is being "too inclusive." But true collaboration means leaving a lot of baggage at the door. It means coming to the table—yes, really sitting down and talking face-to-face—with an open mind and a commitment to solving a problem in an honest way. And a commitment to finding the best possible solution to the problem, even if that solution doesn't necessarily benefit (financially or otherwise) all the partners at the table. This truly is not easy.

Why Is Collaboration So Important?

Because most of us don't really understand collaboration, we tend to be skeptical about its importance, sometimes viewing it as mere jargon. But it is important to collaborate for two reasons. First, the more people with expertise and diverse points of view who are sincerely committed to developing a solution to a pressing problem, the more likely it is that the solution—the program—will be well developed and of a high quality. Second, the more individuals and organizations involved in developing the program, the more individuals and organizations will actually support the program, agree with the need for it, and agree that the program they have worked out is really likely to meet the need. And the more people who believe in the program, the more likely they are to promote it, recruit participants, and give it good publicity by enthusiastic word of mouth. And, just maybe, support it when the grant ends.

What Makes Collaboration So Difficult?

Most people think they want to work together, think they're collaborative, and think collaboration is a good thing. But it isn't easy to leave our preconceived notions, our long-held beliefs, at the door without learning how to do this. It isn't easy to replace our usual roles, responsibilities, goals, and expectations with an entirely new set. For instance, if you represent a not-for-profit organization that works with children, you've probably adopted a particular approach to youth development that you think is the best way to help children achieve their greatest potential. But a new partner may have a completely different—but also very successful—approach. Does one of you have to forgo your tested views in collaborating with the other? Is it possible to incorporate both views? Is there an underlying philosophy that could help you both be comfortable with the details and outcomes of the program?

You and your counterpart, as directors of your respective programs, are both accustomed to making decisions, solving problems as they arise, promoting the program to outsiders. Who will do this now?

And there are other problems, as the following questions indicate.

The Money I Can Get from This Grant Is Barely Enough for My Own Program. Why Do I Have to Share It with a Partner?

This is a very good question, but there's a problem—a big one—inherent in it. Sometimes we only think about collaborating to work on a grant proposal, not to work on significant problems that confront us every day, whether there's a grant to apply for or not. Talk about the need for a culture change, a paradigm shift! Collaboration must become a way of life—a natural response, not just a grant response.

For years, government agencies, schools, nonprofit organizations, colleges, and so on would independently design programs or promote the same old programs—and submit them to the grantmakers. And often they won the grants. Then grant seekers were told by funders to collaborate on grant proposals and share resources after grants were won. Public schools were required to include parochial school students in their grant-funded programs. City agencies were told to show which not-for-profit organizations were involved in program development. Nonprofit organizations were told they had to partner with each other, and with businesses and religious institutions, not to mention government agencies. And everyone felt like throwing their hands up and crying, "Uncle!"

You don't always do it for the money. The greatest shock about collaborating on a grant was that—gulp—not every partner would automatically receive grant funds from every partnership grant. Collaboration cannot only be about money. If it were, we would probably need a new word to describe it. Collaboration must be seen as a strategy to make things better by working together in a sensible, methodical manner. But that strategy can include something for everyone—well, maybe not everyone, but for several of the partners. For example, in a welfare-to-work consortium, the lead agency (funders always expect one agency to receive the check and be responsible for administering the grant) may get less money to operate the program itself but a bit more for administrative costs. Or one partner may take on an element of the program for which it is especially prepared (perhaps a school or a nonprofit GED program handles the literacy component) and refer participants to a second partner for another element (say, job training), to another for child care, and to still another for job placement. Each partner may receive a different amount of funding, depending on the cost or the partner's ability to contribute in-kind services or other support. If the economy is strong, some partners may be able to absorb their piece of the project into their own ongoing operations. A long-term collaborative approach can ensure that as different grant opportunities come along, the other partners will benefit, with the full support of those who get funding in this round.

But sometimes you have to say no. Despite all the benefits of collaboration, there still may be times when a collaboration for a particular grant just doesn't make economic sense to any of the partners. Sometimes a small organization will feel a larger partner is going to soak up all the resources and leave the smaller one with the responsibility for its share of the work. A direct and honest negotiation, and perhaps a contract between two partners (in the form of a very detailed memorandum of understanding, which we'll discuss below), may help resolve this fear. A funder may require collaboration in hopes that it will cost less than grants to individual organizations, even when it is clear that the collaboration actually could increase the project's cost. Some grantmakers do consider the extra costs associated with creating and sustaining a collaboration, and may provide a bit more money to support this effort if there are no resources available within any of the partner organizations—or in the grant—to pay for the work involved. Although collaboration may indeed be the best way to get things done in the long term, sometimes the partners have to decide not to pursue a particular funding opportunity. And we think you should let the grantmakers know why.

But We Provide All of the Services That Are Called for in the Request for Proposals. Why Do We Need a Partner?

Another good question. As we just noted, our position is that sometimes you should not pursue a grant that requires a partnership, especially if you believe that the amount of funding provided could not support the program that you and your partners would have to implement jointly. But very often a funder who is asking for a community coalition or partnership is looking for results that a single agency cannot possibly achieve. It is rare that a single agency really offers all of the services that the grantmaker envisions in such a request for proposals. For example, a coalition of health providers, schools, and social service providers may have a better chance to have an impact on children's asthma than health providers alone.

DISCUSSION

Increasingly, government agencies and many foundations are calling for collaborations among not-for-profit organizations, or between nonprofits and businesses within a community, or between community-based organizations and larger institutions such as a university, a city agency, a hospital, a board of education, or a national or regional nonprofit. Some grantmakers tell us that this is especially true when it is necessary to advocate for funding or legislation concerning issues that affect the community as a whole. Sometimes a group of grantmakers themselves form a consortium to pool their resources, again believing that they can have a greater, more widespread impact this way. If a partnership is called for, ignoring this requirement is fatal to a proposal.

All nonprofit organizations of any size should be reaching out to other organizations in their field of interest and/or in their community, even if these organizations have been competitors in the past. They should be discussing ways of working together productively to address issues of mutual concern. It may be necessary for organizations whose programs overlap to rethink which of them will provide which services. All of this takes time, usually much more time than is available between the time a funding announcement appears and the deadline for proposal submission; this is why collaboration should be ongoing and not only grant related.

Although the lead agency in almost all partnership arrangements must be a government agency, a school district, or an organization incorporated as a 501(c)(3) with tax-exempt status, smaller organizations that are not incorporated may be important partners in a project and may strengthen a proposal by demonstrating a true community partnership. This is a good way for small grassroots organizations to become known to a wider audience than just their immediate neighborhoods, which is important to their own fundraising efforts.

If you do not presently have relationships with other community organizations, you should be approaching every sector of the community, from churches to merchants, from tenant associations to civic and immigrant associations, from schools and school districts to hospitals and health centers, to discuss ways you might work together. If there are existing task forces (such as a task force to combat drug use among teens or one to address domestic violence in a certain immigrant community) or advocacy groups that share your interests, join them. If you can't join, see if you can observe meetings or even become part of working groups that may form. If there are none, talk with other agencies about forming one.

City agencies with sites in the community should be approached. Elected and appointed officials at every level of government also should be included in discussions. If you're not a member of the local Lions Club, or Kiwanis, or chamber of commerce, consider joining. The broader and more diverse the representation within a community, and the more convincing the coordination and integration among partners, the stronger the proposal and the better the chances for funding.

And even if you're not currently seeking any funding, you'll be pleasantly surprised at how much support community organizations can provide for one another. Maybe the Rotary Club will throw a holiday party for the children at your day-care center or members of your senior center; maybe a bank will provide a meeting room for a class in English for speakers of other languages; maybe the school board will find money for snacks for children in the after-school program.

How Do We Show the Funder That We've Worked Together on a Grant Proposal?

Some (not all) grant applications that require collaboration also require documentation of the development of a collaborative program. Notices of meetings, lists of those invited, attendance lists, agendas, and other such documents may prove useful; you should start and keep a file.

Letters of commitment (also called memoranda of understanding, or MOUs) spell out the ways groups will work together, provide resources, refer clients, participate on advisory boards, and so on. MOUs are an important way to document a partnership, replacing the bland, redundant "support" letters commending the program that organizations so often attached to their proposals in the past. This also may be where smaller organizations can pin down what they can give and what they most need from the partnership.

MOUs should be included in a proposal package, if they are allowed. They should be considered minicontracts. Normally they will be presented in an appendix (and are discussed in more detail in Lesson 15); occasionally you will be asked to put them into the body of the proposal. In any case, a paragraph or two about the partners should be included in the proposal narrative.

Reviewers generally can tell if a collaborative effort has been thrown together for a particular grant, especially if they are familiar with your community. Again, outreach and discussions about possible joint efforts should begin *now*.

When a collaboration is proposed in a funding request, each partner's activities, roles, and responsibilities should be addressed with the same level of attention, and their interactions must be presented fully and in detail. For example, for the welfare-to-work consortium mentioned earlier, details of each partner's contribution would be described along with the ways in which each partner would identify, refer, and provide support to participants and interact with the other partners in the consortium. Which partner or partners would handle job training? How, and from which other partners, would clients be referred for training? How, and to which partners, would clients be referred for job placement, child care, social services, GED preparation, or college courses?

Government collaborations. For grant seekers representing local government agencies, collaborations often can present a more complicated set of issues. Many government agencies, because they are responsible for specific services like transportation, sanitation, or housing, are inexperienced at working with one another, let alone with "outsiders" such as schools, not-for-profit organizations, colleges, and hospitals. Collaboration among government agencies involves not only potential competition for dollars but competition for credit, for attention, for praise—maybe from the mayor, the governor, the press. If the police department collaborates with the health department to strengthen the latter's application, and this helps win the grant, then where is the police department when the press conference is held? The answer is that all partners should be viewed as teammates, integral to the winning of the grant—and included in the press conference to announce the grant! When a baseball team wins the World Series, the player who hit the tie-breaking home run—or the team manager or team owner—isn't honored alone. All teammates, managers, and coaches are honored together.

Remember the little guys! Many not-for-profit organizations shy away from working with government agencies or with large nonprofit institutions such as universities and hospitals because they are afraid they'll be swallowed up—disregarded and disrespected by the larger, more powerful agencies. And we've seen this happen. It is critical that the larger organizations, which usually take the lead in the proposal process and manage the grants when they are received, work to keep the process and lines of communication open to avoid shutting out the smaller groups. Timely input and ongoing support from those closest to the community can make or break a project.

So, as we've said, learning to collaborate—learning not to act like Big Brother or the King of the Road—is important for government agencies. If you want to solve your compelling problems (and win competitive grants), you have to view not-for-profit organizations of all sizes as real partners. And not-for-profits must, in turn, stop viewing government with the same reserve (at best) or distrust as in the past. State and local agencies must be seen as the valuable resources they are—as partners to enhance grant proposals and provide useful data, statistics, insights, and experience in implementing programs.

As George Bernard Shaw once said, "Success comes from taking the path of maximum advantage instead of the path of least resistance."

POP QUIZ

True or False?

1. Collaboration isn't that hard—we're all essentially team players.

2. Every organization that collaborates on a grant application should, without exception, receive at least some money once funding is approved.

3. If a grant doesn't require collaboration, don't collaborate.

4. City agencies like to collaborate with city agencies, schools like to collaborate with schools; it is when they have to cross sectors that problems rear their ugly heads.

Short Answer

1. The best way to actually prove that you collaborated with other groups on a grant proposal is to include _____ and _____ in your application. (Give two examples.)

2. List five different sectors of the community that might collaborate on a winning grant. _____, _____, _____, _____, _____.

3. What are some synonyms for "collaboration"? _____, _____, _____.

THE EVALUATION PLAN: HOW CAN YOU BE SURE IF YOUR PROGRAM WORKS?

OPENING REMARKS

I was evaluating a grant-funded program designed to help a small number of homeless families in shelters find and remain in permanent housing by providing intensive, long-term assistance.

A variety of measures showed that it was a very successful program. For example, the families remained in permanent housing significantly longer than families without this assistance—and this information enhanced the organization's later proposals. But staff interviews indicated that the staff felt overwhelmed and burned out by the amount of work they were doing and thought there was a need for more staff. A review of the case files showed that they *were* overworked, but not because they had to be. It turned out that in addition to the small group of clients who were their primary focus, they were providing information or short-term help to hundreds of other families in the shelters; they couldn't say no.

Among other recommendations, I suggested that the program managers either rethink their objectives—and possibly hire additional staff to do the short-term assistance—or retrain staff to focus only on the smaller group that was the original target population. —ASF

LEADING QUESTIONS

I Have Four (or Three, or Two, or One) Programs to Run. Who Has Time for Evaluation?

First of all, you'd better make time if you ever want another grant from the funding organization that asked for the evaluation. In the wake of corporate scandals in the early 2000s and the financial-sector meltdown in 2008, Congress passed new laws requiring, among other things, greater transparency and accountability in the private sector, and it has been working to apply these regulations to the nonprofit sector. Although some of these regulations have since been dropped or modified, foundations and government funders (often under pressure from their boards or the legislative bodies that set the rules for government programs) increasingly are looking for proof that their grants make a significant impact in the lives of people and in the community.

Besides, as you'd agree if you had time to think about it, you really *do* want to know whether the programs that keep you so busy are operating the way you want them to, are meeting your objectives—and are worth the effort. Too many people wait to think about evaluation until the report is due, which is a surefire method for creating serious headaches for everyone involved with the program and is no way to measure the success or failure of a program.

Remember: Programs aren't funded and conducted to look good in reports. They are designed, funded, and implemented to address compelling problems. Well-designed and well-executed evaluations tell you if you've been successful.

The best time to think about the evaluation is when you're first designing a program, when you can select those outcomes and indicators that will satisfy you that the program is working, whether the grant application actually requires an evaluation plan or not. If the information is carefully and systematically collected, and it convinces you that you're getting the results you intended, it almost certainly will be sufficient to convince the funder—and potential funders—as well. And every grant proposal should discuss how a program will be evaluated. It's common sense (we hope) to describe to a funder how you will know if the program is working and what you'll do if it's not. Don't let the absence of an evaluation requirement stop you. Your evaluation plan can be addressed, at least briefly, along with your measurable objectives or in your program description. The key to any good relationship with funders is transparency; you need to keep this in mind as you plan.

My Staff Members Work Hard. They Know If Programs Are Working. Why Do They Have to Have Someone Evaluating Them?

People don't like the feeling that someone is looking over their shoulders, monitoring everything they do. But this really is not what an evaluation is about. Almost all program staff members and managers we've ever met are interested in how well their program is doing and whether their teenagers or seniors or children or students of English for speakers of other languages are getting something out of it. More importantly, staff want to know whether the participants are getting what staff members *hope* they will get out of it. And almost all staff members and managers truly want to know how they can improve their programs. The purpose of an evaluation is not to judge an individual worker but to consider the entire program and determine what works, what doesn't, and how to fix what needs fixing—and sometimes, as in the evaluation described in the Opening Remarks, to reduce the amount of work a staff person is doing!

I Work for a City Government Agency. Of Course We Know How to Run Grant Programs. But Federal Applications Ask for Such Complicated Evaluation Plans...

If a government agency is giving grants for hundreds of thousands of dollars—often millions of dollars—of taxpayers' money over one, two, or three years, why wouldn't it expect to see the most rigorous, methodical evaluation plan? Proposal writers, like program staff, sometimes take offense at the whole notion of evaluation, as if the funder is prying or being just plain nosy. The evaluation plan should be viewed as an important element of the proposal, linked in an orderly way to the objectives and the activities planned to achieve the objectives. As the program is developed, the evaluator should be involved in the process of identifying realistic, measurable objectives.

Whoa... You Said "Evaluator"! Do I Need to Hire—and Pay for—an Evaluator?

The answer to this question depends on your organization's capacity to develop meaningful evaluation plans and conduct meaningful evaluations, whether you are a not-for-profit organization or a government agency or a school district. Federal or state grants often require that the applicant spend a specific percentage of the grant funds on evaluation activities. That's usually a big hint that you should work with an outside evaluator—whether it be someone from a local university, a research organization, a state or city agency that conducts evaluations, or an individual consultant.

Most evaluators who work with government and nonprofit agencies understand the grants process and are willing to help develop the proposal (and the evaluation plan) "on spec," meaning they get money only if the grant is funded, even if they donate considerable time to the planning process. If the evaluator expects to be paid to participate in the development of the proposal for a grant, this is probably not the right evaluator for you. (At least, it wouldn't be the right evaluator for us.) It is reasonable for not-for-profit organizations and government agencies to try to find competent evaluators who do not view a grant as a cash cow. Evaluators should be as much a part of the program development team as every other partner, helping to define and refine the objectives in measurable terms and devising a comprehensive plan that will be included in the grant proposal.

Some evaluators—especially if they are from universities—also may be willing to donate space for meetings and activities, recruit student interns, or provide professors' expertise for all facets of the program. In this way, the evaluators become real partners—collaborators—not just hired hands. And remember, colleges and universities are often eager to work with and support nonprofits and municipal agencies for many reasons—an important one being to build good will in the community. Even if you are a grassroots organization just getting started, you might want to approach a local college for help figuring out evaluation and other strategies for your program.

The cost of conducting the program evaluation should be outlined in the budget; sometimes a separate evaluation budget should be attached, explaining how many people will be conducting the evaluation and in what capacity, along with other relevant details. The evaluator should be able to help with this too.

DISCUSSION

An evaluation, like a needs statement, can range from the simple collection of information on a few indicators (e.g., attendance, demonstrated improvement in a skill, or other concrete measures) to extremely complex research projects that can assess the long-term outcomes of the program or compare it with other programs to determine which is most effective. Evaluations generally are of two types: process evaluation and outcome evaluation. Whenever possible, it's smart to use both, as did the evaluation in the Opening Remarks.

Process evaluation. Process evaluations, sometimes called *formative evaluations*, are used to assess the functioning of the project and provide feedback to allow for program corrections. Process evaluations consider such questions as whether activities are occurring when and where they should, who is receiving the services, how well they are being implemented, whether they could be done more efficiently, and whether participants are satisfied.

Process evaluations generally make use of qualitative methods, which might include focus groups, personal reports, observation notes, case files, surveys, and interviews. You might use this type of evaluation during the first year of a new program, or you might maintain some form of process evaluation throughout the life of the program to keep it functioning at the highest level.

Outcome evaluation. As the name indicates, *outcome* (or *summative*) *evaluations* measure outcomes, program effectiveness, and the program's impact on the problem that it is designed to address. The questions that outcome evaluations raise include whether program objectives have been achieved, whether the target population has changed as a result, whether unanticipated results have occurred and whether they are desirable, what factors may have contributed to the changes that have occurred, how cost-effective the program is compared with others with the same objectives, what impacts the program has had on the problem, and what new knowledge has been generated.

Outcome evaluations generally, but not always, are formal in approach and designed according to professional research procedures. They use primarily quantitative methods but may draw on systematically obtained qualitative data to help explain the research findings. Such evaluations probably would involve "before and after" measures of attitudes and/or behavior and/or knowledge of members of the intervention group (the group that experiences the program) and at least one control or comparison group (which does not receive services, at least until a later time).

Which specific data collection methods are used depends on the nature of the evaluation and the questions to be answered. They may include standard attitudinal or behavioral measures that have been tested on similar populations, or they may be developed and tested for the specific target population. Questionnaires, observations, systematic collection of data from various sources, and similar techniques may be used.

Keep in mind that a program's impact on a broad population or community might require multiple measures over time and might be well outside the scope of your project or your ability to evaluate. It may take the resources of many researchers to determine what factors even need to be examined to determine the real outcomes. You should be comfortable describing the need for long-term evaluation to the funders, and perhaps suggest additional funding to conduct such an evaluation or that this might be the subject of a different grant.

Okay, Evaluation Is Useful. But How Much of the Evaluation Design Do I Have to Put into the Proposal?

At the most basic level, unless you're writing a proposal for a large grant that requires an external evaluation—in which case the evaluator will write the section—you often just need to let the reader know that you care about outcomes, want to know if you've succeeded, and have thought carefully about how you will know if you've succeeded. If you can make the case that collecting a few pieces of information, and looking at changes in those indicators between the beginning and end of a program, will tell you whether the program has worked, and if that information clearly relates to your objectives, the reader probably will accept this as a reasonable effort at evaluation.

Some examples might include the number of adults who were hired for jobs after completing a job training program and, if you can follow them over time, the number who remain in the job; children's reading scores before and after a semester of tutoring in an after-school program; or the number and percentage of teenagers' acceptance to college after the college-bound program, and the number and dollar value of scholarships they receive. A longer-term measure might track whether they stay at the college and whether they graduate. You might use a standardized format to obtain older persons' feelings of depression or loneliness before and after they've engaged in a discussion club for a few months.

How Do I Decide What to Include?

We can't tell you exactly what to include, of course; it depends on your program and your resources. But here are some basic principles that underlie the evaluation section of a proposal and will be at the back of a reviewer's mind.

- *The linkages between the activities (program components) proposed and the expected outcomes of the program must be clear and explicit in the evaluation design.* This linkage is spelled out in the program objectives. Here's an example: By the end of the project, 80 percent of the 21- to 24-year-olds who participate in a comprehensive work-study program will pass their GED exams. The GED scores of the work-study participants will be collected and analyzed.

- *"Dosage," the actual amount or level of services provided, can influence outcomes.* For example, children who participate for two hours several times a week in a tutoring program may show better results than children who participate for an hour once a week—or may not, which has implications for program planning. Another word for dosage is *intervention:* What (and how much of the activity) is actually received by the target population that will likely yield a certain result that can be measured.

- As suggested by the last example, *negative findings can be just as important as positive results* because they help in understanding why a program did not work and how it might be modified to be effective. Why continue providing many hours a week of tutoring when one hour is sufficient?

- *Qualitative data (informal interviews, for instance) can be useful* in determining the effectiveness of an intervention, especially when quantitative data (e.g., scores on standardized tests) are not appropriate or available. Qualitative data also can supplement quantitative data to explain the results and make the evaluation even more comprehensive.

Reviewers will look at the evaluation section to see if it answers several important questions beyond the obvious ones: How did the project work? Were the specific objectives achieved? Which ones were or were not? Were the activities that you planned actually conducted the way you planned? (You may have planned for four workshops to take place in the evening but revised that plan when too few people wanted to come out after dark. Instead, you ran the workshops on Saturday mornings, and you provided child care so people could attend—which greatly improved attendance.) Were there any unexpected world, national, or local events that seemed to affect the success of your project? What did you learn from them? Did the staff members who were hired to run the project follow the job descriptions stipulated in the proposal? Was there community and/or organization buy-in—and if so, how do you know? Could the project be replicated by other organizations in your town or across the country as it is, or should elements be changed for replication purposes?

This Can Be Serious Stuff

As we discussed earlier in this lesson (and in Roundtable 1, at the beginning of the book), funders increasingly want to know their grants have a real impact on the problem they're intended to solve. Many grants, especially those from the federal government or large foundations, may require systematic outcome evaluation of the funded project, using validated and reliable measures (as opposed to homemade quizzes and surveys), to demonstrate whether the program has had an impact, and why it had or did not have an impact. In many cases the funding agency expects, or even requires, that the grantee hire an external evaluator, and tells you in the guidelines to build in the costs for the evaluation. But even in cases where the evaluation is done "in house," it should be as rigorous as possible.

If you think you may be interested in seeking funding to test a model program that you have created (or are replicating), you should establish a relationship with a college or a consulting group that has experience with the funding agency or experience evaluating the type of program proposed. As we said before, the earlier an evaluator becomes involved, the more useful the evaluation plan will be and the stronger the proposal is likely to be. Ideally, the evaluator will help you formulate realistic goals, achievable objectives, and even appropriate activities that can be expected to lead to the results you hope to see. The relationship between you and the evaluator is a special type of collaboration.

POP QUIZ

True or False?

1. Evaluation is only necessary for large government grants.

2. Process evaluation looks at how many, how much, how well, and how often.

3. A large, multiyear grant should have only an outcome evaluation to tell you what the program's impact was.

4. If a grant application requires an outside evaluator, you have to hire a consultant to help you with the evaluation section of the proposal.

5. An evaluation has to be a formal process using an academic research approach.

6. An evaluation considers only statistical data.

7. Whew...the grant application doesn't require an evaluation plan, so I'm off the hook.

8. The best time to think about evaluation is at the very beginning—when you first begin designing the program.

9. Small demonstration projects don't need to be evaluated.

10. Frankly, you should always work with an outside evaluator, even if you are applying for a $5,000 grant.

Short Answer

Describe three important things that you can learn from an evaluation.

THE BUDGET: HOW MUCH WILL IT COST ... AND IS THE COST REASONABLE?

OPENING REMARKS

As I was reading a proposal that a municipal government agency was about to submit to a foundation, I noticed that the budget seemed awfully high for a relatively modest project. Nothing in the program description or objectives seemed unusual, and I was anxious to see what in the world was going to cost all that money. Was there a conference in Maui that 10 staff members would attend? Was the commissioner planning to buy an SUV or something? When I finally got to the budget narrative, I saw it right away. The project director of this relatively modest little program was expecting to be paid an annual salary of $120,000. No one preparing the proposal had a problem with that amount of money...hey, it's a grant, right? (P.S. They changed the salary but they didn't get funded.) —EK

LEADING QUESTIONS

How Do I Figure Out How Much Money to Ask For?

We're pretty far along in this book, yet we haven't focused on the budget...hmm. We've alluded to the budget in every lesson, emphasized its importance, but only now are we focusing on it. Don't for one minute think that you should wait this long to focus on your proposal's budget. You should be considering costs as you lay out your objectives, design your program, build your collaborations, and think about staffing, evaluation, and everything else.

The budget must be consistent in every respect with what you've said you are going to do. Many proposal writers provide excellent needs statements or program descriptions but offer budgets that appear inflated at one extreme or inadequate to carry out the necessary program activities at the other. Some proposal review criteria include points for what is called the *appropriateness* of the budget. The individuals who will be reviewing your proposal often have run programs or agencies like yours, although not necessarily in your city or town. They already know what's realistic and will react favorably toward your proposal if your budget does not overstate or understate the amount of money you will need to do the job. To develop a realistic budget and explain all proposed costs, you need to know the following:

- Exactly what staff and other costs are required to do the job?
- How many people—professional, clerical, full and part time— must be hired to implement the program?
- What skills, education, and experience will each project staff member need to have?
- What is the usual salary that such a background can command?
- Who will manage the program, and will you need to allocate part of that individual's salary to the budget? Why?
- Do you need to pay rent? For how much space? Why do you need that space?

- Is any local or out-of-town travel involved? For what, and how often, and what will it cost?
- What equipment and supplies must be purchased for the program?
- Are there any costs involved in staff training?
- Will there be any stipends for participants?
- Do you need to hire consultants? If so, what will they do, and how much time will they spend on these activities?

The in-kind column. You also have to decide what you *don't* need funds to pay for. Can your agency's secretary create and distribute the newsletter you'll develop to publicize the grant-funded program? (Does your organization even *have* a secretary?) Can managers donate any time to making sure the program is working well at the beginning? Do you have volunteers or interns available? Can your own staff conduct training for new staff? Again, be realistic. If adding responsibilities to the workload of existing staff will burn them out—don't do it!

Once you've addressed all the things you need to know, there are two key budget questions you need to ask.

Is the amount of money I'm asking for really sufficient to achieve the objectives I've proposed? This is an important question because your objectives often get lost in the shuffle of the activities you're planning. Why are you developing the after-school or weekend reading program? If you hope to increase reading scores, you probably want to hire licensed reading instructors, who command a relatively high hourly rate. If you hope to get children excited about books but have no intention of measuring reading scores before or after the program, then you may be able to hire young, enthusiastic college students who would expect to earn significantly less per hour—or even volunteer. Remember that the proposal process works backward and forward: When you craft your objectives, you must keep budget parameters in mind. If the grantmaker is providing a finite amount of money for a lot of required activities, make sure that you don't set unrealistic, unattainable objectives.

Is the amount of money reasonable or outlandish—or somewhere in between—for the things I want to do? The question is much more than a nuance or a matter of semantics. Grant seekers sometimes view grants as opportunities to hire additional staff and purchase equipment and supplies that couldn't be afforded otherwise. Others may "lowball" their cost projection in order to win a grant. But reviewers of government proposals and foundation program officers have been around the block, and they are looking for a budget that's pure perfection—a Goldilocks budget: not too high, not too low, but *just right*. What would a reviewer say about a $3,000 computer, when perfectly good PCs are available in the stores for under $500? Is $45,000 a reasonable yearly salary for a master's-level bilingual social worker in my area, or do I have to allow at least $20,000 more?

We Don't Have Any Money to Pay for the Guy Who Keeps This Place Clean. Can I Ask for His Salary in This Proposal?

Probably not. But it's a very good question. The issue of who will fund support services such as secretaries and custodial staff is discussed endlessly by grantmakers as well as grant seekers. Most funders rightly want their money to be spent on activities that directly benefit the intended target population. But many grantmakers are becoming aware that unless somebody pays for the person who cleans up, or answers the phone, or handles payroll, or maintains the files, or tracks and orders supplies, these jobs will fall on higher-paid professional staff, often to the overall detriment of the funded programs and intended recipients.

So if you can show that the custodian plays a role in the operation of the program for which you are requesting a grant, or provides a less costly service than you could otherwise obtain, you may be able to receive the portion of his salary that is directly attributable to that role. For example, say you run an after-school arts and crafts class at your community center, and you have to leave the room clean for the senior citizen exercise class the next day. You might require your art teachers, who are paid $20 to $30 an hour, to spend an extra half hour to an hour cleaning up each day, or you might make the case to the grantmaker that it is more efficient to pay a custodian $15 an hour to do this. Clearly this doesn't solve the problem of where the rest of the custodian's salary comes from, but it does help a bit. The key is to make your case. Don't try to slip unexplained expenses into the budget.

Local government agencies and school districts do not generally have to ask for funding to pay custodial salaries. They usually can provide cleanup, clerical support, and other important services as part of their everyday activities as an in-kind contribution. Usually the grant-funded program is a drop in the bucket compared with the overall municipal agency budget. That's why it is smart for government agencies to be very generous with in-kind contributions. Grantmakers of all kinds (government and foundation) might have a difficult time sympathizing with a city department of health or department of education that claims it has no one on staff to type some letters or to clean up at the end of program activities. Nonprofits, on the other hand, which often need every penny of the grant money to survive, must be responsive to specific funders' requirements about what they will and will not fund.

So—what IS allowable? All grant seekers want to know what is an allowable cost and what isn't. Is a custodian allowable? Rental space? Construction costs? Ambulettes? Vans? T-shirts? In most cases the best way to find out what you can and cannot use grant money for is to read the application package carefully. (You've heard this before?) Some federal grant applications are very specific. They may, for instance, require applicants to spend a certain percentage of the funding on a yearly evaluation and another set amount on a particular program element (for example, a certified literacy instructor). If the application says nothing about what you can and cannot use the money for, and you're not certain, call or email the funder. Don't automatically assume any element of your program will—or won't—be an allowable expense.

But We Really Need a Full-Time Custodian. Couldn't I Pretend We Need a Few Extra Youth Workers but Pay for the Custodian Instead?

In a word, *no!* Even if doing this were ethical, it's just plain stupid. As we've said before, whether at foundations or government agencies, the program officers responsible for the grant you are applying for are very well aware of what it takes to run a program for 50 children or 200 elderly people or 12 physically challenged teenagers. In many cases they've been there themselves, running programs and writing their own proposals for funding. In other cases they've been reviewing proposals and visiting and evaluating programs for many years. They know the realities and they know the tricks. They can be very supportive if they see a strong, honest case for the costs of your program and very annoyed if they think you're trying to fool them. We stressed the importance of transparency in the lesson on program evaluation. It is equally as important to have a transparent budget.

DISCUSSION

Much of what we discuss in this lesson is just common sense. If you've ever prepared a budget for your organization, you probably are familiar with most of the terms and examples we're providing here. Just remember that each budget item must be calculated and described in a way that clearly and adequately addresses program needs for staffing and other costs—and demonstrates that each and every activity can be properly performed with the amount of money specified in your budget.

The key to developing your budget is to think through all of the real costs of operating the program and to show exactly how each budget line relates to program implementation. Even if you are not required to present a formal budget narrative (a section in which you provide a verbal description and justification of each budget item), the budget must flow from the proposed activities and reflect realistic estimates of what is required to implement the program. It should be comprehensive and detailed enough to demonstrate that you fully understand and can justify all likely costs. And, working back and forth between the budget narrative and the program, you should be sure that every item that appears in the budget or budget narrative is accounted for in the text of the proposal.

The budget reflects the program. There may be several different ways to develop programs and budgets that address the same objectives. For example, an organization might plan a program to tutor 100 sixth graders after school during the course of a year. The budget could reflect one of several different choices you could make for implementing the program. You might use 50 tutors (each working two days a week with two students) or 25 tutors (each working one day a week with four students). The tutors might be volunteers who are given transportation costs, or they might be paid by the hour, or they might be given a flat stipend for the year. Whichever strategy is selected (and justified in the needs section and the program description), the costs of each strategy will differ, and the costs must be explained in some detail in the budget narrative. How much you spend depends on what you're trying to accomplish, and how.

As to the form and content of the budget, not surprisingly, grantmakers require varying degrees of detail. All budgets won't look the same. Federal funding agencies (which tend to provide a lot of money) and state and local agencies (which may provide less but still have to account to taxpayers and federal funders) expect detailed budgets, with a separate line showing each budget item and calculation of costs.

The budget narrative. Budget *narratives*, or budget *justifications*, describe the budget in words and justify the expenditures, item by item. In a narrative, you will relate each budget item to the activity it supports. One sentence usually is enough for each item. Again, even if the narrative isn't required, developing one helps you make sure you haven't left anything out. You may think it is obvious that a clerical assistant will maintain program records such as attendance, reading scores, surveys, and so on, or that the youth workers will organize and oversee the basketball games—or that the basketball program needs to buy basketballs—but you still must explain these things to the funder. If equipment such as a van, desks, printers, file cabinets, and so on is required, its purpose should be clear in the program narrative, and the budget should indicate how many, what type, and the unit cost. (We know a grant writer who actually calculated how many crayons and jars of finger paint would be needed for a preschool art program. This may have been carrying things a bit too far—but it did show the funder that the staff knew what it was doing.)

Foundations want to see program budgets with projected income and costs. In the past they did not usually require a formal budget justification, but some foundations are moving in this direction. Even if a formal budget narrative is not requested, be sure that all of the items in the budget relate to activities described in the program narrative. Whether you are approaching a government or private grant-maker, the numbers in your budget should be as specific as possible. Rounding out a budget item to the nearest hundred or thousand dollars suggests to the funder that you're trying to take a shortcut, which is not smart; showing the exact cost of six basketballs demonstrates that you've researched costs and thought about the program in detail.

Sections of the Budget

Program budgets generally focus on four areas. At the end of this chapter (page 216), we'll show you a very simple sample budget for the literacy program we talked about earlier; it will cover all four of the areas discussed here. All program budgets will have a similar breakdown, though some funders ask for more details or a different format. Some government budget forms run to several pages, and we're not going to review them here. It goes without saying that you should follow the directions and call the program officer if you don't understand an instruction. But all budgets need the following information.

Personnel services (PS) (also called *personal services*) include the costs of all project staff (usually not by name, but by title) and the percentage of their time or the number of hours that they will work on project activities. Unless the grantmaker specifically rules it out, you also may include all of the time that one or more managers can reasonably be expected to devote to the program, whether in setting it up, recruiting, training, supervising the program director, conducting outreach, maintaining partnerships, acting as liaison with the funding agency, and so on. In most cases this will be expressed as the proportion of the managers' time allocated to the program, based on a full-time salary.

Staff should be broken down by full time or part time, year round or seasonal. Although we are oversimplifying here, full time means any employee who works full time for the agency, even if not all of her time is allocated to the specific program. Part time, for budget purposes, generally means any employee who works less than 21 hours a week. The reason for this distinction is that staff members who work 21 hours or more a week normally are entitled to every benefit the agency offers, whereas part-time employees are entitled only to what is required by state or local law, so the calculation of fringe benefits differs between the two groups.

Each budget line presents one or more staff members with the same title. For example, for the literacy program we described earlier, one line would show the annual costs for a project director at 50 percent of full time (she devotes the other 50 percent to a different program), at a specified annual salary; another line would show the total annual cost for three teachers of English for speakers of other languages, each at 15 hours per week over 40 weeks, averaging $30 per hour; and the third line would show a clerk to maintain student records at 50 percent of full time at a salary of $22,000 a year.

Staff whose positions will not be funded by the grant still should be listed if they are working on the project, and their salary should be shown in a separate column as an in-kind donation. It would be a mistake to leave in-kind contributions out of the budget. The funder needs to see the grantee's commitment to the project as well as the total cost of the project, for replication purposes. Salaries for a multiyear budget should reflect anticipated cost-of-living and contractual increases if the funder allows it.

Fringe benefits (e.g., Social Security, unemployment, health and disability insurance, vacation, holidays, pension) are shown on a separate line and should not be combined with salaries. Because different organizations have different packages of benefits, fringe is estimated as the appropriate percentage of the total cost of salaries. As noted earlier, it may be calculated differently for full-time staff, who receive all benefits in your package, and part-time staff (less than 21 hours a week), who may receive only the legally mandated benefits.

Other than personnel services **(OTPS)** (or *other than personal services*), as the name indicates, describes all costs associated with the project that are not staffing costs. They may include the program's share of rent (for the number of square feet it occupies, or for rental of meeting space when it can't be donated, a gym, etc.); its share of liability insurance or an agency-wide audit; supplies such as paper, photographic materials, sports equipment; and travel. This category also includes consultants—perhaps a theater teacher who comes in to produce a play, a human resources trainer, or a program evaluator, anyone who provides services but is not a regular employee. Of course, you will recruit volunteers and student interns whenever possible; if you pay them stipends, these are an OTPS cost; if you do not pay them, you can show the in-kind value of their work.

If out-of-town travel is planned (say, to take a group of high-school students to visit colleges or for staff to go to a professional conference in another city), the budget should show the actual or estimated train fare or airfare, the cost per mile for a car, actual or estimated daily cost of hotel and meals, conference or training costs, and so on. Make sure they're allowable expenses under the funder's guidelines. Also, be sure that such costs are in line with any regulations your organization or government agency may have on the books; for example, many organizations have maximum amounts you can spend on a hotel room or a meal.

Indirect costs (also called *overhead* or *administrative overhead*) are agency-wide costs that cannot be reflected in the program budget but are required just to keep the doors open—the fiscal, human resources, and development departments; utilities; rent, custodial, security, and clerical costs not allocable to any program; and accounting, legal, and insurance costs. This line usually is expressed as a percentage of the total program budget and of course will vary depending on the size and complexity of the organization. The funder may limit the amount that can be charged as overhead, and as a result you may receive much less than your actual costs. In some cases this may be negotiated. Some federal agencies, for example, may instruct you that the maximum overhead you can request is 5 percent or 10 percent of the total budget. However, once you receive a grant, you may go through a process that shows your actual, audited costs in detail, and win an agreement from the funding agency for a higher "negotiated rate" for the following year. Once you have a "federally approved indirect cost rate," you may be able to use that for grants from other funding sources. It's always worth asking.

Getting help. If you are framing your grant proposal budget for the first time, it may seem very technical and intimidating. But it should be no more daunting than doing your household or personal budget. Once you do your first budget, the others will be much easier. And we'd be surprised if there was no one in your organization or on your board who handles financial matters. Of course, large organizations—government agencies, school districts, citywide or national not-for-profits—have entire departments that handle budgetary matters. These specialists will be happy to work with you on your proposal budget or prepare it for you. (They are money people. They want you to bring funds into the organization!) If you are a small grassroots organization applying for foundation funding and you need assistance with your budget, ask for help from someone on your board with financial know-how (if there isn't such a person, there should be) or see if there is a university nearby that has accounting students willing to help, either for free or a nominal fee.

Or call the grantmaker. The program officer may have some good suggestions about where you can go for technical assistance.

You must be brutally honest about your budget. If you fudge here and there—and the grantmaker finds out—well, you know the rest. If you innocently underestimate your proposal costs, you'll find yourself trying to conduct the grant program on a shoestring, which is neither fun nor easy to do. And if you underestimate costs, you decrease your chances of achieving your objectives. So be careful.

Sample Budget for Literacy Program

Personnel Services (PS)	N. hrs./ week	N. wks.	Annual Cost	In-kind
Project director, 50% of full-time				
at $38,000/year	17.5	52	$19,000	
ESOL teachers (3), 15 hours/week				
each, at $30/hour	45.0	40	$54,000	
Records clerk, 50% of full-time				
at $22,000/year	17.5	52	$11,000	
Subtotal Personnel			$84,000	
Fringe at 21% (full-time staff)			$ 6,300	
Fringe at 10% (part-time staff)			$ 5,400	
Total Personnel			**$95,700**	
OTPS				
Books, supplies, and materials,				
90 students at avg. $12/student			$ 1,080	
Printing/photocopying publicity materials			$ 500	
Room rent, 200 sf at $14/sf				$ 2,800
Volunteers (3), 15 hours/week at				$18,000
estimated value of $10/hour				
Total OTPS			**$1,580**	**$20,800**
Project Subtotal (PS + OTPS)			**$97,280**	**$20,800**
Administrative overhead at 10%			$ 9,728	
Project Total			**$107,008**	**$20,800**

POP QUIZ

True or False?

1. I'm desperate for a new copier for our executive offices. I should include one in the budget of the basketball grant I'm writing, right?

2. I'm desperate for new laptop computers so my students can communicate with other children throughout the world. The funder says no equipment costs. But if I explain carefully why they will improve reading scores, it's okay to put the laptops in the budget anyway.

Short Answer

1. If a reading instructor is working for free on a grant-funded project, what does this mean and how do I show it in the budget?

2. What is the difference between PS and OTPS in a grant proposal's budget?

3. Give two examples of OTPS expenses.

LESSON 13

SUSTAINABILITY: HOW WILL YOU CONTINUE THE PROGRAM WHEN THE GRANT FUNDS RUN OUT? (AND YOU'D BETTER NOT SAY, "I WON'T!")

OPENING REMARKS

A complex federal grant application that I worked on, which was funded collaboratively by the US Departments of Education, Justice, and Health, asked applicants to explain how "short- and long-term strategies will allow for the systematic development of infrastructure that builds organizational, community, and individual capacity to sustain outcomes beyond the life of the grant."

"How are we going to address that mouthful?" everyone wondered. "Where do we begin?"

Sustainability—plans for keeping programs and organizations up and running once the grant period is over—is a topic writers are asked to discuss in grant proposals. Grantmakers, it seems, don't like to think that the grant-funded activities will end the second their money runs out. They want some assurance that additional funds will become available to maintain the program. And can you blame them? —EK

LEADING QUESTIONS

But If I Had Enough Money, I Wouldn't Need to Apply for a Grant in the First Place!

Obviously, if money were no object, all the programs in the world would be created, enhanced, expanded, and sustained if successful. In the past, foundations assumed, often correctly, that a successful program would be picked up and replicated by a local or state government agency.

But now funders at every level, from foundations to the municipality to the state and federal government, assume that you will find someone other than them to maintain a program after their grant ends. Federal agencies assume that local government, or perhaps businesses or individuals, will step in to keep a really good program going. Local government agencies hope the state will take over the funding, or that clients will become eligible for entitlement funding such as Medicare or Medicaid or federal disability insurance, or that clients will be happy (and able) to pay fees for services received when the program works well. We know that this is a catch-22.

Whether in tough economic times or a flush economy, it is important to show a grantmaker (and reassure yourself) that at least some of the program elements, if not the entire program, will live on.

Show that other grantmakers are interested in the program. Earlier we suggested that you keep on file a list of current funders of the agency and your programs. Your program budget could show actual income from other grants as part of the total support of an existing program, or it could show all the other grants for which you're applying to support a new program. (Increasingly, funders are thinking carefully about how realistic you are in projecting such income, and they're talking to each other, so make sure your list isn't mostly fantasy.) If you're a government agency, you should describe the tax-levy support that the locality already provides, or any external government funding stream that is or will become available, in order to demonstrate the stability of the program.

Explain that long-term government support will be available once you've developed the program. As we've said, foundations always have liked to provide seed money for new programs that they expect the local or state government to take over if they prove to be successful. But, of course, there is no guarantee that this will happen.

Nevertheless, if you can mention government funding streams that may be available once the program is established, you should do so. One example is an employment program for out-of-school youth. As we write, there still is federal money, usually through a state or local government agency, for such programs, but the guidelines require the grantee to serve fairly large numbers of young people. If you feel you're not ready to jump into such a large-scale effort, and you want to start small and then expand once the program is up and running by applying for the government grant, your request may fit right in to a foundation's "sustainability" criteria.

In a health program, you may know that most of your prospective clients will be eligible for reimbursement through an entitlement program or through private insurance. You may be able to show that once your program has reached full capacity, it will be supported through this income.

Explain that you plan to sell services to supplement a program. If you are seeking a grant to develop a curriculum and run a program, say, for using the arts to engage children in reading or STEM skills, show how you could market the curriculum to other children's programs, or even to children's museums, in order to sustain the program. Or discuss how, if you win a grant to provide special skill training to your home care staff, you may be able to sustain the program by selling training slots to other organizations that want their workers trained but don't have all the resources to do it. If you can demonstrate that your business-oriented approach will work, the grantmaker may be interested in helping you start up and operate the program until the funding stream is well established. We discuss a number of such initiatives in Lesson 18.

If you are a county or municipal agency, tell the reviewer about prospects that the tax-levy budget will cover the funding once the grant period is over. Be open about any difficulties you may encounter while tax revenues are down, but explain which state or federal grants will be available to fund this program, and describe any success you've had in winning such grants. Be sure you make it clear how and when you will apply.

Show underlying support from a larger program. For example, if your agency operates a teen center with other foundation funding or government contracts or grants, show how the proposed karate program or day camp fits into that structure. If you run a senior center, show how a health grant will provide nutrition courses for the participants. These activities may end when the grant runs out, but because there's an underlying, stable source of funding, it is more likely that you will be able to find other grants or realign your overall program to eke out at least part of what you need to keep a project going.

Demonstrate your organization's commitment to and experience in keeping programs going. Do you have development staff? Describe how that staff will pursue additional funding in the future. Have you been working to diversify your funding? Are you undertaking any entrepreneurial initiatives to bring in unrestricted funds? (See Lesson 18.) Describe your initiatives. Do you have a fundraising plan? Describe it. Have you raised private or government dollars in the past? Explain your past success in raising money to sustain programs that are similar to the one in the grant application.

One organization we know had a program that brought otherwise homebound elderly to a senior center to socialize with each other and with more active seniors. This program started with foundation funding. It always operated on a shoestring, but because an external evaluation showed that it significantly reduced serious depression among the elderly participants, the agency was committed to keeping it alive and had done so for more than 10 years. Support was patched together at various times from small foundation and corporate grants, from bits of government contracts when the funder approved, from in-kind contributions, and from the agency's own general operating funds. Proposals for this program consistently demonstrated the organization's commitment to keeping it going, and this commitment did help to win additional grants over the years. Sadly, the program finally had to be closed because of cutbacks in other funding. So we know you can't keep all of your important programs going—there's just not enough general support available out there even in the best of times. But when it's appropriate and possible, tell the grantmaker so.

Consider asking participants to help. We've all become accustomed to the idea that grants from foundations and government would always allow us to provide free services in communities with great need. The reality of the current grant climate may force us to reevaluate this assumption. In Lesson 1 we talked about fundraising approaches that smaller organizations could use before they were ready to apply for grants. Now, even established organizations may want to look back at some of these alternative income sources.

Of course a bake sale won't sustain a program, but if program participants could run one for the general public every month (or even every Friday), the income could help offset some costs of the program. Although, as we've said before, nonprofits rarely want to ask for contributions from participants in less affluent communities, their small contributions in the form of dues, fees, or in-kind donations can help offset costs. Even in the lowest-income communities, organizations (and grantmakers) have found that program participants can pay modest fees or offer volunteer assistance in return for services. Some organizations have incorporated "pay what you can" contributions into their programs, with some success. If you are thinking about such an approach, explain this to prospective funders as part of your plan to sustain the program—and show how a grant can help you do this without denying services to those who can't give anything.

Show how your community partners will be part of the fundraising process. Everyone interested in the proposed program—especially if it is a collaborative one—and connected to the organization in any way needs to get together to figure out how to sustain grant-funded programs. It may be possible for some of the partners to provide portions of funding in a few years. If they can't, at least you can show how the effort has been made.

Use grant funds for activities and/or resources that have a life beyond the grant period. Training, for instance. If grant funds are used to provide up-to-date training for your organization's staff, then the newly trained people will continue to do excellent work once the grant period is over. Train-the-trainer courses (sometimes referred to as turnkey training) increase exponentially the number of individuals who receive training. If 10 staff members participate in a comprehensive, intensive, grant-funded seminar conducted by a top-flight instructor with vast experience in the field, and each of them turns around and trains another 10, who train another 10... well, you get the idea. You are training dozens or even hundreds of people for the price of one grant-funded training session. But don't get carried away. The funders are aware that you're trying to maximize your grant dollars—to spread them as thin as possible to get the most bang for the buck. But they also can sense when you are spreading the money too thin, and getting no bang whatsoever.

Resource guides also live on when a grant period is over. Funds can be used to develop comprehensive guides that will benefit the community (e.g., an exhaustive listing of all programs in a city or community that provide day-care services, including their requirements, program elements, and ratings). The more comprehensive the resource guide is, the more expensive it is to prepare. But it can be updated easily from one year to the next by simply adding or subtracting a page.

Professionally produced and edited training videos also will have a life after the grant has concluded. While costly to shoot, they may be widely used over many years—more than making up for the price.

A disaster plan is another example of a project that lives on after a grant. Once such a plan is in place, it costs relatively little to update it in future years.

Coalitions that develop and implement projects collaboratively may have a better chance of sustaining projects. You'll have more potential funders as a group than each has alone. If an after-school program is a partnership among the school district, a few not-for-profits, the city's parks department, and a local college—well, maintaining this program may be easier than if one not-for-profit alone ran the program, especially if the partners are pleased with its success.

Is It a Mistake to Request a Grant to Fund a Program That Really *Will* End When the Grant Period Is Over?

This is a difficult question to answer. If you're making a film or writing a book, you may be able to complete it within the grant timetable. But why should a successful program for seniors or teens or young children not be ongoing? If you are very sure that there is no possible source of funding to continue a program, you may feel it's better not to get started and inevitably disappoint the participants when it ends—not to mention having to lay off staff. Remember what we said in earlier lessons about not chasing money if it doesn't fit with your mission? This warning applies to pragmatic considerations as well.

Maybe you're ahead of a trend. But what if you feel strongly that you must start a program to address what you know is a growing need? You may just be a little ahead of a trend. Some years ago, there wasn't much broad funder interest in programs for people with Alzheimer's, but, because of the growing need, some Medicaid managed-care organizations started turning to these programs as a less costly alternative to nursing homes. You might not have been sure that this would happen when you first realized how necessary such a program was, and you probably would have been afraid you couldn't sustain it if you got a grant to start it up. But if you started the program anyway because you knew how important it was, you might be in a good position to sustain it now.

Repeat after us: Get involved with advocacy initiatives. One way to get a sense of what grants are going to become available is to keep in touch with advocacy groups working to create new funding streams to support programs of interest to your organization. In New York State, for example, there is extensive advocacy around a dedicated funding stream for family literacy programs, with a fair prospect for success as of this writing. Don't forget to tell prospective funders about the advocacy efforts.

Go for a demonstration project. Sometimes, when funding is uncertain and the prospects for future funding aren't at all clear, it may be worth pursuing a grant for what is called a demonstration project, a model program that is tested through a rigorous and formal evaluation, which will show the project to be effective or ineffective. If it is effective, it may be expanded and funded through the organization's budget or other outside funding that becomes available just because it has been demonstrated to work. If it is effective in some aspects but not in others, it may be revised and tested again. If it is shown to be ineffective, of course, there is no point in continuing it.

Level with the funder. Finally, as a very last resort, you may have to level with the funder. You may have to say you've explored other prospects for support, but there's nothing out there right now that you can point to. But explain how important the program is, what an impact it will have on people's lives. And show how committed you are to doing whatever it takes to keep it going once it's started.

POP QUIZ

Essay Questions

1. Let's say you want to show that you will sustain a literacy program for immigrants in your community if the Love Foundation gives you a grant to cover the first year. How will you convince the foundation that your program isn't a "one-year wonder"?

2. Explain why you might decide to apply for a grant even if you're not sure you can sustain the program.

Short Answer

Another good word for sustainability is _____.

CAPACITY: PROVING THAT YOU CAN GET THE JOB DONE

OPENING REMARKS

I've received many calls from people who wanted help to get a federal grant. A little discussion revealed that these people were from small grassroots organizations that were running a well-attended recreational program for children in the area, or beautifying and maintaining a neighborhood park, or patrolling their blocks to prevent drug users from doing business there. But they operated by committee, with little or no organizational structure, financial system, or other mechanisms that would have let them handle large sums of money and the complex financial and programmatic reporting that is required by a federal grant. They did not have the *organizational capacity* to manage such a grant. —ASF

LEADING QUESTIONS

If I Work for a Not-for-Profit Organization, What Does It Take to Prove My Organization Can Handle a Grant?

In some application packages, especially from a government agency, you may be asked to address *organizational capability*, *organizational capacity*, or something similar. It's important to be able to demonstrate that you can manage the money efficiently, implement the program as it's designed, and handle the reporting requirements (which for some government grants are substantial). Even when these questions aren't asked, somehow you need to include at least a paragraph with information about your track record in the proposal, because it is one of the things almost all grantmakers really want to know.

Go back to your files. As we've said before, you can save a good deal of time if you have assembled a file of materials like those we described in Lesson 4. You usually won't use all of them, but you can tailor them to a specific proposal. Such a file will give you a much easier time persuading a reader that your organization and staff have just the right kind and amount of experience. Here's the kind of information you want to provide in order to show capacity:

- The organization's history
- Your successes in implementing projects similar to the proposed program
- Your reputation in the community to be served
- Relationships with partners in past and proposed collaborations
- Management and staff experience, qualifications, and awards
- The organization's overall budget
- A description of your organization's fiscal control procedures
- Grants that you have won
- Letters of collaboration or commitment or a chart describing community linkages (which some grantmakers ask for in this section, while some ask that they be presented in an appendix)

Tell them about your organization's relevant history. If you haven't done this already, add to the file that brief history of your organization; its experience in operating all the current programs (the number of years a program has operated, the number and type of clients served in it); any awards or honors the organization or any of your programs has received; brief descriptions of the board members' experience, related or not, and their affiliations; and any honors and awards that board members, managers, and staff have received.

Keep the website up to date. This is an important way to let prospective program participants (and funders) know what you offer, what awards and prizes you've received, how you're celebrating the work of your staff and volunteers, about upcoming events that funders—along with the general public—could attend, and about other relevant news to show how vital and exciting the organization is. Provide telephone numbers for key staff. Post the relevant sections of your 990 tax forms and your most recent annual report, perhaps even your latest audit report; this demonstrates that you operate transparently—you are prepared for anyone to see this information. More and more organizations also have a Facebook page and a Twitter account where followers can see what they are doing; develop this capacity if you can.

Show them your board is involved. You should be able to describe how the board oversees the organization. For example, how often does the board meet? Does it have committees or working groups that meet regularly? What are they, and how do they operate? How often does the board receive reports on programs, and how does it intervene, if necessary, to affect the way the agency or major programs are operating? How does the board maintain oversight of the budget?

Describe your effective fiscal systems. It is extremely important to demonstrate that you have fiscal systems in place to ensure the proper expenditure of grant funds. Internally, how are finances managed? Who oversees your fiscal affairs? What staff do you have to track income and payments, and what controls are there over the receipt and expenditure of funds? Which financial software do you use? How often are budget reports provided to management and the board? Is there a regular external audit? Is there a development office? What types of grants do you apply for?

Present up-to-date audit reports. Foundation funders expect you to submit any available agency-wide audit reports. Regarding their own grants, they generally require reports on the expenditure of their funds, but rarely ask for a separate audit just for their grant. Government agencies do conduct separate financial and program audits, but despite the time they take and the wear and tear on your fiscal staff, this can benefit you in the future. Because government agencies generally have strict accounting and accountability requirements, your organization is considered more stable and credible if you have had financial or program audits and received positive evaluations from other government funders. If you have received government grants, have you been audited? Have your procedures been evaluated? Have all of your reports been on time and accepted by the funder? If so, say so. Any information you can provide that shows that other grant-makers have found your organization to be fiscally responsible and programmatically sound will enhance your ability to win new grants.

Mention any relevant evaluation reports. In the same vein, any internal or external program evaluation reports that you have commissioned can help to demonstrate not only the quality of your programs, but also your confidence in your ability to implement them. Again, it is not usually necessary to submit copies of these documents with a grant application, but it is often useful to describe or refer to them.

If I Work for a Local Government Agency or a School District, What Does It Take to Prove My Organization Has the Capacity to Handle a Grant?

Grantmakers—federal, state, and foundation—have certain expectations about municipalities and school districts that differ from their expectations for not-for-profit organizations. A city's police department or school system is not dependent on a grant to conduct its day-to-day business, but a not-for-profit organization may have to shut down numerous programs if it doesn't receive grant funding.

Because of their size, their responsibility, and the critical services they provide to the community, government agencies are assumed to have the capacity to implement grants...but do they? Although a municipal agency or school district may manage enormous budgets, run numerous programs, and employ huge numbers of people, funders need proof that grant programs will be implemented in precisely the manner and time frame spelled out in the grant proposal. They want to see that cities and school systems are not "black holes" into which money is poured—and immediately lost.

To show organizational capability, municipal agencies and schools should, first, flaunt their resources, brag about their leadership and accomplishments, explain their management structure, describe funding streams, and highlight previous grants they have won (and implemented efficiently). Grantmakers may not specifically ask about hiring and procurement, but they would certainly be relieved to know that grant-funded staff will be hired quickly, without obstacles delaying the process, and that contracts and subcontracts will be efficiently organized. If the city has systems in place to speed up grant spending, don't hesitate to mention them.

A timeline like the one we developed in Lesson 9 is very important to show funders exactly when grant-funded positions will be posted, interviews conducted, staff hired, and staff given the go-ahead to start working. Timelines that show which activities will take place before funding is approved—even before the proposal is submitted—help prove organizational capacity for a municipal government agency or school district.

What's This "Adequacy of Resources" Question?

Whether you are a nonprofit organization, a school district, or a government agency, you will have to demonstrate a few other things to show you can handle a grant. For many government funding opportunities, you will be asked to describe the adequacy of the resources that will enable you to conduct the grant-funded activities. You can't assume that a reader knows anything about how strong and substantial your organization really is, and what wonderful "extras" you can provide.

In some ways this question overlaps with information you may also have to give when you demonstrate the sustainability of a program and the in-kind contributions you will make available. It's okay to be redundant; in fact, if two questions in the guidelines call for a similar response, then you *must* be redundant.

Explain what your physical facility is like and what part of it will be available to the program. Do you have enough computers, printers, scanners? Do you have a library, an auditorium, a gymnasium (with or without sports and exercise equipment)? Also (and this is where a floor plan may be useful) explain how the space is accessible to participants with disabilities. How many volunteers are available to support program activities? What are community partners contributing to the project?

As you can see, the word "resources" here doesn't just mean money. This is where you brag about all your other assets.

A Last Word

Why all this fuss about "capacity"? A good way to view organizational capacity is to think of a couple of analogies. First, would you hire a new member of your staff without studying an applicant's résumé; summoning the person to at least one or maybe many more interviews; calling a number of references; perhaps requesting a writing sample; and "asking around"? Second, if you worked in a university admissions office, would you accept an applicant into the incoming freshman class without looking at grades, standardized tests, a personal essay? Without speaking to faculty at the applicant's high school, checking references, meeting the student?

So it is with funders. It makes perfect sense that they want to know as much as possible about your organization's capacity before sending you a check. They want to make the greatest possible impact with their resources; you need to convince them that you can accomplish what you say you will.

POP QUIZ

True or False?

1. An organization's leadership is critical to a funder's assessment of the organization's capacity.

2. Before I apply for a government grant, I have to make sure my organization has the right fiscal controls in place.

3. Nobody cares where my board members work and how much time they spend overseeing this organization.

4. I should expect to put my organization's detailed history, all program descriptions, and staff résumés in every proposal I write.

5. Government agencies should brag about the resources they can bring to a grant-funded project.

Essay Question

A grantmaker is on the fence. There are two excellent applicants for one chunk of money. Describe all of the things that were included in your proposal that prove your organization has the capacity to implement the grant and therefore should be the one to get it.

FRONT AND BACK: THE COVER PAGE OR COVER LETTER, THE ABSTRACT, THE TABLE OF CONTENTS, AND THE APPENDIX

OPENING REMARKS

When I was a beginning grant writer, I focused only on the parts of a grant proposal that were worth a specified number of points—the items I viewed as questions that called for good answers to get the best possible score. Materials such as the cover letter, abstract, table of contents, and appendix received the shortest shrift—until the first time I actually looked back at a copy of a proposal that I had submitted to the federal government for many millions of dollars. The abstract—the very first impression the funder was getting of my organization (and me)—was a mess. There were grammatical errors. The whole abstract was one long, long, long paragraph. And the information in this endless paragraph was disorganized and unclear. No wonder we didn't get this grant. Now I wouldn't think of sending a proposal off without a perfect cover letter; a crisply written, well-organized abstract; a comprehensive table of contents; and an appendix full of relevant, well-chosen information (if an appendix is allowed, of course). —EK

THE COVER PAGE: MAKING IT OFFICIAL

When you are submitting a proposal to a government agency or a common application form published by a regional association of grantmakers, there is usually a page that takes the place of a cover letter (although cover letters often are included anyway, to be polite). The cover page contains the agency's legal name, address, and contact information (including the executive director or agency head, and a program contact person if different); the employer identification number (the organizational equivalent of a Social Security number); the number or identifier of the grant you are applying for (e.g., the Catalog of Federal Domestic Assistance program number); the amount requested; the project start and end dates; and other items, depending on the agency issuing the application package. You would expect these forms to be standardized (and to the extent that every grantmaker needs similar information, they are). But each state and city will have certain elements that are important to that entity, so we thought it would be meaningless to try to give examples for each. Indeed, even within a single municipality, the cover forms can differ from agency to agency.

One cover page that still is almost universally used at the federal level is Form SF-424, sometimes with a letter prefix representing the agency (e.g., ED-424 is the cover page for applications to the US Department of Education). You can find these forms at Grants.gov, and you can download or print them from a chart that lists them all (www .grants.gov/forms/sf-424-family.html). We're including this form in Appendix 4 because, like the common application forms, it includes almost everything you will see on any government cover form.

THE COVER LETTER: GETTING OFF ON THE RIGHT FOOT

When Do I Need to Use a Cover Letter?

When you are applying for a government grant and there is a cover page, it isn't really necessary to add a cover letter, which probably will be discarded anyway. But for all foundation proposals, even when there is a cover page, and for some government proposals that don't include a cover form, we recommend a cover letter. It should be brief (not more than half a page—one page if it substitutes for an abstract or program summary). It should give a one- or two-sentence statement of what you're requesting in the enclosed proposal and one or two reasons—based on the foundation's priorities and interests—you're applying to this foundation. This is especially important if your organization is new to the foundation.

If you're not including a formal program summary or abstract, use the cover letter for this purpose (see the next section and Appendix 4 for some pointers). In this case, include one or two sentences each about the need, the objectives, the program, the partners (if it's a collaboration), how you plan to evaluate the program, the cost of the program, and the amount you are requesting.

If a program officer has been helpful to you in developing the proposal, you should mention this—and note that you've tried to include information that you discussed with the officer. If you've had a grant from this foundation before, mention how important that grant was to your community. (Remember that grants aren't about you; they're about the needs you are trying to address.)

Keep the letter short, to the point, and polite. And that's it!

THE ABSTRACT: MAKING IT EASY FOR THE PROGRAM OFFICER

An abstract (sometimes called a summary, program summary, or executive summary) is the first thing a reader sees and may be your most important marketing tool. But because you can't really prepare it until your proposal is nearly finished, there's a tendency to rush through it, seeing it as less important than the rest of the proposal. And if a grantmaker doesn't ask for an abstract, many writers assume it's not necessary and breathe a sigh of relief about having one less thing to worry about. But if you can slip a summary like this into your proposal, you really will be a little bit ahead of the game.

Isn't an Abstract Redundant? The Proposal Explains the Program in Great Detail, So Why Summarize?

The abstract gives the program officer something to take to the foundation board, or gives the government agency something to take to its congressional oversight committee to show how the money is being spent (and saves them the work of doing it themselves). The abstract summarizes the proposal in a page or two. It can be read quickly, yet it gives the reader—the reviewer—a good sense of the need, the program, the applicant, the goals and objectives, and the budget. The abstract is a work of art! (Stop laughing. To a proposal writer, this *is* art.)

If you were a funder, you'd want the applicant's abstract to include a little more than just a summary of what the organization (or individual) plans to do with the money, although you might not say so in the application guidelines. As noted, foundation program officers often use abstracts to summarize the proposals they plan to recommend to their boards. Government agencies may use them to demonstrate to elected officials that the grants went to projects that were intended under the legislation that authorized them.

When a funding agency asks for an abstract or an executive summary, it often specifies how long this item should be (e.g., two double-spaced pages; half a page; 250 words) because this, or something similar that the program officer prepares, is the document that is going into the officer's report or recommendations. So within that limited space you must be sure to cover most of the following information briefly. (The key word is *briefly*; you may need to cram each item into a single sentence.) As you'll see, it closely tracks the components of a proposal. (An example is given in Appendix 4.)

- A description of your organization, agency, school district, or school. What are you? Where are you and what area do you serve? What services do you provide? To how many people? How long have you been in existence?
- The compelling problem you are addressing in your proposal. If you have room, you should give a taste—a *taste*—of the research and statistical information that are included in your needs section.
- Description of your program, explaining that it will address the problem you've identified by targeting a specific population and achieving the objectives that you briefly summarize. What activities will you conduct? Who are your partners? If all a funder wants is a two- or three-sentence summary of the program alone, you should be sure that this summary is finely honed and includes all of this information.
- Brief description of your evaluation plan.
- Overall cost of the project; the amount of the request; and, as appropriate, your organization's contribution to the project cost and other funders who are supporting the project through either cash or services.

Sure, it's a lot of information, but you must keep the abstract to the page or word limit the funder indicates. That's why you can't just dash it off at the last minute.

What's the difference between an abstract and a summary? There is none, except possibly length. We tend to think of an abstract as a little more complete and formal in style, and it's the term you may see more often in a government request for proposals. We think of a summary as shorter (often just one paragraph), perhaps less formal, and the term that may be used more often by foundations. But the information contained in each is basically the same.

TABLE OF CONTENTS: THE READER'S TRAIL OF BREAD CRUMBS

If your proposal is only a few pages long (say, up to the five or six pages that many foundations ask for), and if you've provided a well-written abstract or summary paragraph, you won't need a table of contents. But for larger requests and longer proposals, such as those for national foundations and government agencies, this road map can be very helpful. It tells the funder that you've covered all the items in its application guidelines or in a request for proposals. It helps a reader or reviewer flip back to something read earlier to check a fact or answer a question. It's useful to the reader, and anything that makes the reader happier is good for you. We suggest that you take the time to create a table of contents, even if the guidelines don't require one.

Think back a minute to Lesson 3, on application packages. Remember that we said you should answer all the questions and address all the instructions, in the same order in which the grantmaker lists them? We suggested that you use an outline. Subheads would include the keywords mentioned in the instructions, to demonstrate that you are responding to the required topics. So it should be pretty easy now to create the table of contents: Just go back and list the titles of the major sections. (Don't get carried away and make the table of contents three pages long; you can stop with the major subheads.) Include the titles of appendices or attachments too, so the reader can see instantly that they're all there and where to find them.

And the reason we're mentioning this at all—you may be thinking, "a table of contents, oh, come on!"—is because it's another intangible: something that makes your proposal better but is not necessarily mentioned in the guidelines or application. A table of contents will allow you to check that you've answered all the questions and that your subheads show continuity and are relevant. And as you prepare your table of contents, you'll notice if any of the sections of the proposal seem a little skimpy and need more work.

THE APPENDIX: IT'S NOT JUST A USELESS ORGAN

You say you have only five pages to make the case for a large foundation grant, and there's important information about awards and honors your agency has received that you have to stuff into those five pages to prove you are the stellar organization the foundation is looking for? You say you've developed an extraordinary partnership with four other organizations in the community to solve a problem you've all been wrestling with on your own, but you don't have space in the proposal to do more than describe the partners in a few words? The appendix is not a useless organ. Here's where you get to show off without occupying vital space in the proposal narrative.

Aren't Appendices Filled with Extraneous Material That Nobody Ever Reads?

We think this is the wrong way to look at it. The appendices let you demonstrate a lot of things that don't fit into the body of the proposal. For example, the narrative may mention that you have a diverse board of directors, but the list of the names of your 15 or 20 board members, with their business titles, other nonprofit affiliations, and so on, paints the picture more concretely. The list also allows funders to determine whether there is any connection with board members that may enhance the prospects for a grant or whether there is a potential conflict of interest. For example, some corporate foundations prefer to give grants to organizations with which their employees or employees' families are connected; others—and some government funders—avoid this type of connection. Or you may talk in the capacity section about how financially stable and enduring your organization is; the audit report in the appendix documents this. As we said in the last section, if you include a list of appendices in the proposal's table of contents, readers will know where to look for whichever pieces of information they consider most important. And there are lots of things they consider important. The appendices for foundations and those for government agencies overlap to a very large extent, but foundations sometimes ask for a bit less information. We'll start with the foundations. By the way, if you did the homework we suggested in Lesson 4, all you'll have to do now is go into your computer files and select those that the foundations request.

Attachments for Foundation Proposals

What should be attached to a foundation proposal? Whatever they ask for! You will notice that as you read foundation guidelines—especially the common application formats published by some regional associations of grantmakers—the foundations usually refer to *attachments*, not *appendices*. At the risk of being boring, we have to repeat: Start with the guidelines and make a phone call if anything isn't clear.

The common application formats have a section in which they list attachments. Even if you're not using one of these formats, it makes sense to have a section at the end of your proposal—however short—in which you list the attachments in the order in which they appear. Following are the attachments that are most often requested:

- *Documentation of not-for-profit status:* Almost all foundations ask that you attach the 501(c)(3) and IRS determination letter.
- *Agency budget for the current and often for the previous fiscal year:* Some foundations also ask for the projected agency budget for the next fiscal year.
- *Project budget*
- *List of other funders for the project*
- *Most recent audit report*
- *Tax return Form 990*
- *Most recent annual report:* Foundations understand that many nonprofit organizations don't publish an annual report. But you should note this when you describe the attachments, so the reader doesn't think you just forgot it.

- *Brief biographies and/or résumés of key staff:* Normally what's expected is a page with one-paragraph summaries of the experience and qualifications of the executive director and/or senior manager responsible for the project; the project director, supervisor, or coordinator; and any professional staff members who are critical to its implementation. Some grantmakers want to see the résumés too.

- *A list of partners if the proposal is for a collaboration:* Foundations don't usually ask for commitment letters or contract letters, but it may be worthwhile to include them if you've developed them. Nor do foundations usually require attendance lists or minutes from partnership meetings, but if this is an important element of your proposal, you may be able to strengthen your chance of winning a grant by documenting the development and current operations of the partnership.

- *Other attachments:* Some foundations want to see a cover letter or form signed by the executive director. As we note for government proposals, you should get this well in advance of the proposal submission date. Foundations sometimes like to see a few (a few!) news articles about the organization, or the executive summary of an evaluation that's been done on the program to be funded. Most foundations do not want to see PowerPoint presentations or videotapes. If you happen to have a video that you think effectively documents the program you want funded, and if the guidelines don't prohibit it or request it, call first to see if there's any interest in seeing it.

Attachments for Government Agencies

As we have said so many times that we're sure you're sick of hearing it by now—but we'll keep saying it—the single most important activity in preparing an application is to check and recheck what the guidelines say the funder wants. Most government application forms or announcements tell you exactly what you must attach. Some recent applications have stipulated how many pages long the appendix can be, without even hinting at what information should be included. The types of attachments that you might include are exactly what you would submit for foundations, with a few additions.

- **Certifications and assurances:** Most government agencies require that you agree to a number of conditions that become part of the contract once you win a grant. Examples include agreements that you are or will be in compliance with all relevant laws, such as fair labor standards and equal opportunity laws; adherence to environmental standards; disclosure of all lobbying activities; maintenance of a drug-free workplace; and so on. Most of these forms have to be signed by a board member and/or the executive director, the agency head, or the school superintendent, so get them completed well in advance of the day the proposal has to go out. More than once we've chased around getting the right signatures at the last minute, when, of course, all the people we needed were at important business meetings, at funerals, or out of town.

- **Documentation of partnerships:** If the proposal represents a collaborative project or a partnership, documentation for a government proposal is usually much more stringent than for foundations. Here you must include memoranda of understanding (MOUs) between and among the partners. These, as we have said earlier, are minicontracts specifying what each partner will have as its responsibility and will receive from the other partners. MOUs that are required for certain government grant proposals are almost always studied by the applicants' lawyers to make sure the promises included are reasonable—and legal. If a city police department or mental health department signs an MOU saying that it will "provide services in a community in the manner described below," you can bet that the legal departments have looked it over once, twice, and even three times. Don't put an MOU into a proposal unless you fully understand all the ramifications. In addition to MOUs, minutes of partners' meetings often are required as proof that the partnership is real and ongoing, and not just an on-paper collaboration.

- *Letters from elected officials:* Foundations don't care at all about political support for your project, and a letter from an elected official may actually offend some. But it's sometimes a little different for government agencies. Although a support letter from your city council member, state senator, or member of Congress is not enough to get a proposal funded, it won't be seen as inappropriate pressure, and it could give you just the tiniest push if other applicants with equal scores don't have such letters. And staff of elected officials may, when it's appropriate, follow up with a phone call on your behalf if they have sent such a letter. At least a week before the proposal is due (longer if possible), send an abstract or executive summary of the proposal to the official's office, with some indication of the comments that would be most useful (some staff like to see a draft or a sample letter). The office may write directly to the commissioner or secretary of the agency receiving the proposal, or may send the letter to you for inclusion in the proposal package. It should go without saying, but we'll say it anyway, that if you want letters from more than one elected official, and they ask you for a draft, the letters should not be identical!

- *Resources in the community and what services these resources are providing (resource mapping):* Government grantmakers are interested in knowing exactly what is going on in a target community so they can see precisely where the proposed project will fit in. As they see what is going on, they look for gaps in services that the grant, if funded, will fill.

- *Résumés of actual or "typical" staff for proposed project:* Understanding that job announcements for important grant-funded positions may have to be widely posted in a fair and impartial manner once funding is approved, government grantmakers often are willing to look at a typical résumé of a well-qualified project director, for instance, rather than the résumé of the person who will be hired. Showing that you've given a lot of thought to the qualifications of project staff is reassuring to funders!

- *Curriculum vitae (CV).* Universities, hospitals, and independent researchers who run labs not connected to any institution are often the applicant for research grants. Such proposals generally name the lead researcher or project director by name and include the person's curriculum vitae in the appendix. The CVs for research grants are often many pages long, detailing the researchers' previous projects. (See the Glossary in Appendix 3 for how a curriculum vitae differs from a résumé.) If other researchers on the team are known, their CVs should be included as well.

- *Job descriptions of all full- and part-time grant-funded staff:* Include the duties and responsibilities of all staff members, how much time they will put into the project, and, if possible, to whom each member will report in the organization's structure. Also, describe the duties of staff members who will work on the project as an in-kind contribution of the applicant—people who will participate in project activities but whose salaries are not paid for by the grant.

POP QUIZ

True or False?

1. The project cost should never appear in the abstract of a grant proposal.

2. A table of contents should only be included in a grant proposal if it is mentioned in the application.

3. The average length of a comprehensive abstract is five pages.

4. If you get letters of support from elected officials, you should make sure they are presented at the very front of your proposal.

5. Foundations never expect to see information about a not-for-profit organization's board of directors in the attachments.

6. A good rule of thumb for your abstract: Use as many words as you need as long as you're completely clear.

7. Government grant applications usually don't specify how many pages the appendix should be.

8. All grantmakers expect at least some attachments or appendix material included in the grant proposal.

9. Another word for "appendix" is "attachment."

Essay Question

Write a sample cover letter to a foundation to accompany a proposal.

THE "PET PEEVES" ROUNDTABLE

BEFORE GOING ON to the components of a grant proposal with our panelists, we asked them to respond as holistically as possible to a full proposal. We asked what three things a proposal writer could do to get their attention and make them want to give the grant (and we asked which single thing was most important). Then we asked about pet peeves. Their responses are scattered throughout the roundtables, but first let us share with you an insight from one of our panelists: "The key is for the person doing the proposal writing to have passion for the organization. Everything else can be taught."

What Did the Grantmakers Really Like?

The roundtable for Part I should have given you a good idea of the panelists' likes. Nearly every grantmaker said that what they like to see is that you've done your homework, read the guidelines, and understand the foundation or government program priorities. Almost all of them said they looked for a good idea, a good program, and clarity—and brevity—in the expression of the idea. Government funders were more concerned than most foundations about a formal statement of objectives and outcome measurement (although, as we've mentioned before, the foundations too are increasingly interested in outcomes or impact).

And What Were Their Pet Peeves?

Laziness. Perhaps you can guess what the most common pet peeve was. As should be clear from the earlier roundtables, nearly every grantmaker talked about applicants who didn't do their homework. Foundation representatives were annoyed by applicants who didn't know what the foundation did, hadn't read the guidelines, and didn't even know who the current program officer or foundation director was. "Scattershot," "shotgun," and "over the transom" were some of the disparaging terms they used about proposals that apparently had been sent out at random and with no thought.

Incoherence. The other major complaint was about proposals in which the applicants hadn't made it clear what they wanted to do, how they were going to do it, or how the budget had been arrived at. "I sometimes read a proposal and can't see where it's going," was an annoyance expressed by one grantmaker, who could have been speaking for all of her colleagues. "If a proposal is a real mess, it's a reflection of a lack of coherence in the program."

But they might forgive some errors. The panelists were less hard on some aspects of the proposal that we thought might be poorly received. Spelling errors, poor writing (as long as the concepts are clear), and other stylistic problems are not necessarily held against the applicant—but they are noticed. We thought maybe we shouldn't even mention this fact to you, though. In more recent interviews, funders were clear that they could not take poorly written proposals to their boards. A few foundation officers said that in the past they might have helped with rewrites for small grassroots organizations or new immigrant groups who were just learning the grants process— and perhaps the English language. But they now find they don't have the time for this kind of help. So unless you know the specific person who will review your proposal and that person's likes and dislikes, you just can't risk submitting a sloppily written proposal.

How Should the Need Be Shown in the Proposal, and How Important Is It Really?

"Beginning grant writers tend to base their proposals on their ideas rather than on a real need," said a funder. "To show need is very important…yet there's an amazing lack of statistics included in proposals—and when they are included, they are often dated and out of context."

Another funder suggested that "you use a commonsense approach to identifying need." Unlike her colleague, she doesn't want to see a lot of data because she is fully aware of which communities have the greatest need in the geographical area funded by her foundation. But do tell her about new needs in your community that require attention. "We know the territory pretty well," agreed a panelist. "We don't want to see proposals overladen with demographic proof. Be smart. More is not necessarily better. But we want to be sure that a grant applicant understands the community it [the organization] represents."

You see—more is better when it comes to reading and studying guidelines, but it is not better if you haphazardly adorn your proposal with statistics that are overwhelming and irrelevant. Clearly you have to find a balance between failing to describe a problem and throwing in the statistical kitchen sink. One way to deal with this may be to include (brief) compelling stories that demonstrate the need. "I like to see some anecdotal data about how a program touched the lives of people, along with some relevant hard data and statistics," said a government funder. "I prefer a bigger picture view showing the organization's understanding of its role in making positive things happen," explained a foundation grantmaker, "rather than, 'our community has the worst so-and-so.'"

Most panelists suggest that your needs statement will be different if your proposal is being sent to your local bank (which knows the neighborhood as well as you do), a small foundation in your community (which also knows the terrain), or to a large national foundation or federal government agency (both of which may be unfamiliar with your neighborhood or community). As one of our panelists said, "Be smart about it (which is always easier said than done). And be clear (which is also easier said than done)."

"Applicants usually understand their needs," said a government grantmaker, "but being clear about them is another story." In other words, whatever information you include to make the case for a need, be sure you organize it well, state it clearly, and show how it is relevant to the program you want to implement.

Do Grants Always Go to the Communities with the Greatest Need?

The answer to this question surprised us a bit. Communities with the direst need aren't always the ones that get the grant. Most funders want to be sure the money will be well spent, so they look for strong organizations doing important things, wherever they are located. When pressed on the subject of need, they admitted that, as much as they may want to, it is very difficult to give grants to organizations that aren't likely to be able to implement and sustain the program, no matter how compelling the problem and how underserved the community.

"We fund underserved communities first and foremost," said one foundation panelist. But, another explained, "we don't give money just to spur community involvement—even if it is a very low-income community. We only give money to a community that can already demonstrate a commitment to making things better."

Another funder said that her foundation gets an idea about something that it thinks should happen and then searches for a "fertile community where it is likely to happen—meaning one with key leadership in place, a track record, and a desire to extend good work that is already going on." Still another said, "We give money to the strongest people and the strongest program—not necessarily the one that is in the lowest-income areas."

On the other hand, "if we fund in 'good' neighborhoods, the amount of money we give is far more modest . . . in fact, we'll generally use a challenge-grant approach (which requires the grantees to find additional funders)," another of our panelists explained. One funder offered this hint: "If you are in a wealthy neighborhood or community asking for a grant, be modest. But geography doesn't automatically knock you out of the box."

Does the Nonprofit Status of a Group Matter?

The nonprofit status of an applicant matters, even if it has a wonderful program in a very needy community. "Sometimes a group will come to us and say, 'We don't have a 501(c)(3), but we feed hundreds of hungry people every night,'" a foundation grantmaker said. "It's frustrating because some groups have access—they know how to get help with that sort of thing—and other groups—like this one—can't manage it." Foundations usually can't give grants to organizations that don't have their paperwork in place, no matter how great their need is and how many people they serve, so it is easy to see why this funder may be frustrated.

And Now for Those Measurable Objectives...Do We Really Need Them?

Generally, the need or problem section of a proposal is followed by the objectives you hope to achieve in order to solve the problem you laid out. In Roundtable I we discussed the increasing emphasis grantmakers are placing on outcomes and impact. Because every program planner and proposal writer tends to have a difficult time arriving at suitable objectives, we asked our panelists about the importance of objectives and for suggestions about how to develop them.

"Measurable objectives—very important," said one funder. "I need to see benchmarks so I can sell the proposal to the board and senior staff." A government funder explained that the most important thing an applicant can do is "be results oriented," which is what objectives are all about. "What do you want to do—what are the gaps—and what services will you provide to fill in the gaps? This is important," said another funder. "There is a lot of research out there that can help you. Be realistic. Don't say you'll increase reading scores by three grade levels through a summer recreation program for children!"

"Frankly, I don't care how many widgets you made, I only care if the widgets made a difference—and how they made a difference," warned another government funder. This grantmaker is not quite so interested in how many people you served as how well the program worked. "Objectives weren't important to us until [recently]," said a panelist. "Our board didn't require them. But now, we don't just fund from our heart—we need to support groups that will make an impact."

"If you're having a problem setting up appropriate measurable objectives," suggested a grantmaker, "work with your program officer... or someone who can help you." One of our panelists pointed out that because organizations often need help in understanding outcomes, his foundation funds training in how to identify them. "We believe that nonprofits should come up with the outcomes they hope to achieve. It isn't up to us to tell them."

We Understand That Measurable Objectives Are Important. But What If We Don't Achieve Them? Will We Have to Give the Money Back?

"Once in a blue moon, if you've aimed too high, the foundation will ask for the money we gave you back," admitted one of our panelists. But this probably would happen only if the organization hasn't seriously worked at reaching the outcomes. "If you've engaged the community and really made an effort, we probably won't ask you to return the funds." Another said, "We want organizations to succeed. We don't want to take money back. If grantees keep the foundation informed about what's going on... we can help you," said a panelist.

Keeping the funder informed may be the key to what happens if the program isn't successful. "I like to see how grantees deal with challenges. Tell me, 'We thought this would happen, but then this happened. Luckily, we had a Plan B, a Plan C, and help from friends and supporters,'" explained a grantmaker.

One funder suggested, "Large foundations can be understanding if you weren't successful doing what you said you'd do. Smaller foundations can't afford to be as flexible." Organizations often can rely on help from funders in figuring out how to restate the objectives to be more realistic, how to achieve the desired outcomes, and why things went wrong. A government grantmaker said, "It's a new ballgame once you get a grant. The highest scores on the proposal are not necessarily the highest performers. The extent to which an applicant overstated its objectives might be revisited once the grant is actually being implemented."

To summarize: Of course funders are more concerned when you don't even try to achieve your objectives than when you try hard and fail to achieve the results you hoped you would. And they all want to see evidence that you've learned something when you haven't quite succeeded.

Oh, and they like to be kept in the loop as you're attempting— or even struggling—to achieve your objectives. No one—not you, not us, certainly not grantmakers—likes surprises. If you're having trouble with your grant-funded program, make sure you talk to the funder. Not only can you get moral support, you can also get tangible help.

The Program Is the Key, Right? So What Do Grantmakers Really Look for in the Program Description?

First, you need to keep in mind that program officers can recommend grants but generally don't have the final say about whether a proposal gets funded. Provide enough information so that they can make your case: "I need a very detailed program description because that's what I'm selling to my board. Your program description gives the program officer the power to make your case by using your words." A government grantmaker described a conversation with an applicant who had gotten a mediocre score on a proposal—and no grant—and was upset because she had received grants for the same program before. "I sat down with the criteria and her application, and called her back and said, 'This is not a good application.' She hadn't clearly and cleanly explained what they wanted to do."

Concerning the program's importance, the grantmakers also said, "The first thing we look at is your program—whether it reflects best practices, sustainability, and measurable outcomes." "The program should be a blueprint for everything." "A good program is the key: What is it you plan to do?"

And what do the grantmakers look for in a proposal that convinces them that it's a good program? "The fewer questions I have about a program as I'm reading a proposal, the better the program is explained," one panelist said. Others noted, "I look at what and who: What is the program and who is the leadership?" "We want to see an explicit theory of action." "Be clear and concise. Build your case: Why is the program excellent, and why is it likely to accomplish what you hope it will?" "Make a good case that the proposed program is consistent with your organization's line of business. 'Stick to your knitting,' which means focus on your core line of work." "The project design should be clear and concise: We are going to implement this and this. We are going to manage it this way and that way." And watch your language. Funders told us, "Program staff are committed to doing a great job running their program.... But they don't learn to sell their program. They learn jargon instead." "I hate pseudoscience babble," one panelist said. "I hate phrases like 'myriad approaches.' Just tell me what you're going to do." "I want to read a proposal and say, 'I want to hear more.'" "I want to know that transformational work is going on."

Above all, one grantmaker said, "Be reasonable. Doable. Implementable. In line with your organization's vision."

And How Important Is Collaboration? If I Collaborate, Am I More Likely to Get a Grant?

Grantmakers talk about collaboration, but grant seekers argue about it. "What is it exactly?" "It's more trouble than it's worth." "It's easy for you to like it—you don't have to do it." As we noted in Roundtable I, grantmakers are thinking much more intently about the benefits (and drawbacks) of collaboration. We asked them to elaborate.

One funder said, "Collaboration is not necessarily a means to an end." But others disagreed. One said, "We encourage collaborations at times when resources aren't abundant." "We fund community development, which works much better with collaboration. We give preference—for financial and policy reasons—to collaborative approaches. They're critical," she added. Her colleague agreed: "Collaboration is essential. Sometimes it isn't about collaboration, but mostly it is. Get together and talk!" Another panelist said, "We actually ask applicants who they are coordinating with.... We want to make sure they're connecting with other groups to provide the highest-quality services." A funder added, "collaborations are important—both formal and informal ones. Be open to forming relationships that may lead to forming pragmatic collaborations."

But we know it's hard. Whether they preferred to see collaborations or not, grantmakers agreed that it's very difficult. As one said, "We like collaboration, but from personal experience, it takes a lot of work." "Sometimes collaboration makes sense...but it is difficult—especially when you're bringing together groups that have different cultures. It's messy," said another.

In fact, the grantmakers recognized that collaboration should emerge from the community itself rather than being required by the funder. "It's nice when two or three groups get together and approach you rather than your telling them to collaborate," said one. "Collaboration is beneficial but it shouldn't be funder driven—and it's awfully hard work," said a foundation grantmaker. "We help people collaborate...but we don't expect them to do so. We actually fund people to work on collaborations—funders need to be sensitive to the difficulty." "We don't force it but we're interested in collaboration," said a funder. "We've seen groups forced to work together who don't like each other."

"We haven't seen much collaboration," said another funder. "But our board would probably appreciate it. We'd be willing to give more money if the groups explained that they were asking for the extra money so they could actually collaborate."

Government funders like it even more. Government grantmakers were even more committed to the concept of collaboration. One government funder said, "It's the best way to get things done. No single entity can do it all. Individuals we're concerned with have very complex needs—housing, primary health care, mental health care, child care, transportation, rehabilitation programs. The very stable, very creative and sophisticated organizations have multiple funding streams and established relationships, sharing information and working together. There's not enough money or expertise to make it happen any other way."

Government agencies are finding ways to collaborate with one another and with community-based organizations within the limits of their procurement regulations. A city government official told us, "Three nonprofits got in touch with us about applying for a federal grant that required collaboration between the city and nonprofits. We did a quick mini-RFP and sent it out to those three organizations and seven others we knew were working in the field. We lifted questions straight from the federal grant application and asked the nonprofits to respond. We got proposals back and had them reviewed just as we would any other. The review team unanimously selected one group, and we put that organization into our grant." This meant that once the city agency won the grant, it could start the program immediately without having to go through another protracted contracting process.

This panelist also told us that more agencies within city government are collaborating, including agencies that are not directly under the mayor's control, such as district attorneys' offices and others. And most important, "Forward-thinking commissioners and agencies are just interested in getting the money into the city. They understand that they don't have to be the grantee, and that they can work with whoever is the best applicant."

Another government funder advised us that "collaboration is becoming more intense. To have a comprehensive impact on communities, you need a coordinated effort. It used to be acceptable to have a bunch of letters of support with different executive directors' signatures. Now there's been a paradigm shift: Create partnerships at the beginning of the project, not right before you're mailing out the grant proposal!"

How should collaboration work? A government panelist reminded us that "collaboration has the word 'labor' in it. 'I've got the costumes, you've got the stage—let's put on a show.' That's collaboration!" His colleague commented, "I see project staff as the key to building collaboration…an entrepreneurial person is needed." And a foundation panelist noted, "To do it well, someone must be in charge to nurture the collaboration…for the care and feeding of the partners…to facilitate the partnership."

One government panelist spoke of foundations as well as nonprofits when discussing collaboration. "There is a lot that foundations can offer without writing a check. They have information on best practices, research they've funded, a perspective outside the specific geographic location. They can donate space for meetings, sit on advisory boards, provide personal contacts. It rounds out the process."

And collaboration's not going away. Most funders seem to agree that working together to solve a problem, help clients, and conduct a comprehensive, effective program is better than working in isolation. But doing it—and doing it well—is another matter altogether. It's probably safe to say that collaboration is a goal, but we haven't reached it yet. Clearly it is on the minds of grantmakers, though. A funder's last words on the subject: "Generally, like it or not, collaboration is not going away anytime soon."

The Program Is Great, but How Can I Prove My Organization Is Capable of Implementing It?

As grantmakers are deciding whether to fund your project, they wonder about your organization's ability to do what you say you're going to do. It is one thing to talk the talk (and write up the write-up) and another thing to walk the walk. We asked our panelists to address "the Big Three"—capacity to implement the program, capacity to sustain the program once the funding cycle is over, and the adequacy of your budget to conduct the activities efficiently.

Leadership was a key to grantmakers' decisions. "I don't necessarily need to know the person in charge of an organization personally, but I want evidence of a track record....Who supports it, who funds it?" "For us, leadership is everything. Does the leader have the vision and capability to run the organization?" "We look for the proof that you have the ability to deliver what you say you will: staff and track record."

Collaboration, or at least the organization's solid place in the community or its relationships within its program area, is another indication of potential success. "If the organization is plugged into a network of other groups we fund, there is at least a context that helps us believe that the organization will do what it says it is going to do." "I want to know who will help the organization if things go wrong." "The size and length of time an organization has been around is not important. What is important is the ability to do what it says it will do—which is why we encourage applicants to form partnerships to build up their capacity." "Show that you've reached out to all the stakeholders the program is expected to impact."

A few grantmakers are willing to help by giving grants that can strengthen the organization: "My foundation gives capacity-building grants." Others look for a signal that the group is not overreaching: "We believe in an agency that knows what its niche is."

Sustainability Is Another Story. How Can I Prove the Program Will Live On When I'm Not Even Sure Myself?

Convincing grantmakers that you will sustain the program when there are no more grant funds is a monumental challenge. More than a monumental challenge, which is why we discuss it throughout this book. We asked our panel how important it is to show you'll sustain the program when the grant runs out, and how applicants can believably and convincingly address the issue of sustainability in their proposals.

"I like to fund programs that are transformative," explained a foundation funder, "but they don't necessarily need to lead to self-sufficiency. I like to see a certain level of democracy, where the beneficiaries of grants turn around and help other organizations."

Diversify funding sources. Several panelists commented on the diversity of funding sources as one way to ensure sustainability. One grantmaker explained, "I am willing to understand that sustainability is a long-term process [rather than a program-by-program effort]— but some organizations don't have diversified funding sources and a healthy individual donor base." "No matter what kind of group you are, diversify your funding," warned a funder. Another said, "We need a sense of the organization. Is it planning for future financial stability? We like to see an economic plan for the future, although we know it's complicated. It gets back to leadership and vision." For the current edition, we asked grantmakers for their opinions on social enterprise, or social entrepreneurship. Some organizations use such business initiatives, developed in support of their mission, as part of a long-term plan for sustainability. The panelists generally were very positive, but with some caveats; their responses are presented in Lesson 18 and Funders Roundtables I and IV.

Build capacity. "Build a development staff," a member of our panel suggested, "and align programs of the organization in an orderly way to secure additional, diverse funding." Another foundation funder said, "Look at other donors, earned income, show that you're thinking about sustaining the program, and that you have some understanding about sustainability." And one suggested, "Be creative about sustainability. Do board development. If 10 of your board members raise $1,000 each, it's a lot easier than getting a $10,000 grant." "Look at grants as building blocks for financial sustainability—but not as the only building block." "Don't be dependent on only one sector for funding. If you are, foundations—or, at least, my foundation—will be concerned."

Don't count on getting the grant renewed. Perhaps we should not have been surprised at the reversal of a long-held assumption in philanthropy that foundations stimulate new programs, and government sources take over to support those that are demonstrated to work well. A federal government grantmaker said, "Everyone in Washington expects grantees to have everything figured out once the federal investment runs out. Even if a grant doesn't require it, show that you've thought about sustaining the program or project. Remember: Programs are no longer funded into perpetuity…there is diminished entitlement." Another government funder is willing to give seed money to get a project started—but he wants to know, "What are your plans to sustain?"

"When there is a large community buy-in, there is likely to be sustainability because the community partners [i.e., local government or businesses] will take the project over," a federal government panelist said. "We expect programs to be institutionalized by the end of five years. We might reduce funding in the third and fourth year."

"The best way to ensure sustainability is to build relationships," a funder said. "Many cities are 'smokestacked.' No one talks to anyone. The schools don't talk to the police who don't talk to…." "Leverage resources—build public-private partnerships," suggested another grantmaker.

Which Leads Us to the Budget: What Do Grantmakers Look For?

"Too often grant writers obviously don't understand the financials of their organizations," said a foundation funder. "Trustees of foundations tend to be business people, so the financial aspects of a proposal are really important to them. They'll ask, 'Why are consulting fees so high?' They'll ask questions about overhead costs." "It's funny," another panelist said, "newer, less experienced groups don't build in overhead—and they undercut themselves. Larger groups, on the other hand, exaggerate their overhead costs. And everyone tends to underestimate in-kind contributions in their proposals."

"A pet peeve of mine is when the budget isn't transparent. People like to bundle things together to leave themselves some room," explained a government grantmaker. "In one proposal I read, the applicant used the word 'modalities' in the budget (with no explanation)—and spent two-thirds of the grant to pay for this thing called 'modalities.'" "I also don't like to see a disproportionately small number of staff included in the budget—it makes me think that someone is trying to pull the wool over my eyes," he added.

"Sometimes we get a budget that looks like it's for a different proposal," complained one grantmaker. "Half of the grant money is going to an arts organization and they didn't mention a word about the arts organization in the narrative. The budget should be able to stand alone as a representation of the proposal."

Another funder complains, "I hate it when budgets make no sense. And I loathe the 'blah-blah-blah syndrome'—when grant writers sort of go blah, blah, blah instead of just telling us directly what they plan to do with the money. Keep the budget simple." As a government panelist advised, "It all goes back to writing a clear proposal. Our application format has a proposal narrative and a budget narrative, and the two have to 'crosswalk.'"

And the funders can't think of any reason you shouldn't have a realistic, straightforward budget. "Spreadsheets and other software packages have allowed people to be more on top of things as far as crafting their budget is concerned."

Other elements of the budget are important to some funders. For example, "I like to see what I think of as 'added value' in the budget," said a grantmaker. "Things like in-kind contributions that show how resources are leveraged." "We're always looking at the reasoning behind your budget—your assumptions need to be clear." "Who are the other funders—name them in the budget." This approach also provides references: "Our grants are only for about $25,000 a year—so we hope that the organizations we're funding are stable. Who funded them last year? We call other funders—if we know them—to check the groups out."

As still another reminder about reading the guidelines, another funder said, "Don't slip something into the budget that we say we won't fund (rent, for example). Some grantmakers will stop reading proposals that do that." "I saw a funny one last year," added a government grantmaker. "Our announcement included a small amount for renovation if it was necessary to provide the services supported in the grant. We got an application asking for the entire amount of the grant for renovation! People don't understand: Leasing, car rental, renovation have to be tied to the services!"

Don't shortchange yourself! "Be realistic about what it costs to run a program...don't shortchange yourself," insisted a panel member. "Put it in front of the foundation's eyes—right smack in the middle of the proposal—that it costs money to do all the things you want to do. Don't say, 'We only need $45,000 to pay the salary of a staff member,' when it costs a hell of a lot more than $45,000 to run the program." Another panelist commented, "We don't want to be the sole support of someone's salary because, let's face it, when the grant runs out, there's a good chance the person will get fired. We don't mind paying a part of a salary, or we might be willing to pay the whole amount for a development staff member who will turn around and raise money for the organization." Even if you're just asking the foundation to support that salary, or part of it, show how it fits into the larger program budget.

Realistic. Reasonable. Appropriate. Grantmakers do want your staff to be paid adequately: "We want to see reasonable salaries." "I believe in reasonable salaries and benefits for not-for-profit staff. I hate to see high-priced consultants mentioned in budgets. They get paid an awful lot of money—and then they disappear."

And about being realistic... Another foundation grantmaker expanded on the need to be realistic. "It's unrealistic, for instance, if you have an all-volunteer staff and suddenly you want to jump to 10 paid staffers. Jump gradually if you expect to get funded." Similarly, "It's silly for a group that we never funded before—never heard of, never dealt with—to ask for $100,000 for general support," warned a funder. "People ask for a larger amount of money than we can give them," said a grantmaker. "We need to see a realistic assessment of how you'll do what you said you'd do using a smaller amount of money." One funder said, "We look at the budget of the proposed project in the context of the organization's entire budget to make sure it fits and makes sense. The budget and the proposal narrative should be completely linked." And, "We don't nitpick about salaries—but we like to fund groups that have done everything possible to be fiscally smart. Are you getting donated space and services? What else are people contributing?"

One last thing on the topic of budget. A funder warned, "I have a dialogue with grant seekers and ask why certain items appear in the budget. I look at the program ideas first and the financials second. But I have to warn you—other grantmakers do it in the reverse. They look at costs first... and only after they've analyzed your budget do they look at the elements of your program."

What Do Grantmakers Say About Evaluation? (Please Say, "It's Not Very Important"!)

Sorry, but most grantmakers say evaluation *is* very important. Again, look back at Roundtable I to see how important outcomes are;

evaluation can document those outcomes. "Anyone can design a good program...but will it get good results? The world is littered with good programs. I want to focus on results," said a grantmaker. "Very few program staff actually care about evaluation—but they should use evaluation techniques to help them make changes in the program. No one ever says, 'We haven't succeeded.'"

Although the ability to know if a program is working is important to almost all funders, foundation grantmakers are more sympathetic about the difficulties of program evaluation than are government grantmakers—probably because the latter are willing to pay for evaluation when it's important to them. "So few funders pay for evaluations that it seems cruel to ask grant writers to include them in proposals," said a foundation grantmaker. But "evaluations allow you to retool constantly to improve your program," another funder pointed out. "We'll help people work on their evaluation plans." Perhaps most reassuring to organizations that really don't know how to do evaluation, "We work with less sophisticated groups and are comfortable with simple deliverables. We just want to see that they have some ideas for evaluation."

A government funder offered a very practical warning: "Don't tack on the evaluation at the end. Front-load it—build in the evaluation component at the beginning. Explain what tests and other measures you're going to use to decide if you've achieved your objectives as you write your objectives. Use the evaluation section of the proposal to go into some detail about how you will use and analyze the measurements."

And when you work with an outside evaluator, as required by many government grants, be sure the evaluator understands how important it is to integrate evaluation into the whole program—and the whole proposal. "Sometimes we see evaluations that don't fit in with the rest of the proposal—we suspect that high-priced consultants were probably used," another government grantmaker complained. "Garbage in, garbage out."

We were reassured to hear that grantmakers want to hear about failures too. "We're lenient if you say that your program didn't have an impact, as long as you try to figure out why it didn't work," said another panelist. "Tell us what lessons you learned. What you'd do differently. Say something like, 'We didn't realize the community wouldn't care about such-and-such. Next time we'd approach folks differently.' We love it when you say, 'We bombed this year...but we'll do better next time.'"

Whether It's Called "Appendix" or "Attachment," What Should I Include?

Sometimes the guidelines or application specify what additional material should be sent; at other times, there is no mention of any supplementary information that funders want to see. We asked the grantmakers a question about what appendix material or attachments should or should not be included in a grant proposal if there's no guideline about this.

"In my opinion," said a government funder, "appendix material should be connected to the collaboration in some way. I like 'resource mapping.' I also like to see articles about past successes, past evaluations of the group's efforts, examples of the organization's track record. 'Soft stuff' [such as anecdotal information] is good too, if it is allowed. Also a brief résumé of the project director—I'm interested in human capital. Do you have the right leader?" Another government panelist pointed out that when grantees receive the grant, "All of a sudden they have to start implementing the project...all of a sudden the rubber must meet the road. I like to see letters of commitment and memoranda of understanding that define how often and how much. They really explain how things will get going." And yet another government member of our panel likes the appendix to include "minutes of partnership meetings—proving the partnership is real. Sometimes applicants go way overboard on the support letters," she said. "And they all have the same wording on different organizations' letterheads."

But keep in mind that, especially for foundations, "when there is too much appendix material, there is a temptation to leaf through it and not read anything carefully." "Send what the foundation asks for—and this is like pulling teeth," explained a funder. "We expect to see an audit (our treasurer goes through this line by line)." "Don't send videos—they usually end up in the trash. And just don't send tons of stuff," said another grantmaker.

What Do I Do If a Foundation Doesn't Have Application Guidelines?

Sometimes the answer is a letter of inquiry. As we said earlier, there are thousands of small to middle-size foundations across the country that have no staff or a very small staff, maybe just a part-time person. They don't want lengthy applications or proposals. For example, "We're open to a broad range of presentations," a grantmaker said. "We're looking for something wonderful. Our program officers can ask you to rewrite if need be."

Another grantmaker whose foundation doesn't have a required application said, "I hate long, beautifully written proposals. I don't want to see more than five pages . . . and don't send everything you've got right away. Remember, we're just dating. We're at the beginning stages. I don't want to meet your parents yet." (This is why it's a very good idea to call and check with a foundation before deciding what to send: Do you want a short letter of inquiry, a full-blown proposal, a miniproposal, a paragraph, attachments, no attachments? You don't even have to bother the program officer—the receptionist probably has fielded this question many times before.)

"I like to see a one-page executive summary—even though we don't have an application—followed by a brief proposal," said one funder. "My board is persnickety about putting restraints on applicants, which is why they would never think of asking for an actual application," she explained. "They're afraid they'd miss the discovery of the Matterhorn or something if they reined applicants into submitting a form application, so they really look hard at the executive summary. It is the executive summary that is given to the board no matter what proposal an organization submits."

Many funders said that their process begins with a fairly short letter of inquiry (LOI), which is either accepted or rejected by the foundation. If it is accepted, applicants are asked to send a completed proposal. Sometimes site visits are arranged as well.

"I like a letter of inquiry to start with a 'grabber'—a startling fact, a compelling story, and a program or strategy that deals with the issue," explained one funder. Another grantmaker said that her foundation expects a letter of inquiry after the applicant has carefully researched what the foundation is doing and invited the foundation to see the program. And, "I like applicants to mention in the LOI which other groups are funding them."

If you are asked to send a letter of inquiry, here's some useful advice from a funder: "The LOI should be a brief description of who you are and why you want a grant. It should be simple and show clarity of purpose—and reflect the foundation's guidelines. And don't forget to mention any telephone conversations you may have had with us."

Before We Move On, Let's Go Back to Those Pet Peeves

You've heard what the panelists said about preparing for a proposal, finding the right funder, designing the best program, being clear about what you want to do and how you will do it, and making sure each part of the proposal reflects that design. You've followed their advice and created a great proposal. You're ready to go. Almost. Before you send out that proposal, let's focus for just a minute more on some of the more concrete, less holistic likes and dislikes of the grantmakers. Then comb through the proposal to be sure you haven't hit any sore spots. As with everything else the panelists have talked about, there are some differences of opinion along the way. But here goes.

Language and format. Only one or two of the panelists were unconcerned about the proposal's presentation and formatting. Rather, panelists said things like, "I'm not the page police, but don't go over the page limit and get all wordy." "[I hate] proposals that don't reflect a clearly defined vision." "[I hate] when applicants don't stick to page limits and font-size limits. You're not considered serious. When people try to get around these limits it drives reviewers nuts. If you want to get on a reviewer's bad side, ignore these limits." "[I hate] incredibly long proposals. If we say two to three pages, don't send us 20 pages." "[I hate] jargon. I hate when things get overintellectualized as opposed to a clear, direct description of the organization's mission and the purpose of the grant." "[I hate] jargon and hyperbole. A woman actually said to me that the target audience for her program was 'potentially every child in the world.'" "[I hate] proposals that aren't precise, concise, and sharp."

"Our reviewers go off when there are a lot of spelling errors. 'Don't they know what spell-check is?' they say." "Because of spelling errors, ideas can be unclear and points are deducted from your score." "Lack of proofreading makes me crazy. From a small grassroots organization—that's one thing. But from a large organization—it's unacceptable. Even with computers, terrible errors can occur!" There's an echo in here: "Bad grammar drives me crazy. We're community oriented and know that English often isn't the first language of the writer. I try to understand but it's hard; bad grammar breaks the flow and it's jarring.... It's less important with grassroots organizations, but I just finished reading proposals from groups that are teaching people to write proposals. That's different."

And so on ... A few pet peeves were more personal or perhaps idiosyncratic, but they give a good idea of why you have to be so attentive. "[I hate] name dropping: When someone calls and says, 'Oh, So-and-So said your foundation would fund our project.'" "I hate it when someone says, 'We're the only one doing this program in the entire city, state, country, world, planet' (but I have to laugh)." "I don't like 'menus' of requests: 'We need support for this, this, this, and this. Do any of these things appeal to you?' Make up your mind about what's important to you!" "[I hate] budget costs that are obviously unrealistic—giving someone too much work to do for too little money and in too little time, for instance."

We recommend that even if you're ready to send out that proposal, you should go back to read the guidelines one more time. Listen: "It makes me nuts when you don't read the guidelines. And you don't proofread. They're *my* grant guidelines. I wrote them and rewrote them—then my boss edited them some more and I rewrote them again. Then a consultant reviewed them. And you turn in an error-filled proposal that is obviously a first draft!" "When I was writing proposals, I figured that if a question wasn't clear or wasn't to the point of what I was writing, I could finesse it. But when you're reviewing proposals it's clear in an answer that the proposer didn't like the question, didn't think it was important, or didn't get it. My agency spent months putting the proposal together. You can't finesse it."

And, "We don't accept the common application form—we ask for a letter of intent—yet people keep sending the application." "We include a checklist of things that should be part of a proposal. Only a minority of applicants come close to following the checklist. We go back and ask them to send things they excluded—and they still sometimes don't send them—but other funders don't necessarily have the time and inclination to do this." "[I hate] proposals that have no business being sent to us."

PART III

AND AFTER THE PROPOSAL...

YOU'RE NOT FINISHED YET. After you send off a proposal, you may have one more step to go through in the grantmaking process. Many, although certainly not all, foundation grantmakers (and some government funders) try to make a site visit before they make any decision on a proposal. Lesson 16 gives a few pointers on how to prepare for the site visit.

Whether it's your first grant or your hundredth, you always feel a bit like a high school senior when the response letter or email from the grantmaker arrives. Whether it's a one-time grant for a small but special project or a multiyear grant that will support a large, important program for your agency and your community, that moment before you find out if your grant will be funded is always difficult and exciting (bland words for the emotions you might be feeling). Win or lose, there are things that you, the proposal writer, must do once you get the grantmaker's answer. If you don't get the grant, there are ways you need to follow up. If you do get it, you also have a few tasks to complete before you plunge into implementing it or turn it over to program staff. Lesson 17 tells you what to do next, and how. A new Lesson 18 provides some concrete ideas about diversifying funding and building a business. Our final Funders Roundtable closes Part III and the book.

271

LESSON 16

THE SITE VISIT—PLAYING HOST

OPENING REMARKS

Most site visits involve a program officer from a local foundation spending an hour or two at your office, meeting staff, chatting with the executive director, asking some questions, observing the programs, and visiting with clients.

But when the federal government or a large national foundation makes a site visit, you can bet there's a lot of money at stake (often grants for many millions of dollars), and the funders come with a posse and an agenda. They expect to see certain things and talk with certain people, maybe even the mayor. Getting ready for one of these site visits almost calls for an event planner—the kind of talented, organized person who plans the Olympics for a host city or a political convention to choose the party's nominee for president.

Of course, no such person is brought on board. Unfortunately! —EK

LEADING QUESTIONS

Once I Send in the Proposal, I Can Relax, Right?

Sure, for most foundation and government grants, you can relax until the time comes for you to hear the outcome of the proposal. But a growing number of foundations (very rarely a government agency) aren't comfortable just with the written word. They recognize that excellent proposals can come from organizations that may not be able to manage a grant, especially a large one. They want to see for themselves what your physical space is like, they want to meet the leadership, they want to see programs in operation, they want to meet the partners. And if they have given you a grant before, they want to see what's new, what's different now. There are a few prospective grantees who see this visit as the equivalent of a barracks inspection or testifying before the grand jury or the oral examination for a master's or doctoral degree, but this is absolutely the wrong way to look at it.

We know an organization that went through six site visits in six weeks—and the executive director was thrilled because a site visit is in fact a very good sign. If a grantmaker wants to visit your agency, it's because there is something in the proposal that appeals to the funder. Although a site visit is never a guarantee of a grant because so many other factors affect the final decision by the foundation's board or the government agency, it means that the funder is thinking seriously about giving one. And the site visit gives you an opportunity to strengthen that inclination.

How Do I Get Ready for a Site Visit?

Most preparation for a site visit is little more than common sense, but we'll go ahead and run through our suggestions just to be sure you touch all the bases.

Start with scheduling—programs and people. In the phone call when a site visit is requested, find out exactly what the funder wants to see and how long the visit will last. Part of the visit will be a discussion with the executive director or agency head about the agency, the proposal, and any questions the program officer has about any of these things. But the visitor(s) undoubtedly will expect to be shown around the place and observe what's going on. If you are a nonprofit, the grantmaker may want to meet members of your board. Find out exactly what would be of interest, and schedule accordingly.

If the proposal is in support of an existing program, seeing that program is obviously one major purpose of the visit. But there may be other activities of interest, especially if the grant is for a new program. If the grant is for a program at a senior center, does the funder want to see the exercise program, the nutrition class, or other health-related activities? The painting or music class? Intergenerational programs? Your Alzheimer's group? Clearly, you should set up a day and time when those activities are in progress. At a senior center the funder might prefer a late-morning visit, around lunchtime, usually the busiest time, to get a sense of how many people you serve. In contrast, a late-day or evening visit would give a grantmaker a better idea of your programs for children and teenagers.

If the request is for a general operating grant in a multiservice agency, the funder may hope to see a sample of everything that's going on in the organization. This is hard to schedule if you run senior programs, which normally end by midafternoon, and youth programs, which normally don't start until then. Find out how long the grantmaker would like to stay, to see if it's possible to offer a taste of everything, and ask which would be most important if it's not.

Just as important as the question of *when* is the question of *who* is included. The funder will want to meet the executive director and possibly some board members, other key managers, and especially the person who will be responsible for operating the program for which a grant is requested. Be sure you arrange a time when all or most of those individuals are available, and be sure they're prepared. The grantmaker also may like to meet some of the participants in your programs.

Bring in other players. Although you won't normally schedule the site visit around the availability of everyone who might be involved, ask if the grantmaker would like to meet some of the partners if the proposal is for a collaborative effort. Invite a few of the key players who are available, at least for part of the visit. Of course, if a grant is of the magnitude mentioned in the Opening Remarks, you will schedule the visit around the availability of all partners, or at least as many as possible. (We'll talk a bit in a later section about what the big funders are looking for.) Select a location that makes it easy for partners to attend and at the same time gives the funder the best possible picture of the partnership.

Brush up. It would be very surprising if the grantmaker did not arrive at a site visit with a lot of questions about the agency and the proposed program. Read the proposal again before the visit. Discuss it with everyone who may meet the funder. Be sure you all know exactly how the program will work, who will do what, and what the budget will support. Know how the program will fit into the overall agency mission and operations. Know who the other funders of the program are and how you expect to sustain it when the grant ends.

But the Place Looks So Dingy. Do I Have to Paint the Meeting Room?

You don't have to do anything extraordinary for foundation or government visitors. You can be sure they've seen plenty of dingy meeting rooms, shabby offices, and old furniture. If your agency is large, airy, and modern, you're among the lucky few. Grantmakers know that beyond keeping the place clean, your money goes into programs, not beautification. Just be sure that the Meals on Wheels lunch of beef stew, peas, and mashed potatoes, which was accidentally dropped in the hallway when it was being carried out to the car, is cleaned up quickly so nobody slips. And let all staff know there will be a visitor that day so *they* won't look dingy.

What If the Site Visit Is by a *Very Important* Funder?

All funders are important, and the preparation is the same whether the site visit is being conducted by one program officer whose foundation is deciding whether to give your organization a $10,000 grant or a team of visitors from the federal government whose agency is deciding whether to give your city a $48 million grant. But some elements are slightly different when a very large grant is at stake.

When the big funders come to town, it's usually for a grant that involves one or more local government agencies and may include a few (or a lot of) not-for-profits. They are looking for assurances that your city or town not only will be able to manage a very sizable grant but will do exactly what the proposal describes. Will partners who are from different political parties—say, a mayor and a governor—work together to support costly grant-funded projects? Will government red tape and turf issues among different groups in the city keep the program from running smoothly and being successful? Is there real buy-in—is the program described in the proposal generated from the top down or the bottom up? Were there town hall meetings where community members actually had significant input in the design of the program, or did municipal government officials create the program without any real collaboration?

The site visit is a chance for those funders who are offering whopping grants to see if the written word and the spoken word are consistent, to see if no stone really was left unturned, as the proposal implied. Is there a unified vision? Has space been identified and reserved for grant-funded activities? Is a contracting procedure in place to make sure the program will hum?

Be sure to hold as many preparatory meetings of the collaborating groups as necessary so that everyone is fully prepared and will be able to speak (as much as any large, diverse partnership can) with one voice. And we were only partly kidding about the event planner!

Anything Else I Need to Know?

We think that the most important element in a site visit could be the enthusiasm of the agency's leadership about the organization and the programs it operates. If you usually enjoy showing people around, if you enjoy talking to people about the wonderful things the organization does and the wonderful people it serves, you will enjoy doing this with the grantmakers. And your guests will enjoy it too.

You also need to remember that whether it's a small foundation giving a small grant or big funders coming to town for a visit to determine the outcome of an enormous grant proposal, it's just one of the (many) steps along the way to winning a grant. Being chosen for a site visit doesn't mean that you'll get the grant—not by any means. But proving your capacity to carry out the project and demonstrating your enthusiasm, your commitment, and, as so many funders say, your passion certainly increases your chances.

POP QUIZ

Essay Question

You've applied for $75,000 from the WW Love Foundation to pay for components of an after-school tutoring program for at-risk teenagers in your community. Out of the clear blue, you get a call saying that a program officer from the foundation would like to pay a visit in three or four days. What is the very first thing you would do (after saying, "Sure, we're looking forward to meeting you")? What is the second thing you'd do? The third?

LESSON 17

SO NOW YOU KNOW—WHAT NEXT?

OPENING REMARKS

A community-based nonprofit organization we know applied for a federal substance abuse grant to offer programs for at-risk teenagers. The federal proposal was complex and the instructions sometimes difficult to comprehend. By the time the group submitted the proposal, it had stated the need clearly, set up measurable objectives, and demonstrated a strong, well-thought-out program with an excellent evaluation plan. But it still didn't win the grant. In fact, more than 80 percent of the organizations that applied for this grant didn't win. —ASF

LEADING QUESTIONS

We Did Everything Right (We Think)...and Our Grant Still Was Turned Down. Why? And What Do We Do About It?

Who wins every grant? What not-for-profit organization, local or state agency, school district, college, or individual researcher or artist ever gets every penny? The answer is, of course, not one. We've said before (and the grantmakers support this), if you win one out of every 10 grants you apply for, you are in the Grant Seeker's

Hall of Fame. Most foundation and government funders report that they can fund only 10 to 20 percent of the applications they receive, and the reason is not always because of poor proposals or programs. And, given government budget cuts or changes in funding priorities, the percentages may drop a bit over the next few years.

Throughout the book, we've referred to getting turned down for grant funding—but we've generally "blamed the victim." You know—you must really, really have done something wrong, not followed directions, not studied the funder's guidelines, not answered all the questions, not submitted the grant on time, not gathered the required partners, not, not...

But what if you have done everything right and still get turned down? What if you have identified a compelling need and made a strong case for the program designed to address the need? What if you have demonstrated the capacity to implement the grant and even have strongly suggested how the program...gulp...would be sustained once the grant period was over? With all the right intentions, all the right moves, all the right homework, the program is not funded. Are you going to throw your hands up in defeat (and lapse into a deep depression)? Are you going to call the grantmaker and complain? Write a letter explaining why you should have won?

The mistake is not that you lost the grant; it's failing to follow up in *appropriate* ways to help your chances of winning the same grant next time. Savvy proposal writers look at rejection as a challenge. (Savvy proposal writers must like challenges or they would be doing something else—although it's hard to think of any jobs that aren't challenging these days.)

Wait a Minute: How Do I Find Out If My Program Will Receive Funding?

In the case of grant proposals, the old adage "No news is good news" does not apply. "No news" can sometimes be the worst news possible. It takes longer to hear that you didn't get a grant than to hear that you did—if the funder bothers to send a rejection letter at all. If you are waiting to hear whether you received funding for a federal grant application and you still haven't heard by the time you were told the announcements would be made, it's possible that the agency hasn't made the decision yet—but it's also possible that the winners have been notified and you aren't among them.

The same thing is true for foundations. If you know that the foundation board was going to meet on a certain date but you haven't heard anything by the end of the following week or two, you probably were not successful in this application.

But you want to be sure. Sometimes a government agency website will publish the list of programs that have been funded. Sometimes if you call or email the program officer, you may learn the status of the grant-review process (e.g., that the decisions haven't been made or that the congressional representatives have to be notified first about grants in their districts)—but the officer probably will not tell you whether your project will be funded. If you win a federal or state grant, the contact person listed on the application may receive a very exciting telephone call or letter from the funding agency or an elected official's office telling you the good news. If you do not win, you will eventually receive a very unexciting letter or email from the agency telling you how stiff the competition was and how sorry the agency is that your application didn't make it.

Foundations usually notify you by mail or email. Some actually enclose the check with the award letter; others ask you to fill out a form or sign a letter accepting the terms of the grant and acknowledging formally that you're still eligible for the grant under the foundation's guidelines. Although government agencies and most foundations eventually get around to letting you know you didn't get the grant, some foundations—usually the smaller ones with limited staff—only notify groups that are awarded a grant. Some say so in their publications, others do not. If you're not sure, you should call after a reasonable period has elapsed. But read through the rest of this chapter and Funders Roundtable IV before you call.

Reality Check: Did I *Actually* Do Everything Right?

Sorry, it sounds as if we're blaming the victim again. But the first thing you should do when you find out that your program wasn't funded is to drag out the proposal that you submitted, along with the request for proposals or guidelines, and take a cold, hard look at the whole package. The passage of a good deal of time since you wrote the proposal often makes it interesting—and sometimes upsetting— to read it again. It is smart to try to recognize and acknowledge flaws that you find in your proposal even before soliciting reviewers' comments or discussing your proposal with foundation program officers. But give yourself a little time to get over the shock, sadness, rejection, and, often, embarrassment (yep...those are the feelings when major proposals that you worked hard on for a long time don't get funded), and then ask yourself the following hard questions:

- Does the proposal look as if it was done in a big hurry (which it was)?
- Is the description of the project clear and believable?
- Did I really make a good case for my program?
- Did I follow the guidelines and answer every single question?
- Is there anything I left out or didn't do because I ran out of time?
- Can I make sense out of the budget now, after not looking at it for a few months? Can it stand alone to represent my program?
- Did I make any computational errors in the budget?
- Is the proposal poorly written or filled with spelling errors and grammatical mistakes that make it hard to understand?
- Are the charts that I included clear and helpful or fuzzy and confusing?
- Is the appendix organized and relevant—or did I use it as a dumping ground for any piece of minutiae that I could find?
- Did I correctly spell the name of the person receiving the proposal?

What Kinds of Information Can I Get About My Rejected Proposal?

After reading your proposal over with great resolve and a strong stomach, it's time to find out what the reviewers thought about your work. There isn't much that is standard about the procedures that foundations and government funding agencies use to let you know your scores (if there are scores) or to give you written or oral comments (whether there are numerical scores or not). The key thing is to get as much information about the reasons your proposal was rejected as the funder is willing to give. Politely. And without defensiveness or hostility.

It is possible that the things you now think are wrong with the proposal didn't bother the reviewers in the least. You may feel, after consideration, that your evaluation plan was weak; they might have found nothing wrong with it but thought your staffing seemed haphazard. This doesn't mean that you had a strong evaluation plan (so don't get excited), but only that your reviewers were distracted by other flaws that they saw as more significant. Their feedback will help you when you return to this grantmaker and when you apply to others.

Reviewers' comments: government agencies. Government program officers usually will not discuss a particular proposal with you, although you will find some who are willing to provide this kind of technical assistance for a variety of reasons, ranging from personal style (he's a nice guy whose agency does not prohibit him from talking with you) to policy (the agency operates on a mandate to make technical assistance available as broadly as possible). Most, however, will refer you to the review process.

Most federal agencies and many state and local agencies employ outside reviewers, experts in the field, to read and score all competitive proposals. Some federal agencies send you a packet that includes your proposal's scores and reviewers' comments on its strengths and weaknesses, with reviewers' names and other identification removed. Others do not, especially if factors other than scores are involved in the awards. The cabinet secretary of each federal agency has discretion in awarding most grants (unless the underlying legislation specifies conditions in detail). For example, it is perfectly legitimate for the secretary to reject two high-scoring applications from one city because an even-higher-scoring application from that city did get funded.

Geographical distribution and other fairness issues can play a part in everything from college admissions to grants. This can make it difficult and time consuming to write to each applicant about the exact circumstances that affected the decision on that proposal. For this reason, some agencies prefer to give you a summary of the comments on the telephone.

However the assessment is given, whether it is written or oral, you should always seek information about how you could improve a proposal the next time. Write a simple letter to the program officer, requesting the reviewers' comments. Make sure you give all the identifying information about your proposal so that the program officer knows exactly who you are, including a confirmation number that you may have received after submitting the proposal. If appropriate, follow up with a call. If comments are given over the phone, take careful notes.

Reviewers' comments: foundations. As in everything else, foundations differ widely on how they handle rejections. (As noted, some don't handle this at all; you never hear from them again.) Most foundation program officers routinely reject proposals outside their guidelines; these rejection letters normally are very brief, sometimes stating that they don't fund the kind of program in the proposal, and sometimes simply saying politely that the foundation has made other awards. In most other cases the letter will be similarly polite, saying that there were "many interesting proposals" but that the foundation couldn't fund them all, and wishing you luck in your fundraising. In a few cases you may be invited to apply at a later time. Very rarely, usually when you have a long-standing relationship with a foundation or have been invited to submit a proposal, you may be asked to provide additional information or to revise the proposal before the program officer takes it to the foundation's board.

So—What Do I Ask?

If your proposal is sitting on the desk of the program officer of a foundation or a government agency while you speak, that would be the most helpful to you—but this is rare. It may be useful to set up an appointment for a convenient time to talk to the program officer; you will explain that you'd like to have a few minutes to find out how you could improve the program or the proposal. (Don't be surprised if the individual is willing just to give you a few moments when you first call. Be ready to ask your questions right then.)

Plan for this conversation by having a carefully thought-out (short) list of questions and follow-up questions to ask. The program officer probably will make some preliminary comments. Don't interrupt as the comments are being delivered—just jot down notes that you can address later. The key is to remain calm and cheerful. If you get defensive and argumentative because you feel the person has it all wrong, the conversation will end quickly and will not be very satisfying to you. You also need to be alert to the individual's responses, check periodically to be sure they're comfortable with the time it's taking, and be prepared to cut the call short if they seem impatient. This means you should ask your most critical questions first and know which ones you can omit. These are the types of questions you want answered:

- Can you tell me if there was a problem with the program or with the proposal itself, or if you just couldn't fund it at this time? (If there was a problem with the program or proposal, politely request some suggestions on how to improve it.)
- Did you think the proposal clearly addressed your guidelines, or should we have made that case more strongly? (Make notes!)
- Would you suggest that we apply again? (This is the most important question you need answered!) Is there a time frame for

doing this? (If you aren't assured that you should apply again, ask if there are any other foundations the funder thinks might be interested in the program.)

- Do you have any other suggestions about how we could strengthen either our program or our proposal?

What Should I Do with the Information I Get About My Proposal?

The more feedback you get about your proposal, the easier it will be for you to make an informed decision about how to proceed. If you are seeking support for a new program but the grantmakers feel it's not strong or compelling, you will have to decide whether to drop the project, at least for the time being, or keep going and continue to seek funding once you make certain revisions. If it's an ongoing project that you wanted to maintain or expand, you still may want to rethink it in light of the funders' comments, but you probably will decide to go back to step one, defining it more clearly and finding the right funder.

Why would we drop a project we think is important? Most of the time, you will be hesitant about discarding a project simply because a source didn't fund it, or even because reviewers didn't like it. But once in a while a grantmaker's rejection will make you rethink the whole thing, and you may become convinced that it just isn't a good idea. It may be too expensive in terms of staff, space, or other costs. It may be a one-shot deal that will not have an impact on a wide-enough audience for long enough. It may be too ambitious and unrealistic, especially if you can't sell it to the grantmakers. It is hard to part with a project that you believe in—but it can be a smart, time-saving, cost-saving move that impresses grantmakers in the long run.

What might the funder say to let me know I should just keep trying? If you get high marks and/or warm, positive comments from reviewers or program officers, your project and proposal are probably on the right track. Maybe this government agency was only able to fund the top 15 proposals and you were ranked 18th (out of 567 applicants). Maybe the foundation ran out of money for this round and wasn't able to fund your particular project. Maybe a grant was already committed to a similar project in your neighborhood or town. Maybe the reviewers gave you generally high marks but found your collaboration to be too new and unstable. Maybe the foundation program officer liked your project and proposal very much but knew that the trustees of her foundation wouldn't feel comfortable funding it. Not all of this information will come out in your follow-up calls, but enough will become clear that you'll have a sense that your project has merit and that your proposal is appealing (albeit not *that* appealing) to this grantmaker.

If the foundation program officer says you should resubmit the proposal with suggested changes, find out when the best time would be to do this and what changes make the most sense. If the program officer does not think you should resubmit to this foundation (for whatever reasons), ask for suggestions of other foundations that might be suitable for the project. Even more important, but only if it seems appropriate, ask if you can use the program officer's name when contacting the new foundation and whether the officer would be willing to serve as a reference.

For federal, state, or city grants that achieve high scores but do not receive funding, it makes sense to reapply if the opportunity arises. Although you will probably have different reviewers in the next round, it can't hurt to say in your proposal that you applied previously, received high marks, and have responded to reviewers' comments by strengthening your needs section or by partnering with a local university to strengthen your project. It can't hurt to explain how committed your organization and community are to the project, which is why you are reapplying. The group in the Opening Remarks was funded, with some important program modifications, on its third try!

A Few More Words of Advice and Encouragement

We have one more bit of advice to give you: Mind your manners. Your mother always told you to write a thank-you note when you got a gift. We think that grantmakers who spent time talking with you about your proposal have given you a very important gift that should be acknowledged in writing. Say thanks for their time. Say that you regret not receiving a grant at this time, but that you hope the advice they gave you will help you develop a better program or proposal in the future. Even if you didn't get to talk with a funder, it's usually a good idea to write a letter expressing regret and saying you hope you'll be able to present a better proposal in the future.

Grant writers agree that the horrific news that the important proposal they slaved over for weeks (and weeks and weeks) didn't get funded can rank right up there with the most painful disappointments in their lives. But use the loss as an opportunity to follow that other bit of your mother's advice, "If at first you don't succeed..."

One last thing: In your thank-you letters to funders who were kind enough to give you helpful information about your proposal, invite them to visit your organization sometime. Also, consider sending newsletters and other material that you routinely distribute. Don't inundate program officers' inboxes with paper or emails, but do keep the foundations in mind when you've got something good to show.

AND IF YOU GET THE GRANT...

Winning a grant is the exact opposite of rejection—it is acceptance, appreciation, love. So the first thing you must do when you win is bask in your glory. Congratulate yourself on doing your homework so well; on making heads and tails of the guidelines and application; on writing a clear, comprehensible proposal with a realistic and sane budget. You may be the only one who does this because only other proposal writers can really appreciate the obstacles that have to be overcome in order to bring home the bacon—and everything else the grant is bringing home—to the organization. But once you've won a few grants, you'll need to cut back a bit on the basking and just keep writing, because there's an organization depending on you.

Once you've finished celebrating, you still have a few things to take care of. Again, mind your manners. (We may be stating the obvious here, but we think it sometimes gets lost in the excitement of winning a grant.) If you got a foundation grant, write a thank-you note to the foundation's director (or the person who signed the letter announcing the grant). If it's appropriate, mention any help the foundation's program officer gave you. For a government grant, call or write to your elected officials to say thanks for their help if that's relevant, or just to keep their office informed. Notify any program partners and set up a meeting to talk about next steps.

Plan your final report now! Both government and foundation grant award letters normally will restate the conditions for which the grant is being made and will advise you of the nature and timing of any reports you must submit. *As soon as you hear about a grant award, go back to the proposal and start planning your final report.* With the program staff, review the action plan, timetable, budget, and other elements of the program to be sure they are still appropriate. If there are any problems, concerns, or questions about your organization's ability to implement the grant according to the proposal, now is the time to raise them with the funder. And if you hit snags after you've started your program, again, get in touch with the grantmaker, with a plan for alternative actions that may be necessary. Don't wait until a report is due. And, by the way, congratulations on winning the grant—you must have done a terrific job, and we tip our hats to you!

POP QUIZ

True or False?

1. Always reapply for a grant after a rejection. Your odds have to be better the second time.

2. Once you've been turned down by a foundation, don't bother the program officer by asking a bunch of questions. You'll be written off as a pest.

3. By law, you are not permitted to receive scores on your federal grant proposals.

4. Because the same person won't be reading your federal proposal the next year, don't bother making any changes based on suggestions from reviewers.

5. It is too pushy to ask a foundation grantmaker to suggest other foundations that might be interested in giving you a grant.

LESSON 18

WHEN GRANT FUNDING NEEDS A BOOST, BUILD A BUSINESS! (HINT: IT CAN BE SMALL!)

OPENING REMARKS

One of the best memories I have from my time as a grant writer for the public schools in New York City is of a coffee (and tea and pastry and bagel) wagon that was run by teenagers with severe disabilities (with some help from their teachers). Because the small school these students attended shared a building with the special education administrative offices where I worked, the teachers decided to take advantage of an in-house, enthusiastic market for a small business idea that met their goal of providing job training opportunities for their students. The older teens in the school were the baristas, wheeling the coffee wagon—well, really a big TV table with shelves and wheels—knocking on office doors, politely taking and filling orders, making change, collecting tips. They prepared the coffee, outfitted the wagon, kept it well stocked, and were responsible for keeping it neat (and hygienic). Those of us who worked in the building loved it—not only because we didn't have to run outside to get coffee or snacks but also because we got to really know and talk to the students for whom we were working. Meanwhile, they learned important work and social skills...and made money for supplies, trips, and other extras. —EK

LEADING QUESTIONS

I'm a Not-for-Profit Organization! I'm an Elementary School! Why Do I Need to Think About a Business?

First and foremost, of course, this is a grant-writing book, not a tome required for an MBA. But, as we noted in the introduction and in the opening roundtable on the funding environment, we believe that, for a variety of reasons, many state and local government grants that originate at the federal level may continue to see significant reductions or disappear altogether. Foundations are clear that they will not be able to fill the huge funding gap that is already developing. We don't mean to make things sound too grim, but, to put it bluntly, you need to protect yourself as much as possible by reducing your dependence on government funding by expanding traditional fundraising methods, by finding business opportunities that fit your mission (even small ones like the coffee wagon run by the students described in the Opening Remarks), or by identifying areas in which participants or clients are able to pay fees for services. And, preferably, all of these approaches. As we've said before, even if government funding levels could remain constant, grantmakers at all levels would still expect to see that you are making every effort to diversify your funding.

In this lesson we'll give you some examples of the kind of thinking we encourage you to do.

Some Organizations Are More Equipped to Run a Business, Right? Yes, but...

Before we discuss business approaches to supplement grant funding, we want to acknowledge that there are differences among grant-seeking organizations and that many already operate small or large businesses that we think can serve as inspiration to others.

First, there are large organizations (such as municipal and state government agencies and school districts) that have their own resources and would not be likely to run businesses. They may compete for discretionary federal or state grants, as well as funding from a full range of foundations, but taxes form the base of their budgets and may (at rare times) be adjusted to account for local needs and priorities. In addition, they often receive what is called *entitlement funding*, based on the number of individuals and families in categories specified under different federal laws (such as low-income families or children with disabilities). Some of this funding may be lost or reduced in coming years, and state and local governments will need to adjust to this loss.

The second relatively well-funded group comprises large nonprofits such as universities, major museums, national social service agencies, or large hospital centers. They may receive government and foundation funding through a proposal process (see Lesson 3) but also have significant private resources, often including endowments. Their board members and donors may be affluent, well-connected, and generous. The arts organizations usually are well known to— and well-respected by—a steady stream of residents and tourists who become members, pay entry fees, or make donations to take advantage of whatever is on offer. Medical centers with outstanding reputations attract patients, research grants, and medical students, as well as major donations and "naming opportunities." These larger organizations often operate volunteer-run gift shops, thrift shops, or other businesses (think of the well-stocked gift shops in the Museum of Contemporary Art in Los Angeles or the Mutter Museum in Philadelphia, as well as the stores run by the Salvation Army and Goodwill Industries) and have fairly large development staffs dedicated to raising money. They will probably be able to weather budgetary storms—but if they rely heavily on government funding, they should review their programs and fundraising strategies to identify priorities or areas that need to be strengthened.

The third type of organization is the one of greatest concern here. These are the small to mid-sized nonprofits (and many larger ones, too) that rely on federal, state, or local government grants and contracts won through a competitive grants process, and on grants awarded by state or local elected officials. Some (but not all) of these organizations may be very good at winning foundation grants and support from local corporations, but such support usually cannot sustain an organization over time. Some (but not all) also may receive support from their board members and other donors through events and annual appeals. But they often do not have affluent boards or communities or dedicated fundraising staff.

Think like an entrepreneur. Although the three types of organization differ in many ways, especially in the availability of resources, all need to think entrepreneurially to stay viable. For those heavily reliant on government funding, it is critical that they look at some of the business-oriented approaches taken by larger institutions and come up with creative ideas of their own (we'll provide a few good examples in a later section). For some, a business solution will help keep them up and running. For others, it may sustain or supplement funding for existing programs within the organization's mission rather than sustaining the organization itself.

We're One of Those Organizations That Rely on Government Contracts and We Know We Should Do More—but What Can We Do?

We won't dwell on traditional "non-business" fundraising methods here; there are excellent books and online guides available. We will, however, say that, if you don't do so now, you must find ways to develop and use the following methods no matter how limited your resources are.

- If you have a board, require the members to contribute at least a small amount of money annually.
- Conduct an annual appeal.

- Host at least one fundraising benefit each year.
- Make use of social media for fundraising.
- Continually seek ways to expand your donor base.

However, for most organizations these initiatives, though critical, are not enough to sustain them if grants and contracts dry up. That's why we asked our government and foundation panelists for suggestions about creative ways to support your programs and your organizations. *Their advice boiled down to something often easier said than done: "Think outside the box."*

Where Do I Start?

You are limited only by your organization's mission, your creative thinking about your programs, and your determination to raise money that's not dependent on grants and contracts.

First, be clear about your mission. If, for instance, your organization was established to serve young children, thinking outside the box by starting a bike-rental business wouldn't be likely to fit your mission—unless you were renting out tricycles. But if your organization works with at-risk high school students to help them get into college or find and hold jobs, you might consider renting out bikes to make money. Such an initiative serves your mission while it brings in unrestricted funds: You can use this "small business" to teach teenagers how to run a business, how to plan, set prices, market the business, and provide good customer service.

Then think about what assets you have (people and places) and what can be developed. Every nonprofit and school has assets that are not always considered in the usual approach to service provision. If you have space that is not fully utilized, for example, there are lots of ways to maximize income from your nonprofit's home. Can you rent out activity space or classrooms for meetings, parties, or community events? What are the skills of your participants and community members? They are potential volunteers who may be willing and able to set up and run business projects on your behalf. Maximize your assets!

SOME SMALL AND EASY EXAMPLES YOU CAN TRY (OR ADAPT TO FIT YOUR ORGANIZATION)

Many schools and nonprofits of all types occasionally use business-oriented approaches for fundraising, even if they don't bring in huge hauls—and even if they don't think of them as businesses. Most are more limited than the ongoing business strategies we want to bring to your attention in this lesson, but every bit helps. And some of the limited activities can be expanded—and become ongoing. Here are some examples of widely used fundraising projects that we encourage you to consider.

- *Put teenagers to work.* High school (and younger) students in many places wash cars, mow lawns, shovel snow, and sell cookies or candy to raise money for their sports programs or for trips. Some even run school stores. You saw in the Opening Remarks that young people with disabilities are able (and proud) to participate in a successful small business.
- *Call on PTAs and volunteers to sell stuff.* Although some recent articles have attacked them as sexist, bake sales can be a great way to pay for enhancements to school programs—and by no means is it only the mothers who bake and run the sales. We know of one, which includes dads, that is especially successful selling baked goods outside polling places on election days. But it doesn't have to be cakes and cookies that are sold—sales can and do include everything and anything, including, say, items handmade by parents and children.
- *Plan fun events.* Nonprofits and schools across the country run fairs, Monte Carlo nights, fashion shows, and talent shows to benefit their organizations. Auctions (silent or live, if you have a suitable volunteer auctioneer) are a terrific way to make money. Businesses in the neighborhood are often willing to donate merchandise for auctions—whether it be sporting goods, restaurant gift certificates, or even free legal or tax advice. Local artists,

jewelers, and other craftspeople are glad to contribute their work, especially if it helps them gain recognition. It takes leg work, but you'll be surprised how much volunteers and local businesses like to support the schools and nonprofits in their neighborhood. It's always good for business.

- **Ask older adults for help.** Many senior centers and multiservice nonprofits benefit from the skills of older people who run bazaars and thrift shops, cater events, donate their own handmade goods like quilts and afghans, and hold their own bake sales to raise funds for their nonprofits. Try asking older volunteers to develop their own fundraising projects to help out, and see what happens.

- **Use your kitchen.** Across the country, nonprofit organizations are operating cafés, restaurants, and catering services, some highly professional, others staffed by volunteers. We'll give a couple of outside-the-box examples below, but you don't need to go that far. If your organization has a kitchen that isn't used beyond after-school snacks or senior-center meals, think about asking volunteers—with or without professional help—to run a coffee shop serving breakfast for people passing by on their way to work, or get a local trade school or restaurant to offer fee-for-service cooking lessons or training for would-be chefs. Consider renting the kitchen in the early morning hours to small businesses such as caterers who may need a place to bake or prepare foods.

- **Use your gym.** If your gym is used primarily for after-school and evening programs, consider adding some exercise equipment (maybe using a start-up grant and/or contributions from local sporting goods stores) and offering it to the community during the daytime hours—for a small fee. Market the gym to local businesses, for their employees' use during lunch hours or before work.

- **Use your senior center.** In many communities, there are few public spaces for special events—sweet sixteens or quinceañeras, retirement parties, engagement parties or weddings, golden anniversaries—or else space rental is prohibitive. If your senior center is reasonably attractive—or could be more so with some simple decorations—let the community know that it's available for a reasonable rental fee. Be sure you calculate the costs of doing this—setting up, cleaning up, security—in the rental fee. You may or may not do the catering for the party, but it would be good know some reliable, reasonable caterers to suggest for an event.

- **Rent your space.** We know that for many organizations space is at a premium; you may be desperate for more yourself. But if you're one of the lucky ones with extra space, maybe you can rent out an unused office to a local professional—a lawyer, a writer, or an accountant. Some nonprofits sublet space to smaller organizations. If you're near a bus stop or train station or a commuter parking lot, a local diner or coffee shop might want to set up a satellite counter for a breakfast bar near your front door. You'll need to be sure you won't need the space for at least a year; most businesses won't want to rent for less time than that.

And Don't Just Stop There

If you currently are running any kind of business at all (no matter how small), you may—and you should—feel pleased that you are thinking creatively and bringing in much-needed supplementary money to your organization. But after talking to so many grantmakers and nonprofit leaders about the importance of diversifying funding, we want to suggest that you consider aiming a little higher, a little broader, with your approach to business. We've included a few examples of what we mean in the next section, but we expect that you will be able to come up with a lot more ideas that make sense for your organizations. Meanwhile, consider going bigger with what you're doing now.

If, as we mentioned in one example, you're a PTA that is doing very well selling baked goods at polling places on Election Day, why not do even better by selling not only pastries but handmade goods (jewelry, artwork), and selling them at other times—before and after school, in time for gift-giving holidays—and at other locations?

If your organization is already running a thrift shop or selling crafts, think about maximizing sales by advertising throughout the neighborhood and on social media. Also think about where else and what else you can sell—and about who else can donate and volunteer to help increase sales revenue.

If you work with the teens we mentioned earlier and are running a bike-rental business, consider adding a bike-repair component. Hire a trainer to teach the teens how to repair bikes, which is a good use of your resources. Develop a reciprocal arrangement with a shop that sells bikes: You'll send customers who want to buy bikes to the shop, and the shop will refer rental customers, or those in need of repair, to you. Or, if there isn't a bike shop in the area and your rental business suggests a likely market, grow into that business yourself!

Sometimes simple needs assessments (to find out what your customers and potential customers want to eat, drink, and purchase) and a little publicity in the neighborhood and beyond will lure more and more people to your business.

And one final thought: For-profit businesses, always focused on adding to their bottom line, routinely try to diversify funding by thinking entrepreneurially. Remember when Amazon.com sold only books? Even the smallest neighborhood shops are coming up with entrepreneurial plans to supplement incomes. One hair salon we know of, next door to a hotel that doesn't have room for suitcases, stores luggage at an hourly rate for hotel guests who have checked out but aren't leaving the city until later. The hotel refers departing guests to the salon. (Sometimes the luggage-storing customers decide to get a haircut or a manicure while they're there.) Small restaurants and bars close to the public for private parties that bring in far more revenue than the typical dinner, lunch, or drinks crowd would. Large corporate conference centers are rented to smaller businesses that need space for annual meetings. You can think of many more examples of how even the smallest businesses aim a little higher.

Nonprofits and schools aren't restaurants or conference centers, of course. Still, businesses can provide a model for thinking outside the box. The point is to be creative about new and expanded ways to raise money. But heed the warnings we'll give below. Plan carefully, work flexibly within your mission, go slowly and deliberately, know your market, and make sure you've thought about any risks—but be prepared to take some of those risks. It will be worth it.

OUTSIDE-THE-BOX EXAMPLES THAT CAN START YOU THINKING

Most of the examples of business-oriented fundraising in the last section require little more than someone to coordinate volunteers' training (when needed) and scheduling, organize outreach and publicity, and troubleshoot the operations. But entrepreneurial organizations will explore the process of building a full-scale business that can contribute significantly, not only to the mission but also to the sustainability of a program or the organization itself. This can take a lot of planning and a commitment to finding and maintaining long-term support for a business until it gets off the ground. Like the examples in the last section, some approaches can be small and be implemented in a relatively short time, but in most of the following examples the process took years for the business to become successful. And there are pitfalls, which we'll discuss a bit later.

An Art Gallery for the Ages (Really!)

In New York City, a network of senior centers operates a successful art gallery that is widely known and well respected for the high caliber of the curated artwork on display. Here's the catch—the artists whose work is exhibited must be at least 60 years old! There is a good reason for this. In spite of their talent, reputation, and bulging portfolios, older artists are generally considered, to put it bluntly, over the hill by many in the art world—and they rarely get the opportunity to have their work shown (and purchased). The gallery started small, in an unused space in one of the senior centers, and very soon moved to a location in what was just becoming a trendy area for galleries. The director of the gallery, an artist and former gallery owner, has been instrumental in placing articles about the gallery and interviews with the artists in numerous national arts and general-interest publications. The gallery hosts a well-publicized, well-attended grand opening every month, with new exhibits and, of course, wine and cheese for the guests. The artists and the senior center network share the profits from sales (which are considerable) and, as a bonus, the gallery rents out its space—which is always filled with paintings, photographs, and art installations—for events such as weddings to bring in extra money for the senior centers. **Can you think of any problems in your community that can be successfully addressed by starting even a small business?**

How an Alzheimer's Center Survived

A social adult day care center for people with Alzheimer's and other dementias provided—"for free"—a secure environment, caring staff, daily transportation, stimulating activities, and new friends who shared their experience of memory loss and understood one another's concerns. It also provided no-cost respite for family members responsible for the participants. The center lost government and foundation funding because, given the intensive, costly nature of such programs, it would never be able to "scale up"—serve more people—as the funders had hoped. It looked as if the center would have to close. But instead of giving up, the nonprofit that ran it identified a foundation whose mission was to help programs that might become self-sustaining. A solid business plan (we'll talk about this a bit later) persuaded the foundation that this adult day care program had a chance to do just that. Some families with resources were asked to pay a daily rate that covered costs (and a tiny bit more) for each participant. A creative executive reached out to managed-care companies that coordinated health care for elderly and disabled individuals, and developed contracts to provide services for their eligible clients with memory loss. The managed-care companies realized this would represent a lower cost than placement in a nursing home's memory unit. It was a slow process (over three years), and the organization sometimes still needs to find small amounts of supplemental funding, but the program survives. **What services can you sell (based on what you now provide for free) to keep your nonprofit afloat in bad times . . . and in good times too?**

Business Cooperatives—the Wave of the Future?

A community-based organization providing a wide range of family services in a low-income, largely immigrant community focuses heavily on preparing adults for work and placing them in jobs. The organization realized that there are workers who struggle to get jobs in traditional placements and that developing their own small businesses could be a solution. Over more than two years, with the help of the nonprofit's staff, a group of participants developed a home-cleaning business that has been so successful that other worker-owned co-ops have been created since, including child-care services, pet-care services, and nonmedical care for frail elderly. The workers—most of whom had limited education and English language skills—learned to do extensive market research to figure out how to price services competitively and where and how to promote the business. They identified and obtained needed training to learn not only the best but also the safest methods of cleaning. They incorporated, with the owner-workers serving as the board. They decided that 95 percent of income should go to the workers, the rest to various overhead costs including back-office and customer-service operations contracted on an hourly basis with the nonprofit parent. They've been so successful that they are now providing cleaning services to commercial as well as residential customers—and discussing setting up a retirement plan. Our panel of funders suggests that this model is very appealing to many foundations that want to see nonprofits prepare clients for jobs and financial independence. **Can worker-owned businesses be an option for your organization?**

Selling Skills to Businesses

An organization in a low-income inner-city area started with a program teaching young people to build and repair old, broken computers, and quickly developed formal courses and curricula on a wide range of information technology skills, from the basics to advanced practices. Students also received training in workplace skills such as customer service, teamwork, and communications. Staff were hired to market the program to businesses in a major metropolitan area; graduates were placed in these businesses, in positions ranging from entry-level help desk to software and network development. As the program expanded over several years, a creative leader began to work with businesses to identify skills they needed, and staff designed courses and curricula for specific business needs. This work has resulted in contracts with small and large corporations to provide workers with skills tailored to the needs of the specific employers. The organization still seeks grants for new initiatives but is close to self-sustaining—and has expanded its business to other cities. *Why beg corporations for job placements when you can sell them on talent and skills designed to meet their own needs?*

Food Service—Serve Your Mission as Well as the Public

Talk about long term! One example of what we have in mind is an organization in the Southwest. The organization started with volunteers assisting older area residents—running errands, shopping, and providing for other needs. Over many years the number of volunteers grew dramatically, and so did grant-supported and fee-for-service programs for seniors and families, including home care, skilled nursing, and memory care. No one is turned away for lack of ability to pay, but participant fees make up more than half of the organization's budget. Grants and private donations represent a significant portion of the budget, but an innovative business model provides another sizable chunk. With professional and volunteer help, and over several years, the organization started and promoted a restaurant open to the public; the restaurant eventually was able to stand alone and began offering catering services. And it started a bookstore on the premises, which helps draw customers to the food-service component. Well within the nonprofit's mission, the restaurant offers free and discounted meals to seniors, including free meals on holidays. *Can a café or restaurant—or a bookstore—serve your mission while it fattens your budget?*

CHALLENGES TO THINKING OUTSIDE THE BOX

We don't want to make it sound as if starting a business—any business—is a snap. Even the small and (relatively) easy business ideas discussed earlier are filled with potential obstacles—and some businesses, like restaurants, operate on slim profit margins. When thinking about adding a business component, it is a good idea to look at your organization and ask, "What could we add that would benefit the people we serve, the community, *and* our nonprofit's bank account?" Before you even begin developing a business or fee-for-service approach, think about what it will take to ensure that your staff will commit to it. You may need many meetings and perhaps help from an outside consultant. Some creative programs of all shapes and sizes did not make it, for a variety of reasons. We'll give you just a few warnings here.

Inadequate Planning

One of our grantmakers described an organization that wanted to create a self-sustaining business that would provide mainstream jobs for ex-convicts. They planned to train individuals to recycle ink cartridges and sell them to corporations. What they did not plan for was the intensive personal support the workers needed (basic job skills, help with personal problems that interfered with performance, etc.); the number of staff it would take to meet these needs; and the number of diverse skills that were required for performing the many aspects of this work. They had too many goals and objectives, and could not make the program work successfully. It is critical to consider everything that could go wrong and plan to address each possibility in a practical way before you try to implement any such project. This is one reason we urge you to create a business plan.

Inadequate Resources

As one grantmaker commented, nonprofit organizations often are so risk averse that they refuse to spend money on initiatives that can bring in more support in the long run—say, a development director or a marketing specialist, let alone a business. But if they do decide to take the plunge in starting a new business, they may overlook the need to raise the sometimes frightening amount of money that will put the business on its feet. The business plan must show where start-up resources will come from and project the length of time outside resources will be needed to keep it going.

Lack of Professional Staff

There's a reason successful businesses have well-prepared managers. According to one grantmaker, some business-oriented programs have failed because the organizations did not recognize the need for management skills, marketing experience, or other high-level professional skills. You may be able to start a small pilot program with a few enthusiastic staff members or volunteers (and it's often helpful to start this way), but, if you want to grow a business that has a chance of success over time, you will need skilled assistance. Although we are very enthusiastic about the use of volunteers, you must be sure you do have the right person for the job. If you don't have exactly the right volunteer, you need to budget for a paid manager. And even if you have a dedicated and skilled crew of volunteers, you still may need a part- or full-time volunteer coordinator. Part of the success of the worker-owned cleaning business was that members were able to draw on the parent organization's professional staff for help with bookkeeping, customer service, and other back-office skills. And a significant part of the art gallery's success was its experienced manager, a former gallery owner.

Relying on the Same Volunteers Over and Over... Until They Get Burned Out

One small nonprofit could not afford to hire extra staff to run fund-raising events and activities and had to keep calling on the same people time after time. Eventually these people said, "Enough—leave me alone. I love the organization but I can't do it anymore." When considering diversifying your fundraising—and certainly when you're going to try even a small business approach—think about who will do what. And, if you plan to use volunteers, how you will recruit (and thank) them; it had better not be the same old good guys.

Skipping Steps, Getting Too Big Too Fast

The program we mentioned before—training ex-convicts—tried to do too much at once, according to the grantmaker we spoke to about it. If they had started, say, by providing some basic technical skills and placing workers in appropriate work environments, they might have built a self-sustaining program in stages, adding needed social services and additional skills training that led to the desired business success.

A small nonprofit theater organization had been very success-ful in building a reputation and an audience in a space that seated fewer than 100 people. It was given the opportunity—an offer they couldn't refuse—to move from this space to a rent-free, profession-ally designed auditorium seating many times that number. The op-portunity was irresistible, but, for a number of unanticipated reasons, the theater was unable to draw an audience that could fill the larger space, and ultimately had to close.

Failing to Plan for a Major Change in Your Organization's Culture If You Decide to Charge Fees or Build a Business

Most nonprofit service organizations always have operated on the assumption that their target population needed free services, and in many communities this was and still is true. But even in the poorest communities, some service providers—and funders—believe it contributes to the participants' sense of ownership of a program if they make at least a small contribution to obtain needed services. Organizations often make such contributions voluntary or create a sliding scale that accounts for family income, but staff may resist any efforts to change the status quo. They will argue that charging fees would prevent some current participants from gaining access to services. You may need to focus on ways to change the existing culture and encourage the staff to recognize the need for fees. It may take many discussions and possibly the help of a skilled consultant.

Here's a good example of what can go wrong: A very high-quality college preparation program drew participants from a wide urban area where many families could and would have sent their children to a for-profit college prep program, but of course were happy to have the free service. The organization decided to charge a small fee to offset the cost of the program, with the potential for a sliding scale or scholarships if students could not pay. Many participants did pay, but staff resistance continued to such an extent that government funding was sought and won, and fees were dropped. For now, this outstanding program is fine, but, because staff members were unwilling to think outside the box, it is vulnerable if the grant is not renewed.

IF YOU CAN WRITE A GOOD GRANT PROPOSAL, YOU CAN WRITE A GOOD BUSINESS PLAN

For grantmakers who are interested in projects that can become self-sustaining, a business plan is often required—and one should be created even if the funders don't demand it. This is not a mysterious activity. Even the smallest businesses should have a business plan to make sure all bases are covered. The focus may be a little different from a standard proposal, and you will need some additional information, but *if you can write a good proposal, you can write a good business plan.*

The business plan will address the same issues as a proposal does—need, goals and objectives, program plan, evaluation, and so forth. In both cases the purpose is to show that you know why it's necessary and that you are fully prepared to run the program. The business plan also must show that you have considered all possible contingencies on the way to making the program self-sufficient. We'll discuss a few of these contingencies here; a sample business plan from the Small Business Administration is provided in Appendix 4, and you will find a wealth of information online.

Know Your Market

Most grant proposals focus on the portion of the population that needs the service proposed. You already know your community very well (or should). You probably could write a needs statement in your sleep. In addition, though, a business plan must identify the portion of the population that *could or would pay for it.* The theater company mentioned earlier learned this the hard way. When it moved to a much larger space than it had been using, it assumed its populous suburban community would fill the seats. It had not sufficiently studied its market or its competition: Residents had many theatergoing opportunities in a nearby city.

On the other hand, the art gallery described earlier knew its market very well and picked a location in Chelsea, the heart of the art gallery section of Manhattan, which is one of the major reasons it has succeeded. The school coffee wagon we told you about in the Opening Remarks also knew its market. There were no nearby coffee shops or bakeries . . . and besides, who wants (or has the time) to walk outside and wait on long lines to get a muffin or a cup of tea when a door-to-door delivery service is available?

If you are planning an ambitious fee-for-service program or a potentially self-sustaining business, you will use the same data sources as for a standard needs assessment, but this part of the business plan requires you to become a super data analyst. Go back to all the data you have about the demographics of the community and your service population, its strengths and weaknesses, and dig deeper.

- Are there pockets of relative affluence in a generally low-income area?
- Are there nearby neighborhoods with higher-income residents?
- Do these neighborhoods include a lot of preschool children? Teenagers? Elderly?
- Are the needs of the middle-class or wealthy residents—for child care, youth services, or elder care—similar to those of the low-income residents?
- Most importantly, are there enough existing free or fee-based programs to meet all the needs? If so, why would it be important for you to jump in? If not, what would it take for you to provide them?

Think through all of your current programs and seriously consider how you might structure fees or request contributions. Think about what it would take to expand the number served, how you would advertise and market a service, and what it would mean to your community and organization if you were able to raise money in this way.

Know the Competition

In addition to showing that you know the market for your services (most importantly, that there *is* a market), you will have to demonstrate that you know what other organizations or businesses, if any, already are addressing the need—your "business competition." Who else provides the proposed service, and why are they not sufficient to meet the need? How is your project different or better? Instead of the business strategy proposed, would a merger or collaborative initiative make more sense? Why not?

Learn Marketing

Many government and private funders ask you how you will recruit participants if you win a grant. The same question applies here, but your answer must be much more sophisticated than, say, making presentations at PTA meetings or sending out fliers about your senior center art classes. Marketing is critical to the success of a business or fee-for-service program. You need to understand specific ways to reach your target population, whether through print advertising, social media, a word-of-mouth campaign, public service or paid ads in media outlets that are popular with your community, and more. You may need to consider the cost of a media specialist in your business plan or show how you will obtain pro bono services from professionals. You certainly need to consider other costs of marketing in your budget, including promotional materials and the cost of advertising.

Know Your Path to Success

In a standard grant proposal, you are required to include a program description and indicators of success. How many teenagers will apply to college? How many will be accepted? How many will graduate? But if you want to create a self-sustaining college prep program, you also need to describe all the steps you will take to make it self-sustaining. How many paying students will you need to cover all the program's costs, cover less affluent students, and perhaps make a small profit? How and where will you recruit them? Will you start by adding a small number of paying students to the existing program and build this number over the years? Will you ask current participants to contribute to the cost of the program? Or will you start a completely new fee-for-service program in addition to the current one? How does your program differ from existing for-profit college prep programs, in format as well as in cost? (You can boast a little here about outcomes from your current "free" program.) How will you cover students who cannot pay? If all answers are satisfactory, how long will it take to reach the desired outcome of a self-sustaining program?

You also need to know how a program or business that becomes self-sustaining will benefit the parent organization. For example, if you successfully create a fully functioning bike-repair shop to train youth in your community to run a business, will your organization pay the ongoing business costs, including salaries and overhead, and keep any profits, or will the new business itself handle all costs, distribute profits to the participants, and perhaps include a contribution or payment to the parent organization in its budget?

IN CONCLUSION

Okay, we get it: starting a business or charging fees is not for everybody. You may not see your way to doing anything like this right now. But we must urge you to think seriously about what you will do if that city or county grant for senior services comes to an end; what you will do if state funds for after-school programs are phased out; what you will do if your ESL programs lose their government support. Of course we hope none of this will happen, but we think that at least some of our fears may come true. We wrote this chapter to encourage you to incorporate some of the ideas here into your planning process, or jump off from them to create your own plans for sustainable support. (And this kind of thinking will look great in your next proposal!)

POP QUIZ

True or False?

1. Before your nonprofit can start even the smallest business, you must have a budget of at least $1 million.

2. The largest nonprofits, like medical centers and museums, are most likely to be the hardest hit by economic turndowns.

3. Public schools, unlike nonprofit organizations, are forbidden to use business approaches to supplement funding.

4. If you are a nonprofit, you cannot pay consultants to help start a business; you must rely on volunteers.

5. Some grantmakers today may be more likely to fund non-profits that are proposing business approaches to diversify their funding.

6. An example of a savvy business strategy is for your organization to send grant proposals to foundations in other cities.

7. A high-quality business plan should never be more than one page long.

Essay Questions

1. In this lesson we discussed how some schools and nonprofits are "thinking outside the box" by using creative business approaches to raise funds. If you run an after-school art program for artistically inclined teenagers who live in the Wishbone housing project in Metropolis, suggest two (or more) ideas for a (small) business that could add much-needed funds to the program.

2. Describe a business that fits your organization's mission and that would be reasonable to build and develop with volunteers and a professional manager.

FUNDERS ROUNDTABLE IV

THE "WHAT DO I DO NOW?"
ROUNDTABLE

THE PROCESS OF REVIEWING GRANT PROPOSALS can be sensitive (reviewing or grading anyone or anything can be a little dicey), so for this last roundtable, we asked the grantmakers on our panel to shed some additional light on the way grants are reviewed within their organizations. They also talked about another sensitive topic—what grant seekers should do if they don't win the grant—and the much less sensitive, much happier prospect of what they should do if they do get one. Most grantmakers were positively impressed by organizations that had developed business-oriented initiatives like those we described in Lesson 18. Their comments have been presented in Roundtable I on Grantsmanship and the Funding Environment.

Reviewing Federal Grant Proposals Is Usually a Pretty Rigid Process...Right?

In Roundtable II, a federal grantmaker explained in painstaking detail the elements of the peer review process. He was making an important point about how fair, objective, and serious the process of scoring a federal grant is. His remarks were echoed by another federal funder, who explained that her agency uses a scoring system ranging from 100 (best) to 500 (worst), using "an algorithm so we get a distribution point spread." She noted that nothing but the technical requirements of the application package is ever considered by reviewers and that every section has an allocated number of points. There are panels of 12 to 15 reviewers, each having primary responsibility for up to eight proposals. Each proposal is read by at least three reviewers. Each reviewer scores the sections of the proposal based on the application criteria, and final scores are assigned after discussion. "There are agencies that do it differently," she said, "groups that are not as stringent." But the purpose is the same: to ensure the fairest, most objective review possible.

"If we make a visit," said a government panelist, "the visitors will be able to see if all those letters of support that clogged up the proposal's appendix were bogus or if the partners were really at the table!" But, although a few government agencies do conduct site visits as part of their decision-making process, most can't because of the tremendous costs involved in traveling throughout the country to visit grant applicants. This means that the proposal normally is a make-or-break opportunity for the grant seeker to communicate everything the reviewers can't see in person.

But Can't Foundations Take Other Things into Account in Making Their Decisions?

Looking at the foundation proposal review process, one of our panelists explained her thinking as she winnowed 26 proposals that had made the first cut down to the 14 that would actually receive funding. "It wasn't all about the proposals. We had to turn a solid group down because we ran out of money.... The job is a balancing act. The bottom line is, good groups that fit should get in 80 percent of the time, but there are reasons why not. Here's what I ask myself: Have I spoken to this group at all during the year? Have I turned them down before even though they have done a good job? Do the trustees know and like this organization, or not?" For this particular funder, "whether or not the proposal is well written is the least of it!"

"We're looking for genuineness in making funding decisions," explained a foundation colleague, "even if the proposal isn't well put together."

"The main thing we look for in making a decision is whether the organization has a good leader," said another foundation funder. "And this is something we can tell once we make a site visit." The site visit means a lot—but not everything—to many grantmakers. "If we're interested in your organization based on the material you sent us, we'll arrange a site visit," said a foundation funder. "It gives us a chance to look at the program in action, meet the program director, the head of the organization. But the site visit isn't the be-all and end-all—we check with other funders too."

A grantmaker offered this reminder: "We're not only judging your program, we're mainly judging the fit." There's that word again— *fit*—which is all about how well your organization matches up with a particular grantmaker and its guidelines.

Foundations Can Even Overlook the "Warts"

"I just made a grant to an organization and then learned that the unified picture everyone presented in the proposal and during the site visit was false," said a frustrated funder. "People want to show their best face—they're afraid if they show 'warts and all,' they won't get funded. But that's not necessarily true. If you show your warts, you may get even more money to help you get rid of them!"

It's a hard call for grant applicants to decide just how candid to be—how many warts to point out—during the process of seeking funds. The temptation to hide problems is great, assuming that by the time a site visit is arranged or the grant is ready to be implemented, the problem or problems will be long solved. Our grantmaker who saw a false unified picture during a site visit found out later that the staff was disgruntled, to say the least. This dire staff problem did not bode well for the smooth implementation of the project.

Other problems that you may feel nervous about sharing with potential funders could include fiscal questions, hiring and procurement issues, and recruitment difficulties, to name just a few. If these issues are likely to impede the implementation of a grant, you might be better off waiting to submit a proposal until you've got them worked out. And if it will take a grant to get them worked out, you'd better say so.

We're pretty sure from what our panelists told us that they're willing to work with an organization that levels with them. They may not be so forgiving of an organization that deceives them, and the next grant may be much harder to get. In fact, one of the foundation funders told us that it could take a change of leadership before she'd give a grant to such a troubled organization. It is our suggestion that you be as honest as possible when applying for a grant.

Decision Making Isn't as Easy for Grantmakers as We Thought

In a way, government funders, with their elaborate review procedures and scoring systems, have it easier than foundations, with their greater flexibility. But both types of grantmakers experience their own challenges. The most difficult is the limited funding available. Even in federal programs, when millions of dollars are granted for specific purposes, the program officers know that the needs are much greater than they are able to meet. As a foundation funder put it, really speaking for all of the panelists, the challenge is that "people who make funding decisions must do so with minimal funds for maximum needs—and with extreme pressure from the board and ultimate responsibility to the community."

In other words, deciding which groups to fund and which ones not to fund...well, it isn't easy.

Let's Look at the Bad News First. After the Gut-Wrenching Rejection, What Should I Do?

It's always hard to receive a rejection letter, even for a small grant. But it's sometimes even harder to try to find out what went wrong. Some grantmakers are reluctant to talk about the reasons for rejecting a proposal, but many told us that they really don't understand why they don't get more calls asking how the applicant could do better next time. "A smart grant writer will call and find out why a project wasn't funded," suggested a panel member. "And sometimes we'll make a site visit anyway."

"We have 'declination' calls with organizations we don't fund," said a panelist. "When you get turned down, get some feedback," said another funder. "Only about 15 to 20 percent of those who were rejected call us back, and many of the ones who call are groups we already know. No more than 10 percent of the other groups— the ones we don't know at all—actually call to see why they were turned down. Yet feedback enhances an organization's chances of being funded the next time." Another panelist agreed: "Very few groups call when they're not funded. I'm impressed when a group calls and asks, 'Can we do something different?' If they tell us their challenges—for instance, 'We're no longer as small as we were, but we're not really big enough to appeal to most funders; what can you suggest?'—they're educating us. We can then tell our board about the challenges inherent in growing." This grantmaker summed up by suggesting, "Tell us your dilemma; maybe we can advocate for you."

Despite these helpful attitudes, it's sometimes (but not always) easier to get information about why a government proposal was turned down than why a foundation proposal was rejected. Although there's no policy carved in stone about how government grantmakers deal with letting applicants know why they didn't get the grant, most of them provide the reviewers' comments. "We routinely send copies of reviewers' comments to the applicants—without the names of the reviewers, of course," explained a federal grantmaker. But, according to another government funder, "Dealing with reviewers' comments varies wildly. Some agencies may be skittish about sending reviewers' comments because they want wiggle room." It is always worth asking.

Foundations vary more than government agencies do in providing feedback, but most are reluctant to be too specific. "If the proposed project is out of our guidelines, we have a form letter saying, 'We don't fund public schools, or the performing arts, or individuals.' Otherwise we use a general letter of rejection," said one of our funders. "For letters of intent," explained a panelist, "we use a standard template for rejection—no specifics, just, 'Your letter was not as highly ranked as the ones we chose.'" Another foundation funder uses the same procedure. "For letters of intent, we send form rejections: 'You're doing great work, but…'" "We don't give comments," said another.

But one grantmaker said, "We call every grant seeker to tell them why they weren't funded, to brainstorm about possible other funders, and to give them advice and technical assistance. After every docket, we call and offer technical assistance."

If We Don't Get "Formal" Comments, What Should We Do?

"Cold calling is hard, but be persistent so you can find out why you were turned down. You need to know whether the answer is 'Sorry, you didn't fit our guidelines and never will' or 'We liked your project but ran out of money,'" said one funder. "When you apply the next time, show us you've gotten better."

"We don't think it's productive to have discussions about why a group didn't get funded," explained a panelist. "It's usually not about the proposal, it's about the program. We turn conversations back to the types of things we're likely to fund, rather than why this particular organization didn't receive funding. If you go into a lot of detail, it takes an awful lot of time. Also, this program that we didn't approve for funding is someone's baby."

This panelist added the following extremely useful suggestion: "A good thing for a grant seeker who has been turned down to say is,

'Were there any questions about the program that I need to address?' A question of this kind gives the program officer an opportunity to say, 'I didn't see so-and-so mentioned.' And this, in turn, gives the grant seeker a chance to ask if there is anyone doing this type of work who may be able to give me some suggestions or pointers." In other words, you can get the funder to help you improve by the next time you come calling.

From another grantmaker: "People call or write polite letters, saying, 'We hope we can reapply in the future.' When they do this, we tell them why their proposals didn't rank as high as some others did. It could make them uncomfortable, but if they're nice...we'll tell them. And if it was a close call, we'll encourage them to apply again in January." "If you call, we can help you. But some call angrily—or, I should say, with thinly disguised anger—and ask why they weren't funded," another grantmaker noted.

Is It Smart—or Obnoxious—to Ask Funders Who Have Turned You Down to Recommend Other Grantmakers?

One funder we spoke to will refer grant seekers to another grantmaker if they call to find out why they weren't funded, but she doesn't do this unless she knows the groups and the funder she's calling pretty well. "I usually fall in love with a couple of new groups that I can't fund every year...and I'll call other foundations on their behalf or let them use my name when contacting other grantmakers," she said. Another panelist said, "I refer groups to other funders all the time, especially when a group is doing such a valuable thing but I can't fund it."

"We don't refer to other foundations—it's too much like passing the buck," explained another funder. "But we do suggest that applicants that have been turned down talk to not-for-profit organizations that are doing similar work."

Before we left this issue of what steps to follow after getting rejected, one panelist speculated on why so many grant seekers don't call to find out why funding was denied. "Maybe it's the power dynamics between those who want money and those who have money. It's similar to kids applying to college. No matter how brilliant and accomplished the student is, the colleges hold all the cards, all the power. And most kids never find out why they were rejected from their first, second, and third choices. They can only guess."

It's clear from talking to our panel of grantmakers that you need to snap out of it—even if it takes joining a support group for proposal writers—and start calling funders to find out why you were turned down, how you might increase your chances of getting a grant the next time, and what other funders might be able to help in the meantime. We understand that old insecurities die hard, but proposal writers and the organizations that count on them can't afford to be insecure. As one of our panelists said, "Grant writing should be one-half job interview and one-half date. The job interview part requires you to be self-promoting and smart; the date part calls for you to be charming and appealing." Easier said than done. But good advice.

Now for the Good News: What If We Do Get the Grant?

Most grantmakers understand that your proposal was an optimistic statement of what you want to do, how you want to do it, and how much it will cost. What may surprise you is that many funders are ready to help you do it, now that you're on their team. For example, a federal grantmaker said, "It's a new ballgame when you get the grant. Not always do the highest scorers become the higher performers. But now we think about start-up issues, and realize that implementation goals might be readjusted."

Don't hide the problems that (inevitably) come up! A foundation funder advised, "Do what you say you're going to do. Report as required, look back at the proposal." The most important thing is that you bring implementation problems to the funder, preferably with a solution. "Think about the reporting when you're writing the proposal, go over expectations with program officers while developing the proposal. It's very difficult to say what you're going to accomplish. If there are problems, keep people informed. Let us know right away. We don't want to take the money back, but if you wait until the grant is over and then have to say you couldn't do it, you probably won't get any new funding." Another panelist said, "We like to hear about internal problems directly...and not read embarrassing (or worse) news in the newspaper. We tend to hang in through good times and bad. Our groups are sometimes up and sometimes down. We'll help. But you have to be straight with us."

And there's sometimes some negotiating to do, some rethinking about what's realistic. As another federal funder said, "Then reality sets in....One of the problems: the person who writes the proposal leaves, maybe a new administration comes into office, plans don't always work out." He described the type of conversation he might have with the grantee:

" 'We can't do everything in our grant.'

'What can you do?'

'X, Y, and Z.'

'Okay, that's a good start.' "

Our panelist says, "It doesn't hurt if they can't do it; it hurts if they're not trying."

So the bottom line is, talk to us. Although we didn't mention the word "communication" to our panelists, the word popped up surprisingly often, and we repeat it throughout the book. Here are some pretty self-explanatory things funders said. "Don't tell us about your problems at the last minute. Communicate, communicate, communicate." "Foster collegial relationships with funders. It will be easier to admit to foundations that problems are brewing. We don't like surprises (who does?). Tell us. Create a climate where people can talk." "Not-for-profits can approach foundations with their problems and needs—and ask for suggestions about how to go about raising money."

CONCLUDING REMARKS

After countless hours of conversation with funders through five editions of this book, it's not easy to sum up everything we learned.

Much to our surprise, not all grantmakers agree on some of the things we thought were "nonnegotiable." For instance, one funder couldn't care less if the applicant spelled her name right. This same funder puts "how well written the proposal is" as her least important criterion for funding. But no panelist was sympathetic to applicants who didn't follow directions.

Some of the intangibles that we thought might be important were important to some funders but not to others. Our advice to grant seekers is not to throw your hands up in the air and scream, "I give up!" Because when you think about it, remember what we said about how different foundations are. Government agencies, too, differ from one another in their missions, budgets, policies, and politics. The same is true for their staffs and for the reviewers who are brought on board for specific grant competitions. Why would everyone think the same way and have the same pet peeves and responses? And although one funder doesn't give a hoot how her name is butchered by prospective grantees, many of our panelists were very put off that people hadn't bothered to check the correct spelling of their names.

So, some rules of thumb: Although not everyone cares about everything, read the guidelines, do your homework, be polite if you call with questions, and make sure you are comfortable with technology and social media. Write the best grant proposal you can, identifying your needs, presenting measurable objectives and activities to achieve the objectives, developing a well-thought-out evaluation plan, and creating a realistic budget. Write passionately about your organization. Write clearly about your organization's ability to implement your program and how you will measure its impact. You should never be greedy—not in flush economic times, not in woeful economic times. You should always think creatively about how to sustain grant-funded projects and diversify your funding sources. (You may want to give thinking outside the box a try!) And no matter what's going on, you need to stay calm, optimistic, and focused. It's part of the job.

APPENDIX 1: TIPS FOR IMPROVING YOUR CHANCES OF WINNING A GRANT

1. ***Find the Foundation Center Library.*** With main libraries in five cities and 450 participating libraries across the country, there is a Foundation Library or funding information center near you. This is your first resource for identifying private funding sources that are right for you.

2. ***Get to know Grants.gov.*** As you'll see in the notes in Appendix 5, this expansive site contains everything you need to know about federal grants.

3. ***Master the latest technology***—the more the better. Technophobes have a much harder time preparing and submitting grant proposals these days, and there's so much more you need to know. Make sure at least one staff member is a "digital native" who can do the research, submit proposals online, and make use of the next two tips.

4. ***Make sure your organization has a website!*** Even a rudimentary one gets your name out there and gives you credibility, and there are apps available that let you create a perfectly respectable site without costly consultants. Consider asking volunteers to help with this—it's really important.

5. ***Take advantage of social media.*** If you don't have them already, add a Facebook page (and keep it up to date), a Twitter account

(tweet about issues related to your organization's work and mission), and other social media to become part of the twenty-first century.

6. *Find the right funding opportunity.* Don't submit a scattershot proposal to all the grantmakers in your area. Do some research to be sure your program is what a particular grantmaker can fund. If the proposed program is not an exact fit with a grantmaker's priorities, you'll only annoy the funder and risk your chances for the next time.

7. *Read the guidelines.* Be absolutely sure that a particular foundation or government grant is appropriate for you. Is your organization eligible? Has this source funded programs like yours? Does this source *want* to fund programs like yours? Does it want to fund in your community? Get your foundation's annual reports, their 990 tax forms, their application guidelines. See what organizations they've funded recently and how much they gave.

8. *Read the instructions.* Answer every question and cover every topic. Grantmakers and reviewers say it is astonishing how often proposal writers do not adhere to the requirements set out in the funding announcement or guidelines. Applicants fail to meet the submission deadline, exceed the specified budget or page limits, present materials in the order they think is appropriate rather than the order requested in the application package, ignore some sections of the application or questions they are asked to address, ignore instructions about format, and make other errors that either lead to outright rejection of the proposal or significantly lower the score.

9. *Get organized...now.* At slow times in your workday, workweek, or work year, prepare a file with all the documents you will need when you get ready to submit a proposal. Items to include are listed in various lessons in this book; basically, they represent information about your organization, your programs, any

publicity you've received, your finances, your management and staff, your participants, and the community.

10. **Update board information regularly; even keep their résumés on file.** Funders often want to see who the board members are and what their skills are. Keep records of how much the board members give financially. Foundations often want to see this kind of support in addition to the skills board members contribute to the organization. Some grantmakers want to know if the demographic makeup of the board reflects the community.

11. **Give yourself plenty of time to prepare the proposal, especially if it's for a government agency.** Rome wasn't built in a day, and successful proposals aren't written in two weeks. Remember that in one study the average time it took to prepare a federal proposal was nearly 80 person-hours—but for those proposals that received awards, the average preparation time was more than 150 hours. We haven't seen any similar figures for local government proposals, but experience suggests it's pretty close. If you can't develop and write a high-quality proposal in the allotted time, wait until next year or the next funding cycle.

12. **Call for technical assistance during the preparation of a government proposal** (e.g., to ask for clarification if application instructions seem contradictory). When in doubt, ask grantmakers questions *before* submitting any proposal! But never put the program officer in an awkward position by pushing for information if the officer indicates that a particular question can't be answered.

13. **Watch your language.** Don't use acronyms! Don't use jargon, either. Both can be annoying and confusing. Be careful to be sensitive (if not downright politically correct) to all individuals, groups, neighborhoods, and communities mentioned in your proposal. To show you understand the grantmaker's own priorities,

use the language in the guidelines or application package as much as possible (and, of course, when it's appropriate).

14. ***Repeat yourself when you have to.*** Although repetition should be kept to a minimum in a proposal, a certain amount of repetition is inevitable in response to an application's questions and requirements for each section. You cannot assume that the reader will remember that an important point has been made earlier.

15. ***Give proposal reviewers a break: Don't write pages and pages and pages of narrative.*** Use charts, tables, graphs, and other illustrative material whenever possible—but only if they are clear, to the point, and easy to read. No need to get fancy.

16. ***Create a checklist.*** At the beginning of the proposal process, lay out a list of everyone you need to speak with, every piece of information you need, every document that has to be collected or prepared, and every signature that you will need. Review it at least once a day, every day—and once more before you submit the proposal.

17. ***Be sure each section of the proposal is consistent with every other section.*** If a statement of need shows a gap in services in the community, the objectives and program description should show how that gap will be filled. If a program activity calls for a certain type or number of staff, this should be explained in the program description, accounted for realistically in the budget and budget narrative, and described in the agency capability or staff expertise section (depending on the specific requirements of the application); job descriptions and/or résumés should be included as requested.

18. ***Use the application package's topics as the headings in your own proposal.*** This will make it easy for the reader to see that you've addressed all the issues the grantmaker considers important.

19. *When designing your program objectives, be realistic.* Aim high, but not too high—and know how you will recognize success. For each measurable objective included in your grant proposal, explain how you will know whether it was achieved.

20. *Get free consulting for the evaluation section of your proposal.* Many academics and freelance consultants will willingly work with you on a major proposal to help frame objectives and research methods for the evaluation, understanding that if you get the grant, they will be paid to do the evaluation.

21. *Get the evaluation consultant involved early.* Working backward and forward among the objectives, the program description, and the evaluation makes for a stronger proposal.

22. *Don't be greedy—but keep it real.* Make sure your budget is reasonable and your math is correct. Funders know if you're asking for too much, or for too little, to make the program work. They will recognize (and not appreciate) inflated salaries and overpriced travel expenses in your budgets.

23. *Think about sustainability.* Tell the grantmaker what you hope to do to keep a program going once the grant runs out. Do this whether the application requires it or not. Talk about other potential sources to sustain the program. And see Tips 24 and 25.

24. *Start a business.* Entrepreneurial organizations are the most likely to survive in any economic climate. Grantmakers are usually glad to hear about any entrepreneurial initiatives you're undertaking to sustain the program *and* the organization (see Lesson 18).

25. *Develop a business plan.* Develop a plan even for the smallest businesses—it will increase your likelihood of success. And it wouldn't hurt to do this for any major new grant-funded program, either.

26. *Develop a marketing plan.* How will you sell your program or business to the community you serve—and recruit the maximum number of participants?

27. *Say thank you.* Write thank-you notes! If you win a grant, say thank you; and even if you don't, thank the funder for considering your proposal. If grantmakers or local politicians visit your organization, let them know how much you enjoyed showing them around and invite them to come again. Thank your volunteers; hold events to honor them and show your gratitude.

28. *When appropriate, include a timeline in your proposal.* It will help the grantmaker understand what you plan to do and when you plan to do it. If there is absolutely no room in your proposal for one extra word, construct a timeline anyway—for your own use. It will keep you organized and your proposal orderly—and will help you implement the project when you get the grant.

29. *Don't stuff the appendix.* You don't need to throw in every press clipping; grantmakers probably won't read them. Be thoughtful about what you think they must see. And if they ask for specific items, make sure you include them.

30. *For a government proposal, include a letter from your elected official.* For a foundation proposal, don't.

31. *Use friends and colleagues for proofreading help and to edit and comment on the proposal at different points in the process.* If the same people keep reading it over and over, many inconsistencies as well as grammatical and spelling errors will be missed. Even more important, ask a friend or colleague to read the budget and budget narrative, and then explain to you exactly what the money is going to be spent on. Ask a different friend or colleague to read the abstract and explain to you exactly what your proposed project is all about. Do this only for the most critical proposals; friends can burn out too.

32. ***Get on mailing and emailing lists.*** Make sure you hear about all the funding that may be available for your community.

33. ***Save newspaper and magazine articles.*** Keep a file of materials describing what your city or town, state, and country are doing in the areas that pertain to your organization's work. Someone, maybe a volunteer, should do this every day so you don't miss a court case, an important speech, a new law that will be relevant to the next proposal. Most of the material will be available online, although sometimes you'll have to pay for subscriptions.

34. ***Get to know your elected officials, and let them get to know you.*** Invite them to see your operation. Let them speak to your participants. Even before submitting a government proposal (whether you work for a not-for-profit organization or a public agency), invite elected officials to be part of your program planning process. Don't wait until you are ready to send the proposal out to ask them for a letter of support or simply to put in a good word for your group or organization.

35. ***Don't ask government or foundation program officers to change their guidelines for you.*** They can't, so they won't.

36. ***Get involved with advocacy groups.*** Find organizations in your community that are working on issues that are important to your clients or participants. Work with them to advocate for policies that benefit the community and to generate new funding sources to meet the needs. This is a long-term approach that can be helpful to officials interested in new solutions in their areas of expertise. And it ultimately may create a new funding stream for the field.

37. ***Advocate for the unmet needs and potential new funding directions in your community or in a particular program area.*** Although there's much more clout if you join with advocacy groups and organizations with a track record in a particular field, you also

can advocate on your own by meeting with appropriate program officers and elected officials to discuss needs and suggest types of funding that would help to address them. Do let the advocacy groups know about your efforts.

38. *If you do get funded, go back to the proposal to be sure you can implement it.* If there are problems, call the funder immediately to discuss what you may need to do instead.

39. *If you get turned down for funding, find out why, and how you can do better next time.* Politely.

40. *The mission comes first!* Always keep your organization's mission in mind. Don't get sidetracked by funding or business opportunities that will take you off course.

APPENDIX 2: PROPOSAL CHECKLIST

Before you send your proposal, review it against the following checklist to be sure you have addressed all the requirements. Note: As you should realize by now, if the application package includes a checklist, it takes priority. But use this one too, just to be sure.

- ✓ I have read and reread the entire application package or foundation guidelines, including all regulations and resources listed or referred to in the package. I would get a very high mark if someone gave me a test on the information included in the application.
- ✓ My grant proposal reflects the priority areas and the requirements described by the grantmaker. I have not tried to sneak in any of my priorities except the ones that clearly mesh with the funder's.
- ✓ I have identified a compelling need for the grant, based on what I know about the community, the target population for the program, and the issues involved.
- ✓ I have brought to the table every partner and stakeholder, and anyone else who is concerned about the need that has been identified and who is likely to be helpful addressing it.
- ✓ I did not break any of the 12 Rules of Proposal Writing that I learned in Lesson 6.
- ✓ Objectives are sharply defined, clearly relate to the compelling need I have demonstrated, are realistic, and are capable of being measured.
- ✓ There are well-conceived and specific programmatic activities for each objective—showing how and why I fully expect the objective to be achieved.
- ✓ The qualifications and relevant experience of staff expected to carry out the activities are explained, and résumés and/or job descriptions are attached if requested or allowed.

✓ I have demonstrated that my organization's leadership, fiscal controls, staff, partners, facilities, and other resources show the capacity to implement the program.

✓ My evaluation plan clearly stipulates how, when, and by whom each objective will be measured.

✓ When appropriate, I have included a timeline that shows we know how to structure the activities to get the job done.

✓ My budget is reasonable in relation to the objectives the project expects to achieve, including number of staff, salary levels, and other resources. I have not tried to sneak in anything—such as a new car or a sofa—that is unrelated to the project.

✓ My budget is neither excessive nor underestimated.

✓ I have shown what resources, such as space, staff time, and equipment, will be available in kind (as a contribution of my organization to the project).

✓ I have intelligently addressed the really hard question of sustainability—how we will continue the project once the grant period is over.

✓ I have explained in my proposal how my organization is—or is working toward—diversifying funding sources.

✓ I have included everything in my proposal that was asked for—and I mean everything—even if I don't fully understand why the grantmaker wanted certain pieces of very strange information.

✓ I have organized the proposal—including my abstract, program narrative, budget, and appendix—exactly the way the grantmaker told me to. No one could ever say that my organization doesn't know how to follow directions.

✓ I did not go over the page limit, and I did not cheat on margins or font.

✓ I'm sending the proposal on time, whether by mail or email, so it will arrive by the grantmaker's deadline.

APPENDIX 3: GLOSSARY

501(c)(3). 501(c) is the section of the Internal Revenue Code that authorizes and defines most tax-exempt organizations, which must be organized and operated for a public purpose. The 501(c)(3) is the most common type of not-for-profit designation. Contributions to a 501(c) organization are tax deductible.

990, 990-PF. Federal tax form used by foundations and public charities (including nonprofit organizations). Available at the Foundation Center Online, these forms usually include lists of foundation grants that have been made during the current tax year and sometimes indicate grants that have been committed for the following tax year.

Abstract, executive summary. A brief (half a page to no more than two pages, depending on funder) summary of the entire proposal, including a sentence or two each on the applicant's history and capability to administer a grant, the need for the proposed program, the objectives, a description of the program and any partners, the expected outcomes, and methods of evaluating the program.

Administrative overhead, indirect costs. A portion of a grant or contract that may be used for nonprogrammatic costs, usually set by a funder as a percentage of the total grant. (See also General operating funds.)

Advisory committee, advisory board. A panel of representatives from all interested organizations and groups in the community who are concerned with a particular program and will help design, support, and oversee it.

Anecdotal information. Informal reports that document or describe, without statistics, conditions that demonstrate a need or that demonstrate the impact of a program on clients. Anecdotal information usually includes compelling stories of individual program participants (e.g., an elderly person who has to choose between heating her home and the medication she needs; the low-income mother who loses her job because she has to stay home to take care of her children during school vacations; the formerly homeless family that now has a home; the child with dyslexia who is now thriving in school).

Annual report. A report issued by an organization (including businesses, foundations, and not-for-profits) that provides a description of its activities during the year and a financial report of its income, expenses, and current status. For grant seekers, foundation annual reports may be a valuable source of information about a foundation's priorities and interests.

Appropriations bill. Congressional legislation that approves spending for a particular federal agency or group of agencies.

Audit. A detailed financial analysis performed by an independent accountant at the end of an organization's fiscal year, or by a funding agency at the end of a major project grant, to assure the public (or the funder) that the organization has handled its money appropriately and in accordance with proper accounting procedures. For not-for-profit organizations, a program audit also assures the funder that the grantee has spent the money in the manner promised in the application.

Best practices. Within a given field, the theories and activities that have been demonstrated to be successful in addressing problems and issues in that field. Programs that have been successfully tested and may be replicated elsewhere.

Bidders' conference, proposers' conference, technical assistance conference. A meeting (or series of meetings) convened by a grantmaker, usually (but not always) a government agency or large national foundation, to discuss a particular funding opportunity and to provide prospective applicants with answers to questions. Normally, questions and answers are compiled and distributed to every prospective applicant, including those who are unable to attend. Increasingly, questions and answers are published on the agency's website. Some bidders' conferences are held by teleconference to allow a wider audience (and to save the costs of travel for the grantmaker's staff).

Block grants. Funds distributed by the federal government to a state or city for broad purposes (e.g., community development block grant), allocated based on population.

Board of directors. Every established not-for-profit organization has a board of directors responsible for setting policy and ensuring fiscal stability. The list of directors, their business affiliations, their home addresses, and any other affiliations should be kept up to date for inclusion in most grant proposals. Many funders expect that the board will reflect the community's population; most funders also expect that all members of the board will make at least a small financial contribution. (See also Development, board.)

Boilerplate language. For grants purposes, boilerplate language refers to standard descriptions about an organization or a program that can be kept on file and essentially pasted into a proposal with minimal adaptation for the new purpose. Boilerplate may include, for example, a description of the agency's history, descriptions of its ongoing programs and its key staff members, a description of awards and honors received by the organization or its key staff, the equal opportunity statement and other personnel matters, and similar topics that don't change significantly from proposal to proposal. Note the phrase "minimal adaptation" above, and keep in mind that the boilerplate may need to be modified to address the interest of a particular funder, as when the proposal writer deletes or significantly abbreviates descriptions of programs for the elderly when preparing a proposal for youth services.

Budget, operating budget. A fiscal plan for an entire organization (usually annual) or a specific program that includes an itemized list of anticipated income (revenues) and expenses. For proposals, the budget must reflect as closely as possible the activities and staffing described in the narrative.

Budget line. An item (line) in a budget (e.g., one supervisor at a specified salary, four teachers at a total hourly cost for a year, travel, books, software).

Budget modification. A formal change in the way grant funds are scheduled to be spent, occurring after the initial approval of the budget by the funding source, with the approval of the funder. Primarily required for government grants and usually described in a standard form required by the funder.

Budget narrative, budget justification. A verbal description of each line item in the budget, describing how the amount was calculated and how the item relates to the program. Almost all government grants require a budget narrative. Most foundations do not require it but should be able to see clearly, even without a separate narrative, exactly how the budget costs relate to the activities to be provided.

Business plan. Similar to but more comprehensive than most proposals, this is a written plan that lays out the need in a community; goals of the business in addressing the need; the capacity of some members of the community to pay for a proposed service (the market) and a marketing strategy to reach them; an analysis of any competing programs or businesses; a program plan including activities to be undertaken to provide services to paying clients, time frames, and staffing; and financial projections of income and expenses to create and maintain the business. It also may include plans to provide services to those who cannot pay, showing how the paying clients will cover these costs.

Capacity, organizational. The organization's ability to manage a grant and ensure that the funded program is implemented successfully. Most grantmakers want to hear about the organization's management structure, the background and qualifications of the managers and people who will run the program, and how the board of directors oversees the agency. The term also includes fiscal systems that are sophisticated enough to handle the large amounts of money in some government grants and the required financial reports that must be submitted. A description of capacity may also include resources like space, volunteers, equipment, supplies, and other assets that will be used in support of the proposed program.

Capital funding. A grant or donation to assist in the construction or renovation of a building or space in a building, or the acquisition of equipment. Generally reflected in a capital budget separate from the operating budget.

Catalog of Federal Domestic Assistance (CFDA). Until recently, a resource that listed all new, existing, and past federal programs. Each federal grant program has a CFDA number that is to be entered on Standard Form 424 (SF-424), the federal cover sheet for the proposal and budget. Although you may still see this term (and the CFDA number still must be entered on the SF-424), at this writing the functions of the CFDA are being phased out by a new database called System for Award Management (SAM), currently reached at beta.SAM.gov. Once this is in place, you will need a DUNS number in addition to the CFDA number. (See also DUNS number, SAM.gov.)

Certificate of incorporation. A document spelling out the organization's purposes and powers in accordance with the laws of a particular state, and filed with the designated office of the state (normally the secretary of state or department of state). When it is filed, the state issues a filing receipt confirming that the organization has legally come into existence. A copy of the certificate of incorporation usually must be submitted with proposals.

Challenge grant. A grant offered by a funder to encourage other grantmakers or individuals to support a particular program or organization. Payable only if other funds are obtained in an amount specified by the donor. (See also Matching grant.)

Collaboration. Two or more individuals and/or groups jointly working out an approach to a problem that is of mutual concern, and developing solutions that make the best use of the strengths of each partner.

Common grant application form, standard application form. Although most foundations now prefer to use their own guidelines or proposal format, the common application form is still used by groups of foundations in a regional association of grantmakers in a given area. It lays out the information, format, and attachments that must be provided by a grant applicant to any of the participating grantmakers. (See also Regional association of grantmakers.)

Common report form. A reporting format required or accepted by a group of grantmakers in an area, usually developed through a regional association of grantmakers. It spells out the information required from an organization submitting an interim or final report on a grant.

Community-based organization (CBO). Any nonprofit organization that is located in a defined geographic area and that has been established to serve residents of that specified area. In contrast, citywide, countywide, or national nonprofit organizations work in large geographic areas, serve a national constituency, and/or focus on specific issues or populations (e.g., the American Heart Association, AARP, Girl Scouts of the USA, Lighthouse for the Blind and Visually Impaired).

Community foundation, community trust. A foundation established for the purpose of managing funds for the benefit of the community in which it functions. Community foundations are designated as public charities by the IRS because they raise money from the public each year. Support is provided by individuals who, either during their lifetimes or after their deaths, want to benefit their particular town, city, or region, but either cannot afford or prefer not to establish a separate foundation. Because donors can specify the areas in which they prefer that grants are to be made, community foundations usually have several diverse priorities for grants and are often a good place to start exploring funding opportunities. Community foundations differ from place to place, but they share several characteristics: a mission to enrich the quality of life in a defined geographic area, and service to three constituencies—their donors, charitable organizations, and the community at large.

Competitive grant. A grant awarded by a government or private funder through a competitive screening process, such as a request for proposals or notice of funding availability, after proposals have been scored by independent reviewers.

Corporate foundation, company-sponsored foundation. A separate, independent foundation created by a large business with funds from the business itself. In most cases the foundation functions like other foundations, receiving proposals and making grants, but giving may be somewhat more tied in to the corporation's own goals. For example, a drug company's foundation may give for medical research; a bank's foundation may give for community development.

Corporate giving program, corporate philanthropy. A grantmaking program established and administered within a business by its own staff and allocated from its own annual budget. Grants go directly to charitable organizations from the corporation. Such programs usually are funded with pretax income, and grants may be even more closely tied to business objectives than are grants from a corporate foundation.

Corporate sponsorships. Direct giving from a corporation to a not-for-profit organization that brings publicity and recognition to the sponsor. Sponsorship can range from support of a Little League team that wears T-shirts with the corporate logo to support of public television with announcements of sponsorship that may be indistinguishable from commercial television advertising. It may include activities such as the purchase of greetings in an organization's fundraising journal or of tables at a fundraising event, in-kind gifts (e.g., computers, food, or furniture), and other assistance.

Curriculum vitae, CV. (Latin for "the course of life.") A detailed, usually chronological, and often lengthy description of an individual's work, including employment and research or academic experience, advanced degrees, publications, honors, and other information that presents the individual as an accomplished professional in one's field. Normally used for academic or research purposes. Compare with résumé, which may include similar information but is generally much shorter (one to two pages), focused on employment and concrete skills, and in outline form.

Demographics. The description, usually numerical, of a population in terms of characteristics such as age, sex, income, race and ethnicity, and national origin. In a proposal it usually is important to describe the demographics of the program's target population in order to provide the reader with an understanding of why the program is critical.

Demonstration project. A project designed (and funded) to determine the viability of new or promising programs or ideas.

Determination letter. A letter from the IRS acknowledging that an organization is eligible for tax-exempt status.

Development. The term *development* is used for most fundraising activities, including foundation research, proposal writing, and all other strategies for bringing money into an organization. These may include, for example, annual and special appeal letters, events such as street fairs, gala dinners, bazaars, benefit golf outings, alumni gatherings, and so on. In very small organizations any such strategies are implemented by an executive director, a board member or committee, or, perhaps, a single staff member devoted to fundraising. As organizations grow, their development departments also grow and become more specialized.

Development, board. Board development is the formal or informal process of training board members in their role as overseers of the organization and their fundraising function. It may be done by experienced board members, the executive director, or an outside board-development consultant.

Direct costs. All budget items that directly support a program, including the salaries of staff and other-than-personnel-services costs such as materials, supplies, travel, and equipment. (See also Administrative overhead, indirect costs.)

Discretionary spending, discretionary grants. All resources that are available to support government functions, purchase goods and services, and issue grants to other entities after debt service and entitlement payments. At the federal level, discretionary spending includes the military, homeland security, education, the IRS, the FBI and CIA, and all other government agencies and programs and their grantees and contractors. (Compare with Formula grants, which are based on the number of individuals in an area eligible for a particular funding source; see also Entitlements.)

DUNS number. Dun & Bradstreet assigns a number (a Data Universal Numbering System number) to every organization that applies. Required for all federal applications and increasingly requested by other government funders. Apply online (http://fedgov.dnb .com/webform for an expedited response). Dun & Bradstreet also can be reached at 844.241.1775.

Earmark. For grants purposes, the inclusion in a government budget bill of a specific amount of funding for a project supported by an elected official. Also called "pork."

Employer identification number (EIN). The EIN is the organizational version of an individual's Social Security number. The organization receives the EIN from the Internal Revenue Service. The EIN is required to open an organization's bank account and must be included in all government and many foundation applications.

Entitlement grants, entitlements. Various federal laws specify benefits that must be paid to all individuals who fall into a certain class. Examples are Social Security, Medicare, and Medicaid. Entitlement benefits may be paid directly to individuals (Social Security) or through states and localities that receive formula grants for the purpose (Medicaid).

Entrepreneurship, social entrepreneurship. See Social enterprise.

Evaluation. A detailed plan for measuring a program's effectiveness and its impact on program participants or the community. The plan describes the kinds of data that will be gathered, the methods for gathering it, and the ways the data will be analyzed and reported.

Executive summary. An overview of a document such as a report or proposal. Often longer than an abstract, it may be distributed in place of the primary document to the public or to specific interested parties.

Family foundation. A family foundation is an independent foundation (see below) in which the trustees, directors, officers, or other decision-makers are members of the family of the original donor, and may be donors themselves. Although some family foundations are very large, use outside trustees, and/or employ professional staff in addition to family members, most are fairly small, and decisions about grants are made by members of the family.

Federal Register. The publication where federal grant announcements such as NOFAs, RFAs, RFPs, SGAs (solicitations for grant applications), rules and regulations, and other notices can be found. Published daily by the Government Printing Office as a paper copy or microfiche, available at or obtainable by libraries, and online in an electronic format that is easily searched by keywords or by agency or topic (https://www.federalregister.gov).

Federated funds. Federated funds raise money each year to support nonprofit organizations. Examples include United Way, Federation of Protestant Welfare Agencies, Federation of Jewish Philanthropies, and local, state, and federal employee campaigns.

Fees, fee for service. Requested or required donations from participants in a given program. At senior centers, voluntary fees may be requested for meals; fees may be required for activities that use outside specialists or consultants, such as exercise or yoga specialists. Fees may cover some or all costs for day care, college prep programs, and so forth. Fees may be required for any programs not funded through grants or contracts, or to supplement such programs when permitted by the funder. Fees may be subject to a sliding scale if participants cannot pay.

Fiscal conduit. An established 501(c)(3) organization that administers a grant for an individual or an organization that is not incorporated or does not have tax-exempt status, or for some other reason is not able to receive a foundation or government grant. The fiscal conduit is responsible for managing and reporting on the money and usually receives a small portion of the grant to cover administrative costs.

Fiscal year (FY). A 12-month period of operation of a given organization under its annual budget for that year. The fiscal year may or may not differ from the calendar year, because an organization can establish its fiscal year for its own purposes. For example, the federal government's fiscal year begins on October 1 and runs through the following September 30. Nonprofit organizations that receive most of their funding from a federal agency may designate the same fiscal year as that entity. The fiscal year is designated by the year in which it ends. A fiscal year starting on July 1, 2019, is called Fiscal Year (or FY) 2020.

Focus group. A group of individuals brought together to discuss an issue. This is a research method often used in marketing to determine a sales strategy. In preparing a proposal or reporting on a program, it is a method that is used to determine the needs and wishes of a target population for the program or to assess the effects of the program on that population.

Format. In grantsmanship, the physical presentation of a proposal, including layout, type size, line spacing, and so on. Whenever an application package or guidelines specify elements of the proposal format, the instructions are to be followed precisely.

Formative evaluation. See Process evaluation.

Formula grant. Federal government funding to states and major localities is based on formulas that account for the number of individuals who are entitled to that funding. They may be based strictly on total population, or they may be based on the number of individuals in specific categories: elderly, youth, people

344 THE ONLY GRANT-WRITING BOOK YOU'LL EVER NEED

with disabilities, and so on. This kind of funding also is known as "entitlements."

Fringe benefits. In a budget, personnel costs above the basic salary, such as vacation, health and dental benefits, unemployment insurance, the employer's share of Social Security contributions, and other benefits. Usually calculated as a percentage of the base personnel costs. Full-time and part-time staff may have different fringe benefit levels, which should be shown in the budget and described in the budget narrative.

Funding opportunity announcement (FOA). A term in current use at Grants.gov, announcing the availability of a federal grant or contract. (See also Notice of funding availability (NOFA), Request for proposals (RFP), etc.)

Funding priorities. Funding priorities are activities that a government agency states in a request for proposals that it intends to fund in a given year. If the RFP states an absolute priority, only proposals that address that priority will be funded. If the RFP describes a competitive priority, applicants addressing this priority may receive additional points during the review process, but they are not required to address it. For invitational priorities, applicants are encouraged to address certain issues, but they do not receive preference over applicants that do not do so.

Funding streams, income sources. Government income is generated from tax-levy revenues, including property taxes, income taxes, and sales taxes. Funds for capital purposes such as buildings, roads, and mass transit generally are raised through bond issues. Funding from higher levels of government may come through block grants, program grants, or formula grants.

General operating support, general operating funds. Also called unrestricted funds, this refers to support for the organization as a whole and for any purpose that furthers the organization's mission. In practical use, it pays for costs that can't be allocated to specific programs. Examples include some portion or all of the costs of secretarial support, rent, building security and maintenance, development staff, a fiscal manager, insurance, and auditing costs. General operating funds may come from a line in the budget called administrative overhead, set at a percentage of the total budget by a grantmaker. Because the administrative percentages allowed often do not cover all overhead costs, general operating funds or unrestricted funds usually must come from individual donations to the organization or from fees or some type of business income. Some foundations also provide grants for general operating support.

Goals. Goals are broad intentions, which may not be measurable (unlike objectives, which are measurable) and, in fact, may never be met. They are the desired, long-term purpose (e.g., ending hunger, improving education) of the program or the organization.

GPO, US Government Printing Office. Publishes the *Federal Register*, the *Congressional Record*, congressional bills, the Economic Report of the President, and many other reports and databases, which are available to the public in print and online.

Grant. An award of money or, more rarely, goods or services to accomplish a purpose defined by the grantmaker.

Grantmaker. Any entity that gives grants, including a government agency, foundation, or federated fund. This also includes not-for-profit organizations (like federations) that receive grants and then re-grant them to smaller not-for-profits.

Grassroots organization. Small, local groups like block and tenant associations, neighborhood-improvement groups, and merchants' associations. Usually led by one or more community residents without a formal organization structure. A grassroots organization usually raises money from dues or contributions given by neighborhood residents, or through group fundraising efforts such as raffles, bake sales, and so on. It also may receive contributions or in-kind goods from local businesses, or may win grant funding as part of a collaboration or through a larger organization that serves as its fiscal conduit.

Guidelines. Broad or detailed specifications published by grantmakers to describe eligible applicants and to alert prospective applicants about the programs and activities that the grantmakers will fund.

Independent foundation, private foundation. A fund or endowment whose primary function is to make grants. Unlike federated funds and some community foundations, independent foundations normally do not raise funds or seek public financial support because their assets are in endowments. Unlike family foundations, independent foundations are not controlled by the original donor or the donor's family. Nevertheless, their guidelines often do reflect the intentions or wishes of the original donor. Some of the largest independent foundations began as family foundations.

Indirect costs. A percentage of total program costs allowable to pay for overhead costs, such as lighting, heat, and wear and tear on equipment, for example. (See also Administrative overhead.)

In-kind contributions. Goods and services that are donated to an organization or one of its programs. Volunteer time is an in-kind contribution; so is food, equipment, space rental, and even staff or management time that are paid for by other programs or absorbed by general operating funds. All available in-kind contributions for a proposed program should be shown in the budget and described in the narrative.

Institutionalization. The permanent or long-term support for or absorption of a particular program by or into another entity in order to sustain it after the end of a grant period. A program may be institutionalized if its support is taken over by a larger nonprofit or local government organization, a business enterprise, a council of churches, or any another entity. (See also Sustainability.)

Job description. Specification of the responsibilities of a particular staff position and the qualifications required for the job. Job descriptions should be created and updated for every current staff position and maintained in a file to facilitate both proposal preparation and advertising to fill the position when vacant.

Key staff. Those managers and staff who are critical to an agency's functioning or the implementation of a particular program.

Letter of commitment. See Memorandum of understanding.

Letter of inquiry. A letter to a foundation exploring the possibility that the foundation will consider a grant for a particular program. For some foundations this is the preferred initial approach; for others it is a way for unknown not-for-profits to introduce themselves. In some cases, the foundation has published guidelines for a letter of inquiry. In all cases, the letter should be treated as a miniproposal, with a brief statement of the need to be addressed, the objectives of a program to address the need, a capsule description of the program, the outcomes to be expected, and the cost.

Letter of intent. A letter to a foundation or government agency indicating an intention to apply for a particular grant. Sometimes requested by a grantmaker specifically for the purpose of determining how many proposals will be received and therefore how many reviewers they will need to hire. Unless otherwise specified, a letter of intent is not a miniproposal; it is a short, to-the-point notification of an intent to apply for a grant.

Letter of support. In the past, a letter from an individual or agency in a community that provided, in effect, a reference for a proposal applicant. It includes a broad and general statement of knowledge of and support for the organization. Most funders no longer accept or review support letters. Instead, they insist on linkage letters, letters of commitment, or memoranda of understanding (see below).

Linkages, linkage letters. Linkage is the term used to describe relationships between and among organizations working together within a community. Linkages tend to be routine and ongoing rather than project oriented, as when a hospital arranges for home care services for patients at discharge or when a school provides space and security for an after-school program run by a nonprofit organization. Partners may refer clients to one another, place staff from one agency at other agencies' sites to provide services that are not provided at those sites, offer training to staff of partner agencies, and work together to assist clients in other ways. For grants requiring collaboration, linkage letters spell out the arrangements in detail.

Local education agency (LEA). The government agency responsible for education in a given community. It may be a school board, a school district, a department of education, or, for some funding sources, a single school.

Logic model. A systemic narrative or visual way of presenting the relationships among all the resources you have to run your program, the activities you plan to conduct, and the outcomes you hope to achieve. This model is popular with many nonprofits and grantmakers.

Match. An amount or percentage of the total budget that a funder may require an applicant to commit to a program if it is funded. The match can be an in-kind contribution of goods and services, cash (including program fees when appropriate), or a combination of both. The funder makes the determination of what is acceptable.

Matching grant. A grant that is made specifically to match or supplement funds provided by another donor, usually as a specified proportion of the total program cost. Often provided as a challenge grant and paid on the condition that the other funds are obtained.

Memorandum of understanding (MOU). A letter, signed by an authorized representative of each organization, from each partner in a collaborative project, specifying the activities and services that the partner will provide and the expectations the partner may have from the other partners and from the grant itself. This should be thought of as a brief contract that will take effect if a grant is awarded. Depending on the complexity of its contents, an MOU may need to be reviewed by a lawyer before you sign it.

Mission creep. An unintended loss of focus on an organization's stated mission when it pursues funding that is not appropriate to the mission just because the money seems readily available.

Mission statement. A brief, focused statement of an organization's reason for being; its overall purpose. The mission is the context in which all the organization's programs operate and for which the programs exist.

Needs assessment. Qualitative and/or quantitative documentation or data organized to demonstrate issues, needs, or problems in a community. This may be as simple as a description of the waiting lists for services at an agency or as elaborate as a statistical analysis demonstrating that the target population experiences more of a particular problem (e.g., crime, drug use, the proportion of teenagers or the elderly with no place to go) than other communities.

Needs statement, problem statement. The section of a proposal that lays out the issues, needs, or problems that a program will address. Normally proposals to government agencies require greater documentation of the problem (crime, substance use, children with asthma, lack of services for youth or the elderly) and demographics of the community (race, ethnicity, income and poverty level, etc.) than do proposals to foundations. Depending on the funder, the needs section also may include research from "the field" and may put your community's problem in the context of the town or city as a whole, as well as your state (and sometimes country).

NOFA. See Notice of funding availability.

Not-for-profit organization. An organization of any size that is incorporated under the laws of the state in which it operates and has been granted tax-exempt status, usually under Section 501(c)(3), by the US Internal Revenue Service. It must have a board of directors, elected officers, and approved financial procedures for managing grants and reporting on expenditures. Known informally as a nonprofit organization.

Notice of funding availability (NOFA). A formal, published announcement by a grantmaking entity, usually a government agency but sometimes a large foundation, that it will accept applications or proposals for a specific purpose detailed in the announcement. (See also Funding opportunity announcement, Request for proposals, Request for applications.)

Notice of proposed rulemaking. A notice published in the *Federal Register* that outlines proposed rules and priorities for certain programs or funding opportunities, and that invites the public to comment on them by a certain deadline.

Objectives. Clearly defined and measurable results (outcomes) that a program is intended to achieve.

Organization chart. A diagram of an organization's structure, showing its internal lines of responsibility and reporting relationships for all departments and programs. Large organizations also may maintain organization charts for individual departments or programs.

Other than personnel services, other than personal services (OTPS). All budgeted costs of a program that do not relate to staffing costs. This budget category may include items such as rent, equipment purchase or lease, consultants, supplies, postage, utilities, and so on.

Outcome, outcomes. The intended, measurable result or results of a program, usually spelled out in objectives.

Outcome evaluation. A process of determining, usually through formal, quantitative research methods, whether and to what extent a program has achieved the results (outcomes) that it set out to achieve. Assesses what a program accomplishes. May require an external evaluator using sophisticated analytic approaches and control or comparison groups that do not experience the program. Also called summative evaluation.

Personnel services, personal services (PS). The section of a budget relating to staffing costs. Each position is shown with the full-time or part-time base yearly or hourly salary for that staff member, and, depending on the application format, the number of hours and proportion of the cost allocated to the proposal request or to other sources. Includes fringe benefits, which are shown on a line separate from the base salaries.

Private operating foundation, operating foundation. This type of private foundation provides charitable services or runs research, social welfare, or other charitable programs of its own. Private operating foundations make few, if any, grants to outside organizations.

Pro bono. (Latin for "for the good.") Often refers to legal services provided for free to an individual or organization but may apply to any volunteered professional help.

Process evaluation. The application of (usually qualitative) research methods to determine whether a program is being implemented in the way in which it was intended to be implemented (e.g., whether it is using the activities it said it would use, deploying staff in the ways it intended, serving the number and type of participants in the way it intended) and providing feedback to program managers to take corrective action. Also called formative evaluation because it helps shape the program. Process evaluation provides a way to understand why outcomes are achieved or fail to be achieved.

Program evaluation. Systematic documentation and analysis of indicators demonstrating that a program has achieved its objectives or intended outcomes. May include both outcome and process evaluation components but need not be complex or formal unless required by the funder.

Program officer, grants officer. The staff member of a funding organization who receives grant proposals and processes applications for a government agency or a foundation's board of trustees.

Program plan. Detailed description of the program's functioning, including activities, time frames, staffing plan and job descriptions, and costs.

Project period. The total time for which support of a project can be approved by a funder. A project period may last for one or more years. If there is a multiyear project period, each year's renewal of the grant probably depends on program performance during the previous year.

Public foundations, public charities. Public foundations raise a significant portion of their resources from a broad cross section of the public each year and redistribute it in grants to nonprofit organizations. Public charity is the designation used by the IRS for an organization that raises funds from the public. Community foundations normally are public foundations.

Regional association of grantmakers (RAGs). As the name indicates, most areas of the United States have a regional membership association that includes many (but usually not all) of the foundations and corporate grantmakers in the area. Some publish membership directories, common application forms, and other information about their members and are a good reference source for grant seekers.

Request for proposals (RFP), request for applications (RFA), solicitation of grant applications (SGA). A document issued by a public or private funding agency, inviting qualified organizations to submit a proposal for a specific funding opportunity. (See also Notice of funding availability.)

Resource mapping. Also called community asset mapping, community inventory, or environmental scanning. Identifies resources and assets available in a community. Among other purposes, enables strategic use of existing resources, facilitates partnerships, identifies gaps or needs for additional resources, and avoids duplication of services.

Reviewers, readers. Most federal proposals and many submissions to state and local government agencies and national foundations are read and scored by outside professionals, called reviewers or readers, acting as outside consultants to the funding agency. Reviewers are selected for their background in the relevant field (e.g., educators or directors of youth programs for proposals affecting children and teenagers; health care professionals for proposals in that field). Normally reviewers will not read proposals from their home state or region.

Reviewers' comments. Most federal agencies and some foundations make available to an applicant (usually only on request) the scores for that proposal, which are provided to the funding agency by the outside readers. The reviewers' names are removed but all comments explaining the scores are shown.

SAM.gov (System for Award Management). SAM is a vast new database managed by the federal General Services Administration (GSA). If you receive a federal grant, you will need to register with SAM. Note that functions of the Catalog of Federal Domestic Assistance have been merged into SAM. Also note that the current address for most information is beta.SAM.gov, which will simply become SAM.gov when the integration of planned functions is complete.

Seed grant, seed money. A grant that is made to start a program, with the intention of leveraging other support to sustain it.

SF-424, Standard Form 424. This serves as a cover sheet for a federal grant application. Information to be filled in on this form includes organization name and address, contact person, name of federal program, CFDA number, name of your project, total budget request, and other items. Sometimes a federal agency will substitute a designation such as ED (Department of Education) in place of the notation SF, but the form is the same.

Site visit. A visit by a funding agency or foundation that is considering giving a grant to an applicant. It gives the funder a chance to assess the accuracy of descriptions in a proposal and to ask additional questions that may help determine whether the agency can manage the grant and accomplish its objectives.

Social enterprise, social entrepreneurship. Business enterprises developed in support of a nonprofit organization's mission that also can bring in unrestricted funds for the organization. An example would be an organization engaged in workforce development that started a bike-rental business or bike shop to train participants to work in and run a business.

Stakeholder. A term applied to any party with an interest in a particular program or who may be affected by the program. In a school program, stakeholders may include parents, faculty, the children themselves, the administration, nonprofit organizations, and local businesses.

Summative evaluation. See Outcome evaluation.

Sustainability. The prospect that an organization will be able to keep a program going (sustain it) after the end of a particular grant. Increasingly a concern of grantmakers at all levels. Applicants should be able to show what resources they expect will be available to sustain the program or how they will work toward that end. Many funders look approvingly at social entrepreneurship as a way of diversifying funding and adding to the organization's ability to sustain its programs. (See Social enterprise.)

Tax-levy funds. Revenues raised through taxes of all sorts (income, sales, property, and other taxes) by government at the local, state, and federal levels to support ongoing operations of the government.

Technical assistance, technical assistance provider. Services provided to organizations to teach or assist them with proposal writing and other fundraising; program planning; organization development and management; financial planning; legal issues; marketing; and other operational matters. May be provided by nonprofit or for-profit organizations, individual consultants, or some grantmakers themselves. Some funders give grants specifically for technical assistance.

Timeline. A chart or narrative showing the month-by-month time frame for the beginning, implementation, and end of each program activity. Some timelines also show activities by each staff person responsible.

Trustee, director. A foundation board member or officer who is responsible for the fiscal well-being of the foundation and for ensuring that the donor's wishes are carried out in the foundation's grantmaking activities. In larger foundations, trustees may depend on professional staff to recommend grants, but the trustees are the ultimate authority.

Unrestricted funds. Money donated by individuals or businesses, or given in general operating grants, to further the mission of an organization. May be spent for any organizational priority or need. Depending on the funder or program, fees for service may or may not be unrestricted.

Waiting list. List of potential users of a service who have requested the service but cannot be accommodated at a given time. In the grants world, waiting lists are one important way to document the need for a particular service.

APPENDIX 4: SAMPLE GRANT FORMS

COMMON GRANT APPLICATION FORM

washington regional
association of grantmakers

Common Grant Application

- Proposals should be typed in 12-point font (Times New Roman or similar) with one-inch margins on all sides
- Pages should be numbered
- Proposals should not be placed in binders or folders; one staple or paper clip in the upper-left hand corner is sufficient

SECTION ONE: Executive Summary (1 page, single-spaced)

1. Application date
2. Organization name and contact information (full address, including mailing address if different, telephone number, and website)
3. Federal tax-exempt number
4. If not a 501(c)(3) nonprofit, provide fiscal agent's contact information and federal tax-exempt number
5. Name, title, telephone number, and email address of CEO or executive director
6. Name, title, telephone number, and email address of contact person for this proposal (if different)
7. Dollar amount of this funding request
8. Total current organizational budget (all requests)
9. Total project budget (project support requests only)
10. Organization's fiscal year (beginning date and end date)
11. Period this funding request will cover
12. Purpose of this funding request, including brief description of the population and number of individuals served, and geographic area(s) that will benefit (as applicable)
13. Signature of executive director or other authorizing official

SECTION TWO: Narrative

ORGANIZATIONAL INFORMATION: All requests must complete this section. If applying for general support, this section should be no more than five (5) pages double-spaced. If applying for project, capital campaign, or capacity building support, this section should be no more than four (4) pages double-spaced.

1. Briefly describe your organization's history, mission, and goals.
2. Briefly describe the role of your organization's board of directors, including how your board carries out its responsibilities for financial and programmatic oversight and fundraising.
3. Briefly describe current activities, recent accomplishments, and future plans.
4. Briefly describe how the population you serve is involved in the work of your organization.

Common Grant Application (*continued*)

5. Briefly describe your most significant collaborations and partnerships with other entities in your field or geographic area.

6. **General support, capital campaign, and capacity building requests only:** What results are you committed to achieving during the grant period? What is the timeline for accomplishing these results? What evidence will prove your success?

PROJECT INFORMATION: Complete only if applying for project support. For capital campaign and capacity building requests, please see appendices I and II. This section should be no more than four (4) pages double-spaced.

1. What problem or need does your project address?
2. What is your proposed solution to this problem or need?
3. What is the plan for implementation of this project?
4. Is this a new project? If yes, how was the project approach developed? If not, what have you accomplished so far?
5. Are there additional partners who you are working with for this project (who were not listed in the previous section)? If so, who are they and what are their roles?
6. What results are you committed to achieving during the grant period? What is the timeline for accomplishing these results? What evidence will prove your success?

SECTION THREE: Financials

Please include the following information, regardless of the size of the request. You may submit this information in the format most convenient to you. Footnotes may be used to explain budget items.

<u>Special note for arts and cultural organizations:</u> Some funders now require applicants to submit organizational and financial data to the DC Cultural Data Project (www.dcculturaldata.org), which generates reports for funders. Be sure to check with the funder you are applying to in order to determine whether this is required.

FOR ALL REQUESTS

Financial statements:

a. For <u>previous</u> fiscal year: organizational budget v. actual, including revenue and expense categories listed below
b. For <u>current</u> fiscal year:
      i. Organizational budget v. actual, including revenue and expense categories listed below
      ii. Organization's year-to-date Statement of Financial Position (Balance Sheet)
      iii. Organization's year-to-date Statement of Activities (Income Statement)
c. For <u>next</u> fiscal year: Organization's projected/proposed/draft budget for the next fiscal year, <u>only if this application is being made during the last quarter of the organization's fiscal year</u>

FOR PROJECT, CAPACITY BUILDING, AND CAPITAL CAMPAIGN REQUESTS PLEASE ALSO INCLUDE THE FOLLOWING:

Financial statements:

a. For <u>previous</u> fiscal year: project budget v. actual, including revenue and expense categories listed below

Common Grant Application (*continued*)

b. For <u>current</u> fiscal year: project budget v. actual, including revenue and expense categories listed below
c. For <u>next</u> fiscal year: project projected/proposed/draft budget for the next fiscal year, <u>only if this application is being made during the last quarter of the organization's fiscal year</u>

Revenue Categories: Please use the categories listed below when developing the financial statements requested above. Not all categories may be applicable to your organization or request.

In addition, please list specific amounts requested from foundations, corporations, and other funding sources, as well as the status of those requests (pending or committed).

Be sure to include all revenue sources, committed <u>and</u> pending. For pending requests, please indicate the date you expect notification. <u>This additional information can be submitted separately from the financial statements</u>.

1. Grants/Contracts:
   a. Local/State/Federal Governments (please list source(s))
   b. Foundations
   c. Corporations
   d. United Way/Combined Federal Campaign and other federated campaigns
   e. Individual Donors
   f. Other (specify)
2. Earned Revenue:
   a. Events
   b. Publications and Products
   c. Fees
   d. Other (specify)
3. Membership Income
4. In-Kind Support (donated goods, services, equipment, non-cash items, volunteer hours)
5. Other (specify)
6. Total Revenue

Expense categories: Include the total amount for each category relevant to your organization. Skip categories where you have no expenses. <u>For project support requests, please show two columns – one listing the total expense and one listing the specific costs requested in this grant proposal.</u>

1. Salaries (total salary budget, number of positions, and whether full- or part-time)
2. Payroll Taxes
3. Fringe Benefits
4. Consultants and Professional Fees (itemize type(s) of consultant(s) and fees)
5. Travel
6. Equipment
7. Supplies
8. Printing and Copying
9. Telephone and Fax
10. Postage and Delivery
11. Rent and Utilities
12. Maintenance
13. Technology (if budgeted separately, specify hardware/software capital spending, maintenance, and/or training)
14. Evaluation

Common Grant Application (*continued*)

15. In-kind expenses
16. Other (specify)
17. Total Expenses

SECTION FOUR: Attachments

1. A copy of your (or your fiscal agent's, if applicable) current IRS tax-exempt determination letter. If tax-exempt status is pending, provide an explanation of application status
2. Most recent audit or form 990 (or that of your fiscal agent, if applicable)
3. A one-page organizational chart
4. Short biographies of staff and volunteers essential to the success of this request
5. List of board members with terms, occupations, and places of employment
6. Current, dated Memoranda of Understanding or Memoranda of Agreement with other organizations for collaborative or cooperative activities, as appropriate
7. **For capital campaign requests only: List of members of the capital campaign/leadership committee**
8. **For capacity building requests only: Current strategic plan**

APPENDIX I: Capital Campaign Requests

Capital campaign requests are designated for the acquisition, construction, renovation, or improvement of a property. If applying for capital campaign support, provide the information requested below, in addition to the organizational information requested in Section Two. This section should be no more than four (4) pages double-spaced. Include information on the following, as applicable to your organization's request.

1. Discuss the need, feasibility, and cost of the capital campaign, and its implications for the organization's ongoing operational expenses.
2. Specify contributions in hand, as well as those that are pending or prospective.
3. Specify loans, including amounts and terms.
4. Include the financial participation in the campaign of the board and the capital/leadership campaign committee (percent participating and total contributed).
5. Specify whether purchase agreements or purchase options are signed or imminent. Specify also whether regulatory approvals (e.g., Certificate of Need, zoning, historic preservation, environmental impact) are in place or are imminent.
6. Indicate if timing is a factor, i.e., if a "window of opportunity" exists that would affect the success of the campaign.

APPENDIX II: Capacity Building Requests

If applying for capacity building support, provide the information requested below, in addition to the organizational information requested in Section Two. This section should be no more than four (4) pages double-spaced.

1. Please provide a brief overview of the strengths and major challenges facing your organization at this time.
2. Please describe the specific capacity issue or need to be addressed with this request.
   a. How was the issue identified? Include information about how the board and other key stakeholders were involved in identifying the issue or need.
   b. Is your organization currently working on this issue? If so, where are you in the process? Have you worked to address this issue previously? If so, what were the outcomes of these efforts? Please identify

Common Grant Application (*continued*)

any current, past, and potential funders of this capacity building project, the amounts you have received or requested, and the status of the request.

3. Please describe the project plan.

a. Describe specific tasks and activities and timeline.

b. Identify key staff or board members who will be involved in the project. Briefly describe what skills and experiences they will bring to the project.

c. Are there specific consultants or groups that the organization will partner with to address the identified capacity issue? What was the process and criteria for selection? If your project includes software, equipment, or other products, please describe the process and criteria for selection.

4. Please describe key outcomes.

a. List at least three specific, measurable short-term outcomes.

b. What will be the long-term impact of this project? How will the project strengthen your organization, enable you to deliver programs or services more effectively, and better achieve the organization's mission? How does it further the goals in your strategic plan?

Note: This Common Grant Application form is developed and produced by the Washington Regional Association of Grantmakers, a membership association of foundations and corporate giving programs that give in the Washington, DC, region. The association's website, www.washingtongrantmakers.org, also includes a sample common report form and guides for using both forms, as well as other useful forms and information.

STANDARD FORM 424 (SF-424)

OMB Number: 4040-0004
Expiration Date: 12/31/2019

Application for Federal Assistance SF-424

* 1. Type of Submission:
☐ Preapplication
☐ Application
☐ Changed/Corrected Application

* 2. Type of Application:
☐ New
☐ Continuation
☐ Revision

* If Revision, select appropriate letter(s):

* Other (Specify):

* 3. Date Received:
Completed by Grants.gov upon submission.

4. Applicant Identifier:

5a. Federal Entity Identifier:

5b. Federal Award Identifier:

State Use Only:

6. Date Received by State:

7. State Application Identifier:

8. APPLICANT INFORMATION:

* a. Legal Name:

* b. Employer/Taxpayer Identification Number (EIN/TIN):

* c. Organizational DUNS:

d. Address:

* Street1:
Street2:
* City:
County/Parish:
* State:
Province:
* Country: USA: UNITED STATES
* Zip / Postal Code:

e. Organizational Unit:

Department Name:

Division Name:

f. Name and contact information of person to be contacted on matters involving this application:

Prefix:
Middle Name:
* Last Name:
Suffix:

* First Name:

Title:

Organizational Affiliation:

* Telephone Number:

Fax Number:

* Email:

Application for Federal Assistance SF-424 (*continued*)

Application for Federal Assistance SF-424

* 9. Type of Applicant 1: Select Applicant Type:

Type of Applicant 2: Select Applicant Type:

Type of Applicant 3: Select Applicant Type:

* Other (specify):

* 10. Name of Federal Agency:

11. Catalog of Federal Domestic Assistance Number:

CFDA Title:

* 12. Funding Opportunity Number:

* Title:

13. Competition Identification Number:

Title:

14. Areas Affected by Project (Cities, Counties, States, etc.):

Add Attachment | Delete Attachment | View Attachment

* 15. Descriptive Title of Applicant's Project:

Attach supporting documents as specified in agency instructions.

Add Attachments | Delete Attachments | View Attachments

Application for Federal Assistance SF-424 (*continued*)

Application for Federal Assistance SF-424

16. Congressional Districts Of:

* a. Applicant [ ]   * b. Program/Project [ ]

Attach an additional list of Program/Project Congressional Districts if needed.

[ ]   Add Attachment   Delete Attachment   View Attachment

17. Proposed Project:

* a. Start Date: [ ]   * b. End Date: [ ]

18. Estimated Funding ($):

* a. Federal [ ]
* b. Applicant [ ]
* c. State [ ]
* d. Local [ ]
* e. Other [ ]
* f. Program Income [ ]
* g. TOTAL [ ]

* 19. Is Application Subject to Review By State Under Executive Order 12372 Process?

[ ] a. This application was made available to the State under the Executive Order 12372 Process for review on [ ].

[ ] b. Program is subject to E.O. 12372 but has not been selected by the State for review.

[ ] c. Program is not covered by E.O. 12372.

* 20. Is the Applicant Delinquent On Any Federal Debt? (If "Yes," provide explanation in attachment.)

[ ] Yes   [ ] No

If "Yes", provide explanation and attach

[ ]   Add Attachment   Delete Attachment   View Attachment

21. ***By signing this application, I certify (1) to the statements contained in the list of certifications** and (2) that the statements herein are true, complete and accurate to the best of my knowledge. I also provide the required assurances** and agree to comply with any resulting terms if I accept an award. I am aware that any false, fictitious, or fraudulent statements or claims may subject me to criminal, civil, or administrative penalties. (U.S. Code, Title 218, Section 1001)**

[ ] **** I AGREE**

** The list of certifications and assurances, or an internet site where you may obtain this list, is contained in the announcement or agency specific instructions.

Authorized Representative:

Prefix: [ ]   * First Name: [ ]

Middle Name: [ ]

* Last Name: [ ]

Suffix: [ ]

* Title: [ ]

* Telephone Number: [ ]   Fax Number: [ ]

* Email: [ ]

* Signature of Authorized Representative: [Completed by Grants.gov upon submission.]   * Date Signed: [Completed by Grants.gov upon submission.]

SAMPLE COVER LETTER

Rosemont Youth Center
101 South Fourth Street
Rosemont, Newstate 11111-1111

[[DATE]]

Mr. Mark Rosenfeld, Executive Director
Rosemont Community Trust
574 East Main Street
Rosemont, Newstate 11111-2222

Dear Mr. Rosenfeld:

I am pleased to submit the enclosed proposal to the Rosemont Community Trust. We are requesting $6,000 to provide an after-school karate program for children from 10 to 13 years of age who are having disciplinary difficulties in school. As you probably are aware, karate engages high-energy children who need a physical outlet, and at the same time teaches respect and discipline.

We understand that in the last year you have given grants to assist several athletic programs for children at this age, and we hope that you will be able to assist us in the coming year.

Please visit our website, *www.rosemontcenter.org*, or call me at (555) 666-7777 if you have any questions. If you'd like to visit, I'd be happy to show you around the Youth Center.

Sincerely,

Judy Morrison
Executive Director

SAMPLE LETTER OF INQUIRY (LOI)

Princeton Community College
67–12 Water Street, Second Floor
Princeton, Newstate 10000

[[DATE]]

Mr. Mark Rosenfeld, Executive Director
Rosemont Community Trust
574 East Main Street
Rosemont, Newstate 11111–2222

Dear Mr. Rosenfeld:

I am writing to ask whether the Rosemont Community Trust would be interested in receiving a proposal for an adult literacy program for Spanish-speaking immigrants.

As you may know, the town of Princeton has experienced a significant in-flux of immigrants from South and Central America over the last 10 years. The US Census Bureau reports that the immigrant population from these countries has increased by 12 percent since the 2010 census, compared to 4 percent for Newstate as a whole. The Newstate Department of Employment indicates that lack of English language skills is the major barrier to employment in our area.

The adult literacy program is intended to provide about 60 immigrants with English skills at a level that will allow them to find and keep employment. At the same time, participants will develop résumés and job-seeking skills and will learn about the cultural expectations of local employers. Three teachers of English for speakers of other languages will offer two-hour computer-assisted ESOL classes at Princeton's computer lab twice a week for 40 weeks. Classes will be limited to 10 to 15 students. The project director, a skilled bilingual employment counselor, will assess students' abilities and interests and will work with each group for two hours on a third day each week, helping each student prepare for employment. All classes will emphasize job-related English conversation.

Students' English will be tested at the beginning of the program and periodically through the year. It is expected that by the end of the school year at least 70 percent of the students will have reached at least an intermediate level of English fluency, will be able to carry out instructions given in English and ask questions in response, will have created an appropriate résumé, and will be comfortable taking part in job interviews in English.

The total cost for this program is $107,000. If the Rosemont Community Trust were to accept a formal proposal, we would request $25,000 of this cost. We have received a commitment from the Barish Foundation for $25,000 and have begun to prepare a proposal to the Rosemont Department of Employment for the balance; we understand that a request for proposals will be issued in about a month and that grants are expected to be in the $50,000 to $60,000 range.

We are very excited about the benefits this program can provide to our new immigrant population. I hope you will consider helping us to develop it. Please visit our website, *www.princetoncc.edu*, or call me at (555) 333-4444 if you have any questions. If you'd like to visit, I'd be happy to introduce you to our staff and show you our new computer lab. I look forward to hearing from you.

Sincerely,

Linda Lamb
Director

SAMPLE ABSTRACT

Sometimes federal government agencies collaborate on a highly competitive grant program that reflects the concerns of more than one agency (for instance, the Departments of Health, Education, and Justice may jointly issue a Request for Proposals). Below is a short example of an abstract that might lead off such a proposal, which would, in this case, provide $2,250,000 per year to winning applicants.

Abstract

The Rosemont School District South, a high-need, culturally and ethnically diverse district (75 percent of the students are non-English speakers whose family incomes fall below the poverty level) on the south side of Rosemont, in collaboration with three city government agencies (the police, health, and youth departments), the Third Street YMCA, the Rosemont South Teen Center, the Community Day Care Collective, the Southside Methodist Church, the Rosemont South Hospital, Rosemont Junior College, the William T. Rosemont Family Foundation, and many other individuals and groups, has designed ROSEMONT ROCKS FOR SAFETY AND HEALTH!

This initiative will build on existing resources and coordinate new partnerships and linkages to create safe and drug-free schools and promote healthy child development for all of the 9,234 students (and their families and caregivers) in the target school district in the city of Rosemont.

To achieve its overall goal of safe and healthy students and ensure system-wide change in the target school district, ROSEMONT ROCKS FOR SAFETY AND HEALTH! will conduct the following activities that are designed to meet the program's objectives:

• Form a cross-disciplinary advisory board to publicize and support the initiative, as well as to take the lead in raising additional funds to supplement and sustain project activities.

- Hire five police officers to patrol the streets near the schools in the target district before, during, and after school hours.
- Provide weekly professional development seminars for all school personnel, conducted by police officers, parole officers, mental health counselors, physicians, and others with expertise in the field of health and safety for children.
- Provide training for parents of schoolchildren, conducted by school staff and outside experts.
- Develop a referral protocol (a memorandum of understanding has been drawn up and signed) among the schools, not-for-profit organizations, hospital, and health care providers to address mental and other health problems affecting students in the target district.
- Expand the school day to include before- and after-school counseling, recreation, and academic programs, both in school buildings and at collaborating not-for-profit organizations for at-risk students.
- Provide intensive preschool counseling and instruction to very young children in the community.

Because the literature (e.g., Smith's 2018 landmark study on school violence) suggests that students in grades 6 and 7 are at the highest risk for violent activities, middle schools will serve as the hub for all project activities—with services radiating out to early childhood programs, elementary schools, high schools, and the community. It is expected that the $2,176,987 program will begin in September 2021.

SMALL BUSINESS ADMINISTRATION SAMPLE BUSINESS PLAN

The following example is from the Small Business Administration (www.sba.gov); their website offers two models, traditional and "lean start-up." We present the traditional model here.

Traditional Business Plan Format

You might prefer a traditional business plan format if you're very detail oriented, want a comprehensive plan, or plan to request financing from traditional sources. When you write your business plan, you don't have to stick to the exact business plan outline. Instead, use the sections that make the most sense for your business and your needs. Traditional business plans use some combination of these nine sections.

Executive Summary

Briefly tell your reader what your company is and why it will be successful. Include your mission statement, your product or service, and basic information about your company's leadership team, employees, and location. You should also include financial information and high-level growth plans if you plan to ask for financing.

Company Description

Use your company description to provide detailed information about your company. Go into detail about the problems your business solves. Be specific, and list the consumers, organization, or businesses your company plans to serve.

Explain the competitive advantages that will make your business a success. Are there experts on your team? Have you found the perfect location for your store? Your company description is the place to boast about your strengths.

Market Analysis

You'll need a good understanding of your industry outlook and target market. Competitive research will show you what other businesses are doing and what their strengths are. In your market research, look for trends and themes. What do successful competitors do? Why does it work? Can you do it better? Now's the time to answer these questions.

Organization and Management

Tell your reader how your company will be structured and who will run it.

Describe the legal structure of your business. State whether you have or intend to incorporate your business as a C or an S corporation, form a general or limited partnership, or if you're a sole proprietor or LLC.

Use an organizational chart to lay out who's in charge of what in your company. Show how each person's unique experience will contribute to the success of your venture. Consider including résumés and CVs of key members of your team.

Service or Product Line

Describe what you sell or what service you offer. Explain how it benefits your customers and what the product lifecycle looks like. Share your plans for intellectual property, like copyright or patent filings. If you're doing research and development for your service or product, explain it in detail.

Marketing and Sales

There's no single way to approach a marketing strategy. Your strategy should evolve and change to fit your unique needs.

Your goal in this section is to describe how you'll attract and retain customers. You'll also describe how a sale will actually happen. You'll refer to this section later when you make financial projections, so make sure to thoroughly describe your complete marketing and sales strategies.

Funding Request

If you're asking for funding, this is where you'll outline your funding requirements. Your goal is to clearly explain how much funding you'll need over the next five years and what you'll use it for.

Specify whether you want debt or equity, the terms you'd like applied, and the length of time your request will cover. Give a detailed description of how you'll use your funds. Specify if you need funds to buy equipment or materials, pay salaries, or cover specific bills until revenue increases. Always include a description of your future strategic financial plans, such as paying off debt or selling your business.

Financial Projections

Supplement your funding request with financial projections. Your goal is to convince the reader that your business is stable and will be a financial success.

If your business is already established, include income statements, balance sheets, and cash flow statements for the last three to five years. If you have other collateral you could put against a loan, make sure to list it now.

Provide a prospective financial outlook for the next five years. Include forecasted income statements, balance sheets, cash flow statements, and capital expenditure budgets. For the first year, be even more specific and use quarterly—or even monthly—projections. Make sure to clearly explain your projections, and match them to your funding requests.

This is a great place to use graphs and charts to tell the financial story of your business.

Appendix

Use your appendix to provide supporting documents or other materials that were specially requested. Common items to include are credit histories, résumés, product pictures, letters of reference, licenses, permits, or patents, legal documents, permits, and other contracts.

SAMPLE BUSINESS PLAN

We Can Do It Consulting Business Plan
This sample business plan is provided by the Small Business
Administration.
Get help starting and running your small business at SBA.gov.
Rebecca Champ, Owner
Created on December 29, 2016

Executive Summary

Product

We Can Do It Consulting provides consultation services to small-
and medium-sized companies. Our services include office management and business process reengineering to improve efficiency and
reduce administrative costs.

Customers

The target audience for We Can Do It Consulting is business owners,
human resources directors, program managers, presidents, or CEOs
with 5 to 500 employees who want to increase productivity and reduce overhead costs. Specifically, we specialize in consulting white
collar executives on office processes such as job tracking, production,
getting the most out of meetings, leadership, financial or hiring best
practices, and other needs relevant to potential customers who serve
in a management role within small or large organizations that may
be bogged down by processes, bureaucracy, or technical experts with
little leadership experience.

Future of the Company

Consulting is a fast-paced, evolving industry. In response to this climate, We Can Do It Consulting will offer other services, including
facilitation and requirements analysis in the future.

Company Description

Mission Statement

To provide quality services to our clients that will help their companies prosper and grow.

Principal Members

Rebecca Champ—owner, primary consultant
Guy Champ—business manager/sales
Sophie Roberts—account manager

Legal Structure

We Can Do It Consulting is an S Corporation, incorporated in Greenville, South Carolina.

MARKET RESEARCH

Industry

We Can Do It Consulting will join the office management and business process improvement consulting industry. Generally, larger consulting firms, such as KEG Consulting, work with international corporations while smaller consulting firms work with both large corporations and smaller organizations, usually closer to home. Consulting firms structured like ours also have a history of working with local, state, and federal government agencies. The consulting industry is still recovering from the economic recession. It was hit hardest in 2009 when the industry shrank by 9.1%. However, as the economy recovers, the industry is showing signs of growth. A recent study stated that operations management consulting is projected to grow by 5.1% per year for the next several years.

Detailed Description of Customers

The target customers for We Can Do It Consulting are business owners, human resources directors, program managers, presidents or CEOs with 5 to 500 employees who want to increase productivity and reduce overhead costs. Specifically, we specialize in consulting white collar executives on office processes such as job tracking, production, getting the most out of meetings, leadership, financial or hiring best practices, and other needs relevant to potential customers who serve in a management role within small or large organizations that may be bogged down by processes, bureaucracy, or technical experts with little leadership experience. To capitalize on opportunities that are geographically close as we start and grow our business, We Can Do It Consulting will specifically target executives within companies in the manufacturing, automotive, healthcare, and defense industries. This will allow us to take advantage of the company's close proximity to hospitals (one of the largest employers in the region), automobile and vehicle parts factories, and government contractors supporting the nearby former Air Force base, now an aviation technology center.

Company Advantages

Because We Can Do It Consulting provides services, as opposed to a product, our advantages are only as strong as our consultants. Aside from ensuring our team is flexible, fast, can provide expert advice and can work on short deadlines, we will take the following steps to support consulting services:

- Maintain only PMP-certified project managers
- Ensure account team members use our proprietary planning and reporting process to stay in touch with customers and keep them updated on projects
- Provide public speaking training for all consultants
- Develop close relationships with subcontractors who can support us in areas such as graphic design, to ensure materials and presentations are always clear and maintain a consistent brand
- All our staff members have at least a four-year degree, with 20% having an advanced degree

- We are a virtual company without a lot of overhead costs or strict corporate rules, which saves time, money and creates a flexible workplace for getting things done

Regulations

We Can Do It Consulting must meet all Federal and state regulations concerning business consulting. Specifically, Code of Federal Regulations in Title 64, Parts 8753 and 4689.62, 65, and 74 and Title 86.7 of the Code of South Carolina.

Service Line

Product/Service

Services Include:

- Business Process Reengineering Analysis
- Office Management Analysis
- On-Site Office Management Services
- Business Process Reengineering Facilitation
- Analytics
- Change Management
- Customer Relationship Management
- Financial Performance
- Operations Improvement
- Risk Management

Pricing Structure

We Can Do It Consulting will offer its services at an hourly rate using the following labor categories and rates:

- Principal, $150
- Account Executive, $140
- Project Manager, $135
- Project Coordinator, $100

- Business Analyst, $90
- Process Analyst, $90
- Financial Analyst, $85
- Technologist, $75

Product Lifecycle

All services are ready to be offered to clients, pending approval of contracts.

Intellectual Property Rights

We Can Do It Consulting is a trademarked name in the state of South Carolina, and we have filed for protection of our proprietary processes and other intellectual property, such as our logo. We have also registered our domain name and parked relevant social media accounts for future use and to prevent the likelihood of someone impersonating one of our consultants.

Research and Development

The company is planning to conduct the following research and development:

- Create a custom technology solution for manufacturers of vehicles such as automobiles or airplanes that helps better track each manufactured piece and its status in the assembly process
- Determine the need for additional consulting services within our market related to tying improved processes to opportunities for increased sales and promotion to potential customers
- Find trends in software solutions that may provide potentially competitive automated services in order to ensure We Can Do It Consulting continues to carefully carve its niche in the marketplace

Marketing & Sales

Growth Strategy

To grow the company, We Can Do It Consulting will do the following:

- Network at manufacturing, automobile industry, and healthcare conferences
- Establish a company website that contains engaging multimedia content about our services
- As the business grows, advertise in publications that reach our target industries

Communicate with the Customer

We Can Do It Consulting will communicate with its customers by:

- Meeting with local managers within targeted companies
- Using social media such as Twitter, YouTube, Facebook, and LinkedIn
- Providing contact information on the company website

How to Sell

Currently, the only person in charge of sales for We Can Do It Consulting is the business manager, Guy Champ. As profits increase, We Can Do It will look to add an employee to assist with account management/coordination. This individual will also provide company social media and online marketing support. The company will increase awareness to our targeted customers through online advertising, proactive public relations campaigns, and attending tradeshows.

APPENDIX 5: NOTES ON SOME USEFUL WEBSITES

There are hundreds—no, thousands—of useful websites that offer information on foundation, corporate, and government grants. We've selected a few that we have used extensively (and others that we use less often but think are representative).

Since we wrote the first edition of this book—in fact, even since the most recent edition—much has changed on the Internet, including the skills of website designers (usually) making the sites more navigable. The sophistication of those who use the web also has also changed, so you need much less guidance. We've updated a lot, deleted a lot, and are listing these sites just to get you there a little faster.

Remember that some websites make it easy for you to find what you need, while others still require patience. Sometimes the information is right up front: You click on clearly visible words such as "grants" or "funding opportunities" on the home page, and the list pops up, or you use a simple search box. But be aware that the links may say something very different from "grants," and the search engine may require other phrases, such as "notice of funding availability." And, especially for state and local government sites, funding opportunities may be buried in a section called "Doing business with…" or something even more obscure; or the search results may include a variety of items that are of interest—but not about grants. Two suggestions:

- First, if your state or locality has an e-grants or grant-alert system, **sign up for it immediately.** Because the categories for these systems are broad (e.g., youth, aging, health), you may get a lot more announcements than just those that are appropriate for your organization, but it's well worth sifting through them to have these announcements come directly to your desk.

- Second, even if an online grant function is available and easy to use, it still won't hurt to **get in touch with specific state and local agencies of interest to your organization** and ask to be placed on their mailing lists and/or email lists.

FOUNDATION RESOURCES

We know it can be disheartening that so many foundations still do not have their own websites. However, the following resources do provide a wealth of information on almost any foundation that may be right for you.

The Foundation Center (Now Called Candid)

The Foundation Center offers a variety of training opportunities and resources for nonprofits, including an extensive grantsmanship library and in-house training to use it. There are Foundation Centers with libraries in New York City, San Francisco, Cleveland, Atlanta, and Washington, DC. The Centers sponsor a network of 450 affiliated Funding Information Network locations in libraries, community foundations, and other nonprofit resource centers across the country, so there is likely to be a center near you. Much of the information at the libraries is free, so it is one of the first places to begin your research on foundations and corporate giving. The Foundation Center also publishes a free online newsletter, *Philanthropy News Digest* (PND; philanthropynewsdigest.org), which provides updates on trends, some current RFPs, and news on issues in philanthropy. The Foundation Center's own website, https://fconline.foundationcenter .org, also contains some free information on grantmakers, but most of the information at this site is by paid subscription. We believe that for many of you this may be well worth the cost. There are currently three subscription plans (note that these may change over time):

- **Essential:** This basic subscription has three payment options: a two-year subscription at $559; a one-year subscription at $399;

and a monthly plan at $49.99 per month (plus sales tax). If you're not familiar with the website, we suggest you try it for a month or two to see if it gives you all you need (which is plenty). It provides information on 100,000 foundations. It allows you to search by location, total giving, and other characteristics, and includes links to the foundations' websites and their 990s. (The FCO site also includes a separate, free search function for 990s.)

- *Professional:* This subscription adds number and amounts of grants awarded and to what recipients. It includes information on 140,000 foundations and on federal and corporate grants, and has maps to show where the grantmakers give. It provides a good deal more information than the Essential package, but costs a lot more too. A two-year subscription is $2,099; a one-year subscription is $1,499; and one month is $199.99 (plus tax).
- *Enterprise:* This package is directed to the largest nonprofit organizations, including academic institutions. Pricing is not shown on the FCO website, which suggests it's way out of reach for most organizations.

As we noted earlier, the Foundation Center recently merged with another nonprofit, called Guidestar, which provides potential donors with a range of financial and other information about nonprofits. The new organization, Candid, maintains both websites, www. fconline.org and www.guidestar.org, but is working to develop a new website combining information from both the original organizations.

The Grantsmanship Center
The Grantsmanship Center (**www.tgci.com**) provides a range of services, including training on grantsmanship and grants management, program development, and other topics that support nonprofit organizations. Information available at this website includes workshops and seminars, publications, and other resources, some free, most for a fee.

https://www.tgci.com/resources/grantdomain: GrantDomain is a subscription database that includes information on foundations, federal grants, and corporate grants. The database is searchable on a number of useful topics and keywords. Subscriptions are $495 for one year, $695 for two years, and $795 for three years. There is a 30-day trial period, with your subscription refunded if you are not satisfied with the database.

https://tgci.com/funding-sources: A separate, very useful funding resource that identifies grant resources by state. It includes foundation, government, and corporate grants. You click on your state on a map of the United States to find a list of top-giving foundations in the state, a list of community foundations, a list of corporate giving programs, and a link to the state's website. This site still appears to be free and available to any user, but again, this could change, so be sure to check.

WEBSITES FOR INDIVIDUAL GRANT SEEKERS

If you search for "grants for individuals," you will come up with a substantial number of for-profit sites that offer to help you. Some may be worth exploring, but we'd suggest sticking to libraries and centers run by nonprofit organizations, educational institutions, and government agencies. Here are just a few websites that may be of interest to individual grant seekers.

- **foundationcenter.org/products/foundation-grants-to-individuals-online.** This Foundation Center site requires a subscription that costs $19.95 a month, but is probably well worth it for anyone looking for grants, scholarships, and fellowships, including students, artists, writers, researchers, and others. Among other information, the database includes application information and tips for searching. Three-month, six-month, and one-year subscriptions (the last at $99) also are available.
- **https://libguides.lib.msu.edu/grants.** Hosted by Michigan State University, this list of links for individuals allows you to search by academic level, population group, or subject. Within any

category, it provides brief descriptions of the purposes of the funding, eligibility, size of grants, and links to the funders.

- **https://grants.library.wisc.edu/memorial/collections/grants-information-collection.** The University of Wisconsin–Madison's grants information collection has a section for individuals.
- **https://www.grants.gov/applicants/registration.html.** The federal government's site allows you to register to submit proposals on your own behalf, search for grants for individuals, and apply online, but the results of a search don't clearly separate individual from organizational grants within a topic. Needs patience.

STATE AND LOCAL WEBSITES

We don't really need to list any state websites in this edition. The best place to start looking for state information is the Grantsmanship Center's link: **https://tgci.com/funding-sources.** This takes you to a map of the United States that connects you to each official state site (and to other resources, including top-giving foundations, community foundations, and corporate donors) via one convenient location.

But getting information about state funding is still far from easy. Almost all state websites are set up primarily to offer information about government services available to residents in each area, so you may have to sift through many of them to find the few that are relevant. In many states and localities, grant opportunities may be found somewhere in the web pages of departments or divisions of the government, so your best bet may be to identify the departments most pertinent to your needs, work from their own websites or pages within the state site, and get in touch directly. Most will put you on their email or other mailing lists for "vendors" interested in grants and contracts. Keep attuned to the broader political and social climate in which you're operating by becoming familiar with all the relevant information available on these websites, not just that pertaining to grants.

FEDERAL WEBSITES

Grants.gov: http://www.grants.gov

Grants.gov is a centralized grant site for the federal government. Although the site is far from complete at the current writing, Grants .gov is intended to replace all or most of the funding information and procedures that until recently have been scattered throughout the various government agencies and official publications. It includes what amounts to a grade-school-to-graduate education about the federal government and the grants process, including a "community blog." Start with grants.gov to learn everything you want to know about any of the federal agencies as well.

And Grants.gov is certainly the first place to look when you are searching for federal funding opportunities. Although most agencies continue to use the *Federal Register*, they now must post their grant opportunities at Grants.gov. You can search for grants without registering, but in order to submit a proposal at this site (as many federal agencies now require) you will have to register. The site includes instructions for doing this.

The Grants.gov home page has a link ("Search Grants") to a form that lets you search by a variety of indicators, including keyword; opportunity status (i.e., whether a grant possibility is currently posted, forecast, or closed at the present time); CFDA number; category (e.g., arts, community development, health); eligibility (e.g., city government, not-for-profit, school district); and other characteristics. You can specify the type of funding (in most cases, "grant"), and the funding agency or agencies that you think will be relevant. But be aware that, even with this advanced search, you still may have to plow through a long list of possibilities. It will pay you to search as narrowly as you can, even if you have to conduct several different searches to be sure you've covered what you need.

The Federal Register Online: https://www.federalregister .gov

When it comes to finding federal grant opportunities, the Federal Register Online still is an important source. Although the federal government has worked to make it easier to access grant information through Grants.gov, and some agencies are using their own websites, the *Federal Register* is still the official daily record of all meetings, notices, regulations, and other functions of the federal government. This information may be useful to you in identifying upcoming grant opportunities, or you may want to comment on proposed regulations or funding opportunities.

The Federal Register Online has some helpful guides at the site itself, under the section called "User Aids." And if you type "grants" in the search box, you'll come to a page that lets you search by type, topic (a *very* long list), publication date, agency, and many other entries. *Grants.gov is easier.*

Catalog of Federal Domestic Assistance (CFDA)

The CFDA has been merged into a new, integrated system called System for Award Management (SAM). As of this writing, searches for CFDA are directed to a site of the General Services Administration (GSA) called beta.SAM.gov, which will become SAM.gov once the system is complete. As noted above, you still can search by CFDA number, but apparently this will be phased out.

EMERGENCY FUNDING

As we were doing research for the second edition of this book, the headlines were full of natural disasters, including hurricanes Katrina and Rita, so we included some information on how to find emergency funds. For the third edition, the emergencies were man-made, in the form of the financial meltdown, and the concern was that many foundations were working with reduced investments. Hoping that such powerful natural disasters on the scale of those occurring at the time of the second edition were no longer a major issue, we considered deleting the section on emergency funding; but then New York, New Jersey, and parts of Connecticut were hit by Superstorm Sandy. Since the last edition, drought and wildfires have devastated the west, and increasingly powerful hurricanes have hit Puerto Rico, Texas, the Carolinas, and Florida. Forecasters predict increasingly harsh periods of storm, drought, and flooding. So whether you are a government or local education agency, a development corporation or another type of not-for-profit, you can use some of the following sites to look for funding if you are involved in disaster relief or are developing disaster plans.

FEMA: www.fema.gov

The federal agency established to help individuals, businesses, and organizations with disaster funding is the Federal Emergency Management Agency (FEMA). Grants are offered for planning and preparedness, disaster relief, and hazard mitigation. You can find multiple resources available for different types of emergency responses to a catastrophic event. FEMA also provides a preparedness guide (*Are You Ready?*). It is primarily for individuals and families, but it may give you some pointers your organization and your participants can use in planning for a number of different types of disasters.

State Emergency Management Offices

The state emergency management offices (SEMOs) are responsible for emergency planning and response. They also disburse FEMA or other disaster funding. They can be accessed through your state's homepage. Your jurisdiction probably also has a local or regional emergency management office that may assist in funding and have other resources available.

Center for Disaster Philanthropy: www.disasterphilanthropy.org

Created by and for grantmakers, this website partners with the Foundation Center and donor networks to "increase the effectiveness of donor dollars" in planning for and responding to disasters. It focuses its funds on mid- to long-term recovery for the most vulnerable populations. The Center does not accept proposals; rather, its members generally reach out to organizations they know can address a given situation. But it is worth reviewing the website to become familiar with its priorities, members' past approaches to disaster funding, and what they view as best practices.

INFORMATION FOR NEEDS ASSESSMENTS, PROGRAM PLANNING, AND EVALUATION

In addition to funding opportunities, government agency websites (federal, state, and local) provide a wealth of information that can help nonprofits and municipal agencies justify needs and develop and evaluate their programs. Take the time to browse all government sites of interest to you, to see what you can use in your programs as well as in your fundraising. In addition to the websites listed earlier, try these:

The US Census Bureau: www.census.gov

This site is a treasure trove for anyone who needs demographic data for any purpose; get familiar with it! In addition to the familiar 10-year census required by the Constitution and reported in exhaustive breakdowns by many demographic variables, the Census Bureau conducts more frequent surveys, including a five-year economic census; the American Community Survey (ACS, an ongoing statistical survey that samples a small percentage of the population every year, giving communities fairly current information to plan investments and services and giving nonprofit organizations a wealth of data for their needs assessments); and annual surveys of business practices by county and zip code.

Small Business Administration (SBA): www.sba.gov/tools/business-plan/1

All you need to know about creating a business plan (and a business) is found at this comprehensive site. It includes sample plans like the one we presented in Appendix 4 and a handy "10 Steps to Start Your Business" guide. It covers much, much more than we can offer in Lesson 18. Among other things, this site offers a sample spreadsheet to help you figure out how much money you'd need to start and run the business.

National Center for Education Statistics: www.nces.ed.gov

This center collects and analyzes data relating to education. For example, it conducts the National Assessment of Educational Progress and the Early Childhood Longitudinal Study, along with many others.

Interagency Working Group on Youth Programs: www.youth.gov

A consortium of 20 federal agencies and programs that support programs and services for youth. "Provides interactive tools and other resources to help youth-serving organizations and community partnerships plan, implement, and participate in effective programs for youth."

State and Local Planning Departments

As noted, some state, county, and city planning offices use the data from the Census or from the American Community Survey to describe smaller areas within their target area. We're most familiar with the New York City Department of City Planning (www.nyc.gov/html/dcp/home.html), which provides all the information a grant seeker needs to support a proposal from any organization in that city. Get in touch with the planning department in your state, county, or locality to see what they can provide.

APPENDIX 6: ANSWERS
TO POP QUIZZES

Lesson 1: Who Am I (and What in the World Do I Want to Do?)

Multiple Choice
1. **a** (Small grassroots organizations should "think small" while they are small.)
2. **b** (The 501(c)(3) proves to funders that you're a tax-exempt organization.)
3. **a** (The key is "not-for-profits of all kinds"; not specific types of not-for-profits.)
4. **d** (Hey—if you don't know who you are, funders won't either.)

Essay Questions
(Example for a grassroots organization) The Elm Street Garden Association is a grassroots organization whose mission is to plant flowers along the length of Elm Street every spring. The association needs money for seeds and plants, and to replace some very old gardening tools this coming spring.

(Example for a larger not-for-profit organization) The Rosemont Teen Center is a 501(c)(3) not-for-profit organization with a 12-person board comprising community residents and a professional staff of one full-time teen-center director and a part-time staff of four youth workers. The center serves 120 teenagers in athletics and arts programs each year, and needs money to hire a part-time teacher to start a drama program.

(Example for a government agency) The Rosemont Department of Health (DOH), an agency in a city of 55,000, addresses all the health and mental health needs of Rosemont's residents. DOH plans to start an asthma initiative for young children living on the north side of the city.

Lesson 2: Wait a Second—What Is a Grant... and Where Do I Get One?

Multiple Choice

1. **d** (So read the fine print in those requests for proposals.)
2. **d** (You'll find a foundation of the right size and shape for you if you look hard enough.)
3. **c** (It's always good not only to do your homework but also to show grantmakers that you've done it.)
4. **c** (So make sure you check out Grants.gov often.)
5. **c** (Getting a track record is an important first step in grant seeking—and starting small makes sense.)

Essay Questions

(Grassroots organization) The Elm Street Garden Association needs approximately $120 to purchase seeds, plants, and gardening equipment. This is an other-than-personnel-services (OTPS) budget item; staffing is done by volunteers. The likely funders for this project are the merchants located at the east end of Elm Street.

(Larger nonprofit) The Rosemont Teen Center's drama teacher will work for approximately four hours each week, for 40 weeks, at $20/hour; the center needs $3,200 for personnel services (PS). The most likely funders for this project are the Rosemont Community Trust; the Johnson Foundation for the Arts; and Mrs. Ann Johnson, director of the community theater company (who may provide a drama teacher in kind).

(City agency) The Rosemont Department of Health (DOH) needs $100,000 to conduct a needs assessment, provide education about asthma prevention and treatment to families and caregivers, and to treat children with asthma at day-care centers and preschools. Approximately $75,000 will be used to pay part-time salaries of physicians and nurses to provide training and care; a consultant from the Rosemont Community College will conduct the needs assessment and evaluate the project ($10,000). The remaining $15,000 will be spent for printing and supplies, resource guides to be given to families, transportation expenses for staff to visit preschools and day-care centers, and games and toys for children who participate in the program. The most likely funders for this project will be the state health department and the US Department of Health and Human Services. The Rosemont Health Foundation may provide some funding for the resource guides, and the Broome Street Toy Shop will provide some of the toys.

Lesson 3: Making (Dollars and) Sense of Grant-Application Packages: What Grantmakers Want

True or False?

1. **True** (No matter what application packages look like, they all contain certain basic pieces of information. Some contain much, much, much more of this stuff than others.)
2. **False** (You can call and ask questions about the application package; different funders have different policies, but most will answer at least some general questions.)
3. **False** (You are expected to answer every question or cover every topic in the grant application. If you don't understand how a question pertains to you or your organization, you can call and ask—but it is possible that the funding source isn't right for you!)
4. **False** (Sure, this is America, but it's up to the grantmaker to decide whether you are an eligible applicant. So you'd better check eligibility requirements before you apply.)
5. **False** (It makes no sense to submit an application that asks for more money than the grantmaker indicates—it means you have ignored the guidelines or not followed directions. If the funder decides to give you more money later—well, that's another story.)

Lesson 4: Getting Ready to Write a Grant Proposal

True or False?

1. **False** (Be prepared to show proof of your not-for-profit status, the names and affiliations of your board members, and other materials the funder might want to see.)
2. **False** (Grants for individuals follow many of the same steps that grants for not-for-profits and government agencies follow. All grants require homework, and all proposals must be clear responses to certain questions.)
3. **False** (Not-for-profit organizations are eligible for—and win—a slew of government grants, so check out that eligibility section.)
4. **False** (National Endowment for the Arts is an example of a government grant for individuals. In fact, foundation funding for individuals can be much scarcer and harder to get.)
5. **False** (School districts should apply for the myriad grants available that will actually help them teach the three Rs as well as science, technology, art, and music—not to mention assist in reducing violence, substance abuse, teen pregnancy, and so forth.)
6. **False** (Individuals can sometimes get a grant without a 501(c) (3). Mostly, though, individuals do need to affiliate with an existing not-for-profit to be eligible for a grant.)

Essay Question

The best ways to prepare yourself for a proposal in advance of a funding announcement are to:

- Develop and maintain solid boilerplate material, including the organization's mission, programs you run, budget, staffing, funding sources and grants, evaluations that have been conducted, and publicity documents.
- Develop and maintain collaborations within your sector (health care, youth, aging, transportation) and across other sectors

(schools, other government agencies, clergy, businesses, and universities).

- (*Government agency or not-for-profit*) Develop and maintain up-to-the-minute files consisting of census data, needs assessments, and other statistics that you can pull out the minute a funding announcement is made.
- (*Individual*) Keep your portfolio of work, reviews, and other relevant materials up to date.

Lesson 5: Intangibles: Things They Never Tell You (About Proposal Writing)

True or False?

1. **False** (Developing and writing a grant proposal is in no way as straightforward as filling out an application for a credit card. In *no* way!)
2. **False** (Okay, maybe it takes a little luck to win a grant...very little. Mainly, winning a grant takes hard work, lots of homework, good programs, great leadership, fiscal responsibility...well, you get the picture.)
3. **False** (Anyone and everyone in an organization may write grant proposals, although in most organizations the task falls either to a program manager or a grant writer.)
4. **False** (Grant writers should beware of internal politics and adapt!)
5. **False** (Being greedy has no part in the grants process. Ever.)
6. **False** (Grant applications never say a word about abbreviations—it's one of those "intangibles"—but you shouldn't use them in your proposals.)
7. **True** (Most grant applications leave all decisions about hiring grant-funded staff up to you. But you must explain the qualifications of staff in your proposal.)
8. **False** (Write well but be quick. Time is of the essence.)

Lesson 6: Writing (Proposals) with Style: 12 Basic Rules

True or False?

1. **False** (Maybe the PC police are out of style, but sensitive language isn't.)
2. **False** (You can never be too organized.)
3. **False** (Let the facts speak for themselves.)
4. **False** (Save your poetry for an anthology.)
5. **False** (But make sure to let the funder know why it is an effective reading program.)
6. **False** (Be selective!)

Short Answer

1. **Rule 4:** Exaggeration. (If the Meridian Mews Center is known all over the world, there had better be some proof!)
2. **Rule 12:** Common knowledge; **Rule 5:** Grammar. (Everyone in the neighborhood respects...)
3. **Rule 10:** Passive voice; **Rule 6:** Spelling. (Meridian Mews Center's program...)
4. **Rule 9:** Adjectives; **Rule 4:** Exaggeration.
5. **Rule 5:** Grammar. (...neighborhood schools and churches for its activities.)
6. **Rule 5:** Grammar. (...their grades and their behavior...)
7. **Rule 11:** Acronyms. (HHS, DOJ, and DOE)
8. **Rule 2:** Write as you should speak. ("awesome" is teen talk)
9. **Rule 3:** Insensitive terminology and slang. (Geezer; old folks; kids)
10. **Rule 9:** Adjectives; **Rule 4:** Exaggeration. (cutting-edge; innovative); **Rule 10:** (We)

Lesson 7: Identifying and Documenting the Need: What Problem Will a Grant Fix?

Multiple Choice

1. **d** (Along with a quality program, the bottom line to winning grants is your documented "compelling need." But many funders also look for continuity of leadership.)
2. **d** (As good as your intuition may be, it just doesn't work as data in a grant proposal.)
3. **d** (Documenting need can take many forms.)
4. **d** (There is no rule of thumb about how many footnotes to include.)

Lesson 8: Goals and Objectives: What Do You Hope to Achieve If You Get the Money?

Multiple Choice

1. **b** ("The literature" suggests that rewards are usually better than punishments, right?)
2. **d** (All these activities promote interaction with others and can decrease feelings of loneliness and depression.)
3. **c** (Both community involvement and police presence make neighborhoods safer.)

Realistic or Unrealistic?

1. **Unrealistic** (The program only lasts for one year; a three-year objective is outside the control of the organization that's running it.)
2. **Realistic** (It's a one-year program and expecting improved attitudes by the end of the year is reasonable; we hope you also expect that participants will get jobs.)

3. **Realistic** (Since the program is for one year, a one-year objective makes perfect sense; because participants' motivation to get a job is high, the 85 percent attendance figure is probably realistic.)
4. **Realistic** (A very reasonable objective for a one-year course.)

Lesson 9: Developing and Presenting a Winning Program

True or False?

1. **False** (Activities are the most important part of the grant proposal—they make the program you are describing believable.)
2. **False** (There is no such thing as too much detail—which doesn't mean repetition—if it makes your program come alive.)
3. **True** (In fact, use the grantmaker's own language whenever possible to ensure that you both are on the same page.)
4. **False** (Funders expect to see exactly as many activities in the proposal as you expect to conduct—and the more the merrier.)
5. **False** (Write in specifics, not in generalities...and don't expect to change your mind. This is a grant, for cryin' out loud!)
6. **True** (Specific activities should be linked to each and every measurable objective in your proposal. You're conducting the activities to achieve your objectives.)
7. **False** (First comes your compelling need, then your objectives, and finally the activities to achieve these objectives.)
8. **False** (Timelines are anything but baloney—they show that the grant program is doable, real, and accountable.)
9. **False** (The proposal should never be vague; if the person writing it doesn't know what's going on, funders will be anything but sympathetic.)
10. **True** (If at all possible, you should do some grant-related work even before you find out if you've won the money.)

Lesson 10: Finding Partners and Building Coalitions (The MOUs That Roared)

True or False?

1. **False** (Collaboration is very hard. We're all essentially team players...as long as we can be team captain.)
2. **False** (It can't always be about the money. Collaboration is about solving problems.)
3. **False** (If collaboration isn't required, think about trying it anyway—it's often a better option for getting things done than going it alone.)
4. **False** (Let's face it. No one likes to collaborate with anyone, whether they're in the same sector or not.)

Short Answer

1. The best way to actually prove that you collaborated with other groups on a grant proposal is to include a memorandum of understanding, letters of commitment, and/or sign-in sheets for collaborative program development meetings in your application.
2. Some different sectors of the community that might collaborate on a winning grant include large and middle-sized not-for-profit organizations, small grassroots organizations, faith-based organizations, businesses, school districts, municipal government agencies, hospitals or health care providers, colleges, and even foundations.
3. Some synonyms for "collaboration" are partnering, cooperating, coalition building, and team building.

Lesson 11: The Evaluation Plan: How Can You Be Sure If Your Program Works?

True or False?

1. **False** (Evaluation is necessary for grant-funded programs even if they are tiny. In fact, all programs should be evaluated whether they are grant funded or not. The evaluation does not have to be elaborate; it just needs to be a systematic way of assessing your program's performance.)

2. **True** (Often called formative evaluation, this type of evaluation allows you to make changes throughout.)

3. **False** (If you wait until a large multiyear grant program is over to conduct the evaluation, it's far too late to make any changes along the way.)

4. **False** (If an outside evaluator is required by the funder, consider working with a university or consultant who will help in the preparation of the proposal and get paid to conduct the evaluation only if the grant is funded.)

5. **False** (Evaluations can use simple before-and-after questionnaires and surveys, as well as more complex measures.)

6. **False** (A program evaluation looks at all kinds of data, from personal interviews and observations to standardized, reliable measures.)

7. **False** (Whether an evaluation plan is required by the grant-maker or not, it should be included. Otherwise, how will you know if you achieved your objectives?)

8. **True** (Too many grant writers start thinking about the evaluation plan just as they are about to submit their proposals. Evaluation methods should be linked to your objectives: How will you know if you achieved them?)

9. **False** (Small demonstration projects need rigorous evaluations to determine if they are worth replicating in other places.)

10. **False** (Frankly, there often is no need to work with an outside evaluator; your staff should know very well what data would provide the information you need to be sure it's working as you designed it.)

Short Answer

Three important things you can learn from an evaluation are whether the program worked the way you hoped it would, whether there were any surprise results that will help you design programs in the future, and which elements of the program were successful and which weren't.

Lesson 12: The Budget: How Much Will It Cost...and Is the Cost Reasonable?

True or False?

1. **False** (Don't include the new copier you're desperate for unless you can show why the basketball program you're applying for needs a copier to achieve the objectives you've set out. Our guess is that the copier probably has no place in the grant proposal.)
2. **False** (If the funder says you can't include laptop computers in your budget, don't. Try to find another grantmaker who may pay for them.)

Short Answer

1. If you are teaching reading as an in-kind contribution, it means that your organization has (or you have) donated your time to the project. The way this is reflected in the budget is to indicate the percentage of your time you spend on the project—say 25 percent of your job is now spent on this program. If your yearly salary is $50,000, you're "donating" a quarter of it to the grant-funded program. Your in-kind contribution is $12,500. This, along with other contributions by the applicant, can be reflected in a column called "In-Kind."

2. PS (Personnel Services) describes personnel (staffing) costs, and OTPS (Other Than Personnel Services) lists everything that does not relate to personnel that you include in the grant's budget.

3. Examples of OTPS costs include equipment that you may be buying or leasing, consultants that you may need to bring on board, and supplies that you need to purchase.

Lesson 13: Sustainability: How Will You Continue the Program When the Grant Funds Run Out? (and You'd Better Not Say, "I Won't!")

Essay Questions

1. To sustain the literacy program for immigrants at the Rosemont Center, the center staff will apply to the state's department for youth and families when it issues a request for proposals for literacy programs next year. Rosemont's development director has begun identifying other foundations that support literacy programs like Rosemont's. The executive director and program staff believe that the local community college will be willing to provide some services in kind once the program has begun.

2. The Edgewood Senior Center might apply for a foundation grant for an intergenerational arts program even if we aren't sure we can sustain it, because it is so important to find ways to relieve the depression and isolation our seniors are experiencing. When the city sees how successful the program is, it may provide unexpected resources that will keep the program running.

Short Answer

1. Some other words for sustainability are "likelihood of institutionalizing" the program. That's a fancy way of saying making it a permanent part of your organization.

Lesson 14: Capacity: Proving That You Can Get the Job Done

True or False?

1. **True** (An organization's leadership says a great deal about the strength of the organization.)
2. **True** (Only an organization that maintains strong financial controls will win the confidence of a government funder—or any other funder.)
3. **False** (Every grantmaker cares about your board if you're a nonprofit organization.)
4. **False** (But you want to include as much history, program, and staff information as possible to highlight your organization's capacity to run effective programs.)
5. **True** (Government agencies should mention the size of their budgets, the grants and other funding they receive, and their history of fiscal responsibility. But brag? We don't like bragging.)

Essay Question

Here's an example of some things you might describe in detail to convince the grantmaker that you're the right choice for a grant for a literacy program:

- The quality, background, and experience of leadership and key staff, and their success in running strong literacy programs (talk about the outcomes of those programs).
- The quality of your facilities and resources. If you have special classrooms and equipment that will enhance the program, say so here.
- The positive evaluations that other funders have given to your programs.
- Any awards that your organization and staff have received.

Lesson 15: Front and Back: The Cover Page or Cover Letter, the Abstract, the Table of Contents, and the Appendix

True or False?

1. **False** (The overall cost of the project should appear in the abstract, along with the amount you are requesting.)
2. **False** (A table of contents should be included whether the application mentions it or not, unless the proposal is very short or, for some reason, a grantmaker says, "No table of contents.")
3. **False** (The average length of a comprehensive abstract is under two pages.)
4. **False** (Letters of support from elected officials should be placed in the appendix.)
5. **False** (If you are permitted to have attachments and the funder doesn't stipulate specific items, certainly include information about your board.)
6. **False** (An abstract should be short and to the point. Don't use as many words as you need to. Use as few as you can to clearly describe the program.)
7. **True** (But sometimes government grants don't even let you include an appendix and, lately, they have required a certain number of pages when they do allow one. You have to be creative in deciding what to attach.)
8. **False** (Not all grantmakers want or will accept attachments or appendix material. When in doubt, ask.)
9. **True**

Essay Question

See Appendix 4 for a sample cover letter.

Lesson 16: The Site Visit—Playing Host

Essay Question

The first thing we will do when a funder calls to set up a visit is to arrange a time when activities of interest to the funder are available and when all the key staff members and partners who will be involved with the program are available. The next thing is to review the proposal to be sure everyone who will meet with the funder is up to speed on the program plan, budget, staffing, and all other aspects about which the funder may have questions. Finally, we will have available all the information the funder might want, such as a list of other funders; our agency budget if we haven't sent it before; and other relevant documents.

Lesson 17: So Now You Know—What Next?

True or False?

1. **False** (Sometimes you should apply for a grant after you've been rejected—ouch, there's that word again—and sometimes you shouldn't. There are many factors involved in your decision.)
2. **False** (If a foundation turns you down for a grant, definitely ask why... but very nicely, of course.)
3. **False** (There's nothing in the law that forbids you to receive scores on federal grant proposals. It's up to the individual agencies, and most do give you the information.)
4. **False** (While the same reviewer probably won't read your grant if you submit it again, the comments may have been right on the money—so why not take them to heart to improve your next proposal?)
5. **False** (It's not pushy to ask grantmakers to suggest other foundations that might be appropriate for your proposal. But don't get pushy if they can't help you!)

Lesson 18: When Grant Funding Needs a Boost, Build a Business! (Hint: It Can Be Small!)

True or False?

1. **False** (A nonprofit is not required to have a budget of at least $1 million to start a small business. There is no budget requirement at all.)
2. **False** (Large nonprofits generally have diverse funding sources that allow them to weather economic meltdowns.)
3. **False** (Many public schools use an array of business approaches. But if you're a teacher, make sure you check with your principal if you have an idea for a small business!)
4. **False** (If you're a nonprofit and are serious about starting a business, especially one that you hope to sustain, it is often a good idea—and a good use of funds—to hire a consultant.)
5. **True** (There are grantmakers who like to fund entrepreneurial nonprofits that are proposing business approaches to diversify funding.)
6. **False** (Generally, a savvy business strategy is to seek grant funding from foundations close to home. They will be more likely to support your entrepreneurial efforts on behalf of the community you both care about.)
7. **False** (A business plan should be long enough to address all the issues as clearly and comprehensively as possible.)

Essay Questions

1. Teenage art students in an after-school art program at the Wishbone housing project can design, create, and sell (following business plans they develop) holiday cards, calendars, masks, and other artwork.
2. A bake shop in a nearby storefront, perhaps with rent donated for a few months by the landlord, selling baked goods made by members of the senior center and parents of children in the

after-school program, using senior center members and teenagers in the youth program to coordinate and staff it. Expand, perhaps using foundation grants, by adding a kitchen and hiring a manager to train and later hire community members to bake and sell their goods. Expand again to add coffee, tea, juices, sandwiches, and a few tables to create a takeout counter and café.

ACKNOWLEDGMENTS

NEARLY 20 YEARS AGO, neither of us had an inkling that we'd write five editions of a book about grants—we were both too busy churning out proposals to even imagine such a thing. It was Christina Farrell who suggested—very convincingly—that we should get busy and start writing, and it was Howie Schuman who helped us (that's an understatement) figure out how to navigate the world of publishing. Without them, and without our agent, John Thornton, there would be no *The Only Grant-Writing Book You'll Ever Need*. For this edition, we want to give a shout-out to Melissa Veronesi, senior project editor, for her patience and responsiveness, and to Theresa Winchell for her careful and thoughtful copy editing.

Many people gave us helpful advice all along the way. Lisa Philp and the late Barbara Bryan, both working, at the time, at the New York Regional Association of Grantmakers (now Philanthropy New York), were the first colleagues we spoke to about doing a book, and they generously brainstormed all aspects of grantsmanship and philanthropy with us. Marcia Brown, now retired from the Nonprofit Coordinating Committee of New York (now Nonprofit New York), and Anne Shkuda, formerly of United Neighborhood Houses, responded to all our questions and generously recommended colleagues for yet another, slightly different point of view.

We are deeply indebted to the ever-increasing list of grantmakers, government officials, nonprofit leaders, proposal writers, and others who spoke about the grants process, over the course of the various editions, with candor, compassion, and eloquence. We want to apologize for listing the following alphabetically and wish we had room to thank each of them individually: Jocelyn Ancheta, Eileen Auld, Plinio Ayala, Alison Bauer, Doug Bauer, Emily Blank, Gale Brewer, Joan Brody, Ronna Brown, Gordon J. Campbell, Cathy Cha, Michael Clark, Denise Clayton, Sybil Del Gaudio, Bill Dionne, Camille Emeagwali, Kanyere Eaton, Jill Eisenhard, the late Peter Eldridge, Susan Epstein, Christina Farrell, Marilyn Gelber, Lorenzo Harrison, Rachel Howard, Erica Hunt, Julia Jean-Francois, June Kress, Tamra Lhota, Paul Lopatto, Kristen Mahoney, Michelle Neugebauer, Paula J. Olsiewski, Catherine Giron Pino, Jennifer Powell, Mike Pratt, Anita Rogers, Karen Rosa, Elmy Savoie, Warren Scharf, Michael Seltzer, Chris Shearer, Pat Swann, Jane Taylor, MaryAnn Tierney, Doug Turetsky, Robert Uyeki, Patty Wineapple, and Judy Zangwill. We have omitted the names of individuals who preferred to remain anonymous, including some who spoke with us about the federal and state budgets, but we want them to know how grateful we are.

The Washington, DC, Regional Association of Grantmakers very kindly gave us permission to publish the common grant application form that it developed and produced. This is one of several Regional Association of Grantmakers common application forms that we think are valuable models for structuring any proposal.

Our warmest thanks to Judy Bernstein, Jocelyn Szczepaniak-Gillece, and Nicole Todini for their help and support on previous editions. Thanks also to Linda Lamb, Mark Rosenfeld, and Judy Morrison for the use of their names, and to Judy and Mark for their comments on Lesson 18.

Nancy Needle has helped us (with all five editions) in ways too numerous to mention. She gets her own paragraph as proof of our appreciation.

And finally, we want to thank our family and friends, who are always encouraging and supportive—especially Mark Rosenfeld (who is still, after all this time, urging us to hold out for the movie rights), and Sylvia Howard Fuhrman, who continues to be an inspiration.

INDEX

Page numbers followed by n refer to footnotes.

ABOUT THE AUTHORS

ELLEN KARSH, now writing and consulting full-time, was director of the New York City Mayor's Office of Grants Administration for more than seven years under both Mayor Giuliani and Mayor Bloomberg, and developed and wrote grants for the New York City Department of Education for five years before coming to the Mayor's Office. She graduated from Purdue University, has a doctorate in special education from Columbia University, and taught for years in the New York City public schools and in area colleges and universities. She has won tens of millions of dollars for the City of New York by writing grant proposals to government agencies and private foundations. In addition to developing and writing grant proposals, she has taught program development and grant writing to thousands of people representing not-for-profits, schools and colleges, and government agencies throughout New York City, using materials and resources that she developed over the years. While working in the Mayor's Office, she was the only public sector member of the City Connect Committee of the New York Regional Association of Grantmakers (now Philanthropy New York), comprising foundations and corporations interested in collaborating (among themselves and with government leaders) to address issues of interest to both the philanthropic community and government. Karsh has written articles—not about grants!—that have appeared in *Newsweek*, the *New York Times*, and other publications.

ARLEN SUE FOX has had many years of experience in program planning and evaluation, writing, and editing (including editing social science textbooks for a major publisher). Her background includes 10 years as the director of research, planning, and evaluation for the New York City Commission on Human Rights and 12 years as a consultant to nonprofit organizations, from small grassroots groups to national organizations including AARP and the Lighthouse. She spent three years as the coordinator of the City Connect Federal Grantsmanship Network, a foundation-initiated project designed to help nonprofit organizations improve their ability to obtain federal funding. In that project, she provided technical assistance and training on the federal grant process to dozens of nonprofit organizations, wrote *Preparing Federal Proposals: An Introduction*, and managed the development of an automated grants-information system that alerted nonprofit organizations to relevant federal and state funding opportunities. Fox has written—and has taught her clients to write—proposals that have brought nonprofits tens of millions of dollars for their programs. Fox retired from Sunnyside Community Services, a settlement house based in Queens, NY, where, as associate executive director for development, she was privileged to create and manage the development department for 10 years. Currently she is writing, editing, and volunteering with United Neighborhood Houses of New York, that extraordinary supporter of and advocate for 40-plus settlement houses and the neighborhoods they serve throughout New York City.